"The authors provide a concise, easy-to-understand vehicle for business leaders to recognize the value of information and how to leverage it."
—JERRY LUFTMAN, Executive Director and Distinguished Professor, Stevens Institute of Technology

"Frank and Magnone have created an insightful and groundbreaking model that will likely be built upon for years to come. As data continues to grow exponentially, useful information remains elusive. The framework presented herein presents a methodology that is critical for separating the knowledge from the noise and then shows how to apply it within our processes to make more effective business decisions."
—JOHN C. RIZZUTO, Research VP, Gartner

"Finally, a book that puts a valve on the overwhelming flood of data coming into today's organizations. From small companies to big businesses—we're choking. Through a simple seven-question approach, this book offers a customer-centric model that can be implemented immediately to channel rivers of data into actionable information. Throughout, the authors sprinkle illuminating anecdotes that drive home the lessons and make us feel normal."
—JAMES ALEXANDER, CEO, Vizibility

"In *Drinking from the Fire Hose*," Frank and Magnone tackle one of the biggest problems facing business decision makers today—how to sift through the multitude of raw data to find 'the indispensable answer.' The seven Fire Hose questions they pose, and the case study examples they present, provide powerful insights for anyone who needs to move past facts to a fuller understanding of the issues they are trying to address. A must-read for anyone who is looking 'to effectively communicate results and inspire action.' This is a very timely and important book, full of sound advice, written by two accomplished business practitioners."

—VINCENT J. CAMA, Ph.D., Chairman of the Board,
Knowledge Systems & Research, Inc.

"It's easy to spend money and collect data—but much harder to figure out what to do with all of your data. Not many organizations are good at that. This book will help you answer the key questions: what information to focus on and what to do with it."

—RAJIV GROVER, dean, Fogelman College of Business
and Economics, University of Memphis, and Editor of
Handbook of Marketing Research

DRINKING
FROM THE
FIRE HOSE

Catherine,

Keep Asking Questions!

Paul

CHRISTOPHER J FRANK AND PAUL MAGNONE

DRINKING
FROM THE
FIRE HOSE

MAKING SMARTER DECISIONS WITHOUT
DROWNING IN INFORMATION

PORTFOLIO / PENGUIN

PORTFOLIO / PENGUIN
Published by the Penguin Group
Penguin Group (USA) Inc., 375 Hudson Street,
New York, New York 10014, U.S.A.
Penguin Group (Canada), 90 Eglinton Avenue East, Suite 700,
Toronto, Ontario, Canada M4P 2Y3
(a division of Pearson Penguin Canada Inc.)
Penguin Books Ltd, 80 Strand, London WC2R 0RL, England
Penguin Ireland, 25 St. Stephen's Green, Dublin 2, Ireland
(a division of Penguin Books Ltd)
Penguin Books Australia Ltd, 250 Camberwell Road, Camberwell,
Victoria 3124, Australia
(a division of Pearson Australia Group Pty Ltd)
Penguin Books India Pvt Ltd, 11 Community Centre, Panchsheel Park,
New Delhi – 110 017, India
Penguin Group (NZ), 67 Apollo Drive, Rosedale, Auckland 0632,
New Zealand (a division of Pearson New Zealand Ltd)
Penguin Books (South Africa) (Pty) Ltd, 24 Sturdee Avenue,
Rosebank, Johannesburg 2196, South Africa

Penguin Books Ltd, Registered Offices:
80 Strand, London WC2R 0RL, England

First published in 2011 by Portfolio / Penguin,
a member of Penguin Group (USA) Inc.

10 9 8 7 6 5 4 3 2 1

Graph on page xxvi: Anderson & Wolff / Wired / Condé Nast Archive. Copyright © Condé Nast.

LIBRARY OF CONGRESS CATALOGING IN PUBLICATION DATA

Frank, Christopher J
  Drinking from the fire hose : making smarter decisions without drowning in information /
Christopher J Frank and Paul F. Magnone.
     p. cm.
  Includes index.
  ISBN 978-1-59184-426-6
  1. Decision making. 2. Management. I. Magnone, Paul F. II. Title.
  HD30.23.F735 2011
  658.4'03—dc22
                              2011013859

Printed in the United States of America
Set in Garamond 3 LT Std
Designed by Pauline Neuwirth

Michelle, my inspiration, North Star, and Lighthouse in this crazy journey called life. With love and gratitude for your constant support.
—CJF

Suzanne, for making me whole and keeping me sane. I don't need poetry with you in my life, and I thank the stars for you every day.
—PFM

To our gang of future crunchers: Alexander Ryan, Lauren Catherine, Luke Francis.

"He uses statistics as a drunken man uses lamp-posts . . . for support rather than illumination."
—ANDREW LANG

Contents

2. Does the data point to that vital piece of information or conceal it?

CHAPTER TWO
Where Is Your Customer's North Star?

Chapter Lessons
1. Uncover your customer's needs and wants in your existing data.
2. Confirm that the numbers you're using amplify the customer's voice, not muffle it.
3. Make sure the customer's voice can be heard and that it's listened to.

CHAPTER THREE
Should You Believe the Squiggly Line?

Chapter Lessons
1. Gain perspective by stepping further away from the data.
2. Bring broader thinking to the short-term nature of business.

>> SECTION TWO INSIGHT

CHAPTER FOUR
What Surprised You?

Chapter Lessons
1. Take a hard look at the numbers on the page, not the numbers you *expected* to see.
2. Use your intuition to spot mistakes and your natural skepticism to look for surprises.

Case Study: Digital Photography

Fire Hose Exercise No. 3: Trench Fantasy Football

Chapter Lessons

1. Employ a simple framework to report your conclusions.
2. Reduce the surface area of your presentations.
3. Present the numbers, but always in the context of other numbers.
4. Be confident enough to leave the "extra footage" on the cutting-room floor.

Case Study: IBM

The Drinking from the Fire Hose Questions

- What Is the Essential Business Question?
  - ▶ Asking the right question is the key to finding the indispensable answer in the mountain of information.
- Where Is Your Customer's North Star?
  - ▶ Shift your view from company-centric to customer-centric.
- Should You Believe the Squiggly Line?
  - ▶ Question the validity of short-term data.
- What Surprised You?
  - ▶ Uncover hidden information and use it to change the dialogue.
- What Does the Lighthouse Reveal?
  - ▶ Identify the risks, barriers, and bridges that surround your business.
- Who Are Your Swing Voters?
  - ▶ Drive growth, increase revenue, and boost satisfaction by looking at your existing customers in a new way.
- What? So What? Now What?
  - ▶ Follow this easy-to-remember sequence of questions to effectively communicate results and inspire action.

How to Use This Book

We're businesspeople first and authors second. We know what it's like to work on the front lines—making decisions, leading teams, and juggling multiple priorities. We realize that your time is limited, and that you have to shift your focus frequently throughout the working day. As a result, we wrote this book so that it can be read in a number of ways—end to end on a long flight, in chapters during your morning commute, or as a guide and a constant reference. With the exception of the final chapters, you needn't have read one chapter before reading another. You might start by dog-earing the table of contents, and get into the habit of giving the Seven Questions a quick look before you sit down at a meeting. Or, if you're not in the mood for a lesson, you might just scan the table of contents and go right to a case study—like IBM's decision to abandon Lotus Script for Java, or iRobot's initial foray into domestic robotics. They're listed by company in each chapter. In short, we've tried to make this book as navigable as possible, just like a well-presented deck based on good information, not meaningless data.

For that reason we've also written *Drinking from the Fire Hose* with multiple cues. We've put the key lessons of each chapter right up front, examined those lessons in greater detail in the pages that follow, and then reinforced them with a short list of "takeaways" at the end of each chapter. We've also used real business-world examples throughout the book, both to reinforce the central point of each chapter and to let you see how and when the questions should be asked—or have been asked—and with what effect.

To make sure this book was grounded in a reality larger than our own, we've also reached out to some of the most talented people we know in market research, business development, marketing, and sales, asking them to pressure-test the lessons in this book and letting you eavesdrop on our conversations with them. There is in fact a significant amount of expert advice packed into this short book, from insights into the Seven Questions themselves to practical advice on applying the lessons to your day-to-day work, something you should be able to do as soon as you put this book down.

A few more practical reminders. You can use the lessons in this book one at a time or in combination, although we think you'll find that one question often leads to another. You might, for instance, find yourself asking one Fire Hose Question at the beginning of a project and another at the end. In short, we use the questions like a jazz musician plays notes in a riff rather than a scale.

Finally, *Drinking from the Fire Hose* is divided into three major sections: Discovery, Insight, and Delivery. No matter which questions you use, the process should be the same. Identify the data you need, use the information it yields to develop insights, and then deliver that information and those insights to decision makers. And in the same way that you know what's good for your business you will know how to apply this book far better than we can tell you. So think of the table of contents as a map rather than a manual.

In short, we've done everything we can to make *Drinking from the Fire Hose* a book that can be picked up over and over again, either to gain some new insight or to reinforce what you've already learned. And once you've gotten through it, in whatever way you thought was best, we hope you'll visit us online at www.firehosethebook.com and let us know what you think about it and how it's changed the way you do business.

Foreword

The old cliché "What gets measured gets done" might have been accurate once, but in today's data-driven, digital world it seems that *everything* is quantified, tracked, and recorded. And to what end? Wasn't having all that data at your fingertips supposed to make you better informed? Wasn't it supposed to make you more confident and more certain of your direction? The new cliché, it seems, is that you can't be too thin, be too rich, or have too much information. Today, instead, it seems that everything is measured, and nothing gets done. In our information-driven global economy, the real challenge lies in keeping your head above the flood of data, learning how to separate information from facts, and acquiring the judgment to use what you find to inspire others to act.

This is especially true because most of the irrelevant information that washes across your desk, laptop, or smartphone doesn't just fall from the sky—it's generated by the company you work for. In other words, because managers don't know *what* they're looking for—that is, because they don't focus on the one indispensable piece of information they need to move a project forward—they blame their confusion on the *volume* of data. Yet even while waving the flag of surrender, most of them *continue* to ask for even more information. And as unproductive and contradictory as this habit clearly is, it's reinforced every day. Why? Because we work in a business culture that *worships* numbers, whether or not the numbers mean anything. Just try showing up at a sales meeting with a two-page spreadsheet or a deck with only seven slides in it. Chances are they'll throw you right out, then start complaining about your "level of rigor."

Drinking from the Fire Hose was written to help break the habit of gathering and presenting too much information, and to give you the tools—that is, the seven Fire Hose Questions—to help others break the habit. People want answers. Just as a prism separates light into parts, the Seven Questions serve as a prism for the information streaming across your desk, thus creating a new spectrum of actionable information. The reason is simple: The right questions expose outliers in the data, draw connections between seemingly unrelated conclusions, and open different avenues of discussion between your colleagues.

This book was written to help you avoid meaningless data, to help you find the information you need, and to help you gain new insights. And strangely enough, although the problem is extremely complex, the solution is relatively simple. From our firsthand experience at both *Fortune* 500 corporations and bootstrap start-ups, we've learned that the solution to the problem involves nothing more difficult than asking the right questions at the right time.

That's what this book is all about. Seven Questions. Seven straightforward, immediately applicable, practical questions. Seven Questions that can be asked from the businessperson's perspective or the customer's. Seven Questions that used together provide a process for the most effective use of your company's data. That process, or approach, is the key to accessing data already locked in your organization and to finding answers that will drive your business forward. The core principle of this book, in fact, is that the person with the right questions shapes the discussion. And by asking those questions, he or she focuses the inquiry, makes better decisions, and helps others make better decisions.

What we're saying is that this book isn't about crunching numbers, or absorbing all the data coming out of the fire hose. It's about keeping yourself from being swept out on the tide of information overload. But it's also about doing more than just treading water and trying not to drown. It's about giving you the tools to face the flood of information head-on. It's about enabling you to quickly dismiss anything but the truly relevant information, about taking the time to think over the information you've gathered, and, as a result, about arriving at fresh insights. Once that's happened, you'll be able to make carefully thought-out, well-informed decisions—and you'll do it in half the time you used to.

We must have considered hundreds of questions before settling on the short list that forms the backbone of this book. And although each question asks for a different set of facts, a common thread connects them all: the search for the one critical piece of information you need to move the project, or your business, forward. Toward that end, the questions are designed to let you know what the customer really wants, what the end user will buy, and how you'll provide it. And once you've answered those questions, the Fire Hose approach will also enable your team to act.

If the data in front of you doesn't help you answer at least one of these questions, get rid of it.

Useless data saps morale. Useful information is energizing. We all know what it's like to sit through tedious, unproductive meetings. Meetings where no one ever asks a question—unless everyone already knows the answer. The Fire Hose Questions aren't like that. They're not like the questions you were asked in B-school. They're the product of decades of combined business experience. They came from our understanding that unless you're sitting at the head of the table—or pretty close to it—it's tough to speak up. From our knowing that it's easier, and safer, just to sit there and nod your head as the slides go by like so many floats in a parade.

And knowing how much courage it takes to be the one person in the room who doesn't just ignore the presentation and check e-mail on their phone, we worked hard to come up with questions you'll feel comfortable asking a roomful of your peers—or senior management. Questions that can't be ignored, by virtue of their obvious, thoughtful relevance. And questions, by the way, to which you don't need immediate answers, because their primary purpose is to make everyone in the room stop and think, and then to shift the conversation into a more fruitful direction. The answers will come in their own good time. In the meantime, we're confident that you'll quickly become comfortable asking these questions, because you'll see that you're doing *everyone* in the room a service—by refocusing the analysis, reevaluating the information it yields, and using it as a catalyst for action.

Learn to ask the right question at the right time, and whether or not you're an expert on research, analysis, or business development, you'll get to the *right* data—that is, the information you need to move things forward. Or, put another way, you'll learn how to drink from the Fire Hose.

Now, let's take a quick look at the real world—that is the business world of today, without the Fire Hose Questions.

It's late morning. You're sitting in a conference room with no windows. The lights are low and the projector is humming. Eight of your colleagues are there with you at the meeting, including the head of marketing, the social-media manager, and a few business development folks. A few of them are checking their e-mail. Three other participants have dialed in on the phone. The meeting starts ten minutes late. Two of the key people couldn't make it and they sent delegates, neither of whom has a real understanding of the issues or the authority to make decisions. Twenty minutes into the meeting, the presenter finally makes it to slide four of a thirty-two-slide deck. At least you can read this one, unlike the first three, which were so crammed with numbers (Figure 1), graphs, and charts, all of them using different colors, that you couldn't figure out what they meant.

You look around the room, wondering whether anyone else is actually following the presentation. If they are, they must be smarter than you. You can't figure this slide out, either. In fact, the moment it pops up, your head starts spinning.

Another slide appears (Figure 2). You can't figure out what the headline has to do with the bar graphs below it. And although each one of them is divided into segments, you can't tell why. The presenter reads every word and every number on the slide. He then veers off on a tangent, and two or three minutes go by before he comes back to the slide. From what you can see, there wasn't much movement in the numbers, but when the presenter points to them as a "directional improvement," heads nod approvingly.

Another slide takes its place. You start to raise a hand to ask for clarification, but then think twice about it. No one else in the room has asked a single question, and the more you think about it, the more you think it's not such a good idea. Everyone else must get it, so what's the point in letting them know that you don't? Besides, it might lead to a lengthy debate, with no obvious answer, and you've got work to do. Finally, someone calls for a "time check," and you and the other five

[FIGURE 1]

3Q Actual and Outlook by Geography

	1Q			2Q			3Q						
	Plan	Actual	Attain-ment	Plan	Actual	Attain-ment	Plan	QTD (Wk 7) Actual	Attain-ment QTD (Wk 7)	Total Validated Pipeline (Wk 7)	Projected Yield (Wk 7)	Geo Outlook	Projected attainment (Geo outlook to plan)
Americas	27.5	20.6	75%	34.1	41.7	122%	25.6	-2.7	-11%	125	33	27.3	107%
US	23.4	19.5	84%	29.3	34.2	117%	21.1	-4.0	-19%	90	24	22.7	107%
LA	1.9	0.6	34%	2.2	3.2	144%	2.4	1.0	41%	28	6	2.0	85%
Canada	2.3	0.5	22%	2.6	4.3	165%	2.1	0.3	12%	8	3	2.6	125%
NE IOT	38.6	24.8	64%	37.8	19.0	50%	30.4	7.0	23%	87	22	36.2	119%
CEMAAS	14.4	5.9	41%	13.5	8.4	62%	13.0	5.1	39%	29	11	17.7	137%
Germany	9.8	12.0	122%	10.7	6.6	61%	11.2	1.5	13%	31	6	13.1	117%
UKISA	7.8	3.8	49%	8.3	0.5	7%	0.9	0.1	10%	14	3	1.7	193%
Nordics	5.0	3.1	62%	5.4	3.4	64%	5.4	0.4	7%	14	2	3.7	69%
SW IOT	31.5	19.0	60%	36.2	43.7	121%	32.0	3.6	11%	67	20	17.3	54%
BeNeLux	7.4	7.1	96%	9.2	4.8	52%	7.4	1.4	19%	7	4	5.2	70%
France	9.1	6.2	68%	9.9	6.1	62%	9.1	-0.9	-10%	41	10	3.8	42%
Italy	7.6	3.8	50%	8.8	23.8	271%	7.3	2.5	34%	11	4	5.6	76%
SPGIT	7.4	1.9	25%	8.3	9.0	108%	8.2	0.2	2%	7	2	2.7	33%
AP	16.7	28.8	173%	16.2	17.5	108%	19.6	2.4	12%	87	33	21.0	107%
ANZ	0.7	0.0	0%	0.8	0.3	37%	0.7	0.0	0%	7	1	1.0	139%
GCG	7.7	5.4	70%	8.6	5.6	66%	7.3	1.3	17%	27	10	5.0	68%
India-SA	0.1	5.3	3789%	0.2	2.3	1533%	0.2	0.1	93%	4	1	1.0	625%
ASEAN	1.8	11.6	342%	0.5	2.1	388%	2.1	0.1	6%	17	7	4.0	194%
Korea	3.3	0.1	2%	2.8	3.6	127%	3.1	0.0	0%	12	3	3.0	97%
Japan	3.0	6.4	214%	3.3	3.6	109%	6.2	0.9	14%	19	11	7.0	112%
WWTop			3.2			3.2				1.7			
WW	114.4	93.3	82%	127.6	121.9	96%	109.2	10.3	9%	366	108	101.8	93%

- Attainment QTD is from Week 7 data – DTL historical average is 25%.
- $13.9M Acme deal from 2Q moved from Division A to Division B resulting in negative QTD attainment in US for Division A.
- "Double counting" of $10.6M in OEM software from General Inc. from 1Q that showed up in July has been reversed out.

people left around the table scramble to identify as many action items as you can in a vain attempt to show that the meeting had some purpose. Someone suggests a follow-up meeting later in the week. You tap your phone to check your calendar: There are eleven new e-mails in your inbox, and you've missed two calls. Another hour shot out of your workday, and for what? All the facts and figures just led to more questions, not answers. In fact, you feel like you know less than when you got there, and the presenter wants to go through the same charade later in the week.

[FIGURE 2]

DTL PRACTICE ACTIVITY CORRESPONDS TO CALCULATED METRICS FOR 1H2011 SALES AND BUSINESS DEVELOPMENT

Activity split by Band and Practice Overall (without overhead and transfer costs)

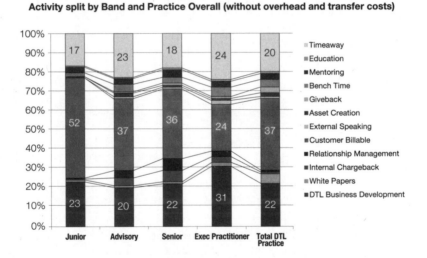

DATA OVERLOAD

By now everyone recognizes the problem, but few of us have figured out how to deal with it. What's more, the *symptoms* of the disease make it even harder to treat. The facts and figures blind us—or, worse yet, they bury us. And even if you manage to stay on your feet as the Fire Hose whips back and forth, soaking everyone in sight, meaningful dialogue and critical thinking are impossible. The promise of the information age, in other words, has given way to the reality of data overload. And every day, as the types of data expand, the frequency of data collection increases, and the total volume of data *explodes*, the stream becomes more powerful. Far from helping us make decisions, the water cannon of information pins us against the wall, creating more questions than it answers and leading to caution and uncertainty instead of well-informed, carefully considered business strategies.

> Everywhere you look, the quantity of information in the world is soaring. According to one estimate, mankind created 150 exabytes (billion gigabytes) of data in 2005. This year, it will create 1,200 exabytes. Merely keeping up with this flood, and storing the bits that might be useful, is difficult enough. Analyzing it, to spot patterns and extract useful information, is harder still. Even so, the data deluge is already starting to transform business, government, science and everyday life . . . It has great potential for good—as long as consumers, companies and governments make the right choices about when to restrict the flow of data, and when to encourage it.
>
> —"The Data Deluge," *The Economist,* February 25, 2010

So we're all overwhelmed by data. That we can agree on. But as the authors of this book, we want to make one thing clear: We're not *anti-data*. In fact, we love numbers—sales volume, retail traffic, market trends, applications, subscriptions, renewals, news bits, reports, blogs, e-mails, articles, etc. That is, we love *good* information. Information that leads to answers. Information presented at just the right time in the decision-making process. To make this clear, we need to devote a few lines to talking about the difference between data, numbers, and information.

Data is facts. In a storm, drops of rain are the data. They fall endlessly. They never stop falling. Like data in the business world, they rain down on everything and everyone. Many of those raindrops hit the ground and disappear; others collect in pools or flow together to form streams. But the data itself is meaningless. That is, it may or may not hold meaning. But even if it does, you won't be able to get to it unless you learn how to tell one raindrop from another.

Numbers are results. They communicate change. They show speed and direction, much like a rain gauge shows accumulation. Those results come from the collection of specific data, data selected for a reason. Numbers may or may not be useful. But they're not random. We think of them as filtered data.

Information is what you get when you analyze numbers. It involves the recognition of tendencies in certain collections of numbers. Information can prove or disprove statements. It can support or discourage plans. It can be *acted* upon.

But information isn't the Holy Grail. Insight is. Insights allow us to see clearly into complex situations, and that's the whole point. Data leads to numbers, numbers to information, and information to insights. Insights, finally, inspire action. Data is just a means to an end. But in our data-driven world, almost all of us seem to have lost sight of that.

The sheer volume of data isn't the only thing that's changed; today's data no longer streams through the same channels it did at the turn of the twenty-first century. In its August 17, 2010, online edition, for instance, *Wired* magazine (Figure 3) charted the expansion and contraction of Internet usage patterns over the past twenty years.

[FIGURE 3]

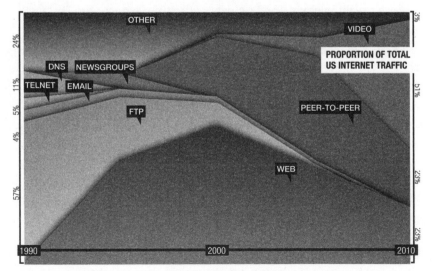

Anderson & Wolff / Wired / Condé Nast Archive. Copyright © Condé Nast.

E-mail, as you can see from the chart, might as well be reduced to a rounding error. And even though there's no correlation between the demand for broadband bandwidth and the usefulness of the material, it's a safe bet that the paths along which data flow *through* the World Wide Web will continue to change. For that matter, with the rise of apps and APIs,* who can say whether traffic on the Internet will continue to flow through the World Wide Web at all? Furthermore, a lot of this data is flowing through infrastructure that was built by entrepreneurs who *hope* they'll be able to monetize it one day. But who, once push comes to shove, will hit the PAY button to watch a home video, a photo library of every moment in the baby's life, or a low-resolution broadcast of a pirated movie?

So while the volume of data will continue to expand, some of the channels that data flows through, and some of today's data sources, will disappear over time. Advertisers and marketers, for instance, might not be able to track Web users' habits much longer—at least not without their permission. And closer scrutiny of some of the newer forms of analytics is almost certain to lead to restrictions as a result of privacy concerns. So even as the volume of data increases, advertisers and marketers can't assume they'll continue to have access to the same data sources they can tap today. Still, while the relevance of this material, no matter how it's transmitted, is open to discussion, its content, its purpose, and the way it was created—in other words, the metadata that describe it—cannot be ignored.

THE DAILY CRUNCH

Most of us have our smartphones in our hands as we drink our first cup of coffee in the morning. And before we embark on the daily trek to the office, we're already thinking ahead to the first conference call of the day. Or to the endless meetings that jam our calendars. Or the follow-ups with vendors or the proposals we've been asked to review—or, most important, the pitch we've been meaning to make for more resources. But as soon as we arrive at the office, even those quickly rearranged priorities come under attack.

*Application programming interfaces.

Did you get a chance to read the report? Have you thought about the expansion, reviewed the presentation, checked the project status? Did you sign off on the budget? Before you've gotten through the first ten e-mails in your inbox, your phone rings.

As you answer a question, you glance at your calendar, trying to remember if your 11:00 A.M. meeting is a brainstorming session, an information-sharing meeting, or a meeting that requires a decision from you. By the time you put the phone down you feel like you're in a batting cage, facing a pitching machine that never stops throwing balls at you. And before long you just start swinging at anything that comes your way, whether or not it's near the plate.

By the middle of the afternoon you feel like you haven't actually *done* anything. And the rest of the day is more of the same. In meetings or on calls, you're faced with one of two things: incomplete data that leads to rambling, pointless conversations, or a mountain of numbers you wouldn't be able to dig through even if you were behind the controls of an earthmover. So what do you do? You work even harder, and before you know it your personal tachometer begins to redline. But no matter how much faster it spins, your engine won't deliver any additional horsepower or results.

You've lost your focus, and your day has lost its purpose. Instead of focusing on the right data, and considering it in light of two or three simple principles, you've done nothing more than keep up with your latest runaway day. And what's worse, it's not as if someone asked you to put the final details on the master plan for "growing the company over the next three years." All you've been trying to do is get your hands on the information you need to make the routine, daily course corrections to keep your team's plans on track.

> Research is to see what everybody else has seen, and to think what nobody else has thought.
>
> —Albert Szent-Györgyi, Hungarian biochemist and
> 1937 Nobel laureate in Medicine

If you continue doing things the way you've always done them, your tomorrow won't be any different than your today. And data overload will continue to bury you and everyone else beneath it. Your inbox will be jammed with even more e-mails "inviting" you to attend another round of presentations, meetings, and conference calls. And every invitation will be accompanied by new facts and figures. And day by day, your desk will be buried even deeper under proposals you have to respond to or surveys you have to evaluate or data on market size, sales trends, growth plans, and emerging segments you have to read.

In other words, seeing what "everybody else has seen" *is* the problem. What you've got to do instead is start by finding the data you *need*. And to do that, you've got to ask the right questions. Only by asking *those* questions—and asking them repeatedly—will you have any chance at "thinking what nobody else has thought."

Again, we're not from some think tank. We've experienced data overload firsthand, just like you have. And we've gotten to the point where we're not going to put up with it anymore, because we're sure there's a better way.

Hence the Seven Questions. And for what it's worth, we didn't pick the questions out of a hat or come up with them over the weekend. They're based on our frontline experiences in the small-business and corporate worlds over the past twenty years. During that time, we've been present at the birth of countless small businesses and we've worked with some of the biggest players in the venture capital community. We've also worked for some of the most iconic brands in business—brands like American Express, IBM, and Microsoft. So when we say that both *Fortune* 500 corporations and poorly funded start-ups suffer from data overload, we're speaking from experience.

Whether we were working on shoestring budgets for new ventures or had millions of dollars to spend on ad campaigns or product rollouts, we know what it's like to be inundated by data on customers, data on the markets, and data on the competition. In fact, as it turns out, one of us was generating the data and the other using it to launch new businesses or further develop existing businesses. One of us designed the studies, and the other analyzed the outputs. Both of us have written business plans, and both of us have made pitches to investors. Both of us have put businesses on their feet, and both of us have watched some of them fail.

We came armed with the key performance indicators (KPI). We pored over forecasts, projections, scorecards, trends, gaps, targets, and pipelines. And a lot of the data was both eye-opening *and* actionable, but more often than not, there was so much of it that we either were overwhelmed or, once we got through it, didn't have any time left to analyze it.

And we contributed to information overload, too. As part of our attempts to launch new products, we built spreadsheets on top of spreadsheets. In our attempts to collaborate, we wrote e-mails with distribution lists longer than the messages themselves. What were we thinking?

Like Michelangelo, we knew there was an angel in the block of marble, but there was so much waste to chip away that we hardly ever got to it. And sometimes, after swinging our mallets for hours, we were so worn out that we forgot what it was we were looking for and smashed through an arm or a leg without realizing what we were doing.

In other words, these questions are already battle-tested. We know from personal experience that they'll work on market research. They'll work on sales data too, and on social-media output. They'll work for marketing, finance, operations, and strategic planning. And they'll work for start-ups just as well as they'll work for global corporate giants.

Our search for the answers in the data, in fact, led us to the first Fire Hose Question, which we now call the *Essential Question*—namely, what is the one indispensable piece of information we need to move forward? And that question led to others. Are we getting hung up on short-term numbers and missing long-term trends? Did we get the results we expected? Do these survey results truly tell us what our customers want? Are we paying enough attention to our existing customers? What, specifically, would attract new revenue and new customers? Where are the bumps in the road? And finally, once we've got the information we need, what do we do next?

To give you an idea of what can happen when you ask the Fire Hose Questions—and someone answers them—let's take a look at another hypothetical meeting.

A MEETING WITH A PURPOSE

It's late afternoon. You're sitting in a conference room with no windows. The lights are low and the projector is humming. Six of your colleagues are there, including the head of market research, the social-media manager, and two of the more successful salesmen in the company. A few people are typing on their phones. Six others have dialed in on the phone. The meeting starts on time. One of the key people couldn't make it, but she sent a delegate with a real understanding of the issues and the authority to make decisions on her behalf.

Twenty minutes into the meeting, the presenter is on slide nine of a twelve-slide deck. At first glance, even before the presenter begins to explain the significance of the numbers represented by the simple pie chart, you've already grasped their significance. Everyone in the room is focused on the slide. People are asking questions. They're engaged.

This is an information-sharing meeting, not a decision-making meeting, so there's a lot of back-and-forth. Every time the conversation slows down, the presenter moves to the next slide. There are a lot of questions, many of them from senior staff. As the presenter gathers answers from everyone in the room, he refers not only to the slides in his deck but also to the company's long-term strategic plans.

The meeting runs over, but no one's complaining. There's another meeting scheduled for the following week—a decision-making meeting—and they want to be sure they know what they want before they get there, and have voice in the final decision.

In the introduction, we'll go over the Fire Hose Questions one by one, then lay the groundwork for the practical applications and the case studies that follow. Before we do, we'd like you to take the following short quiz. Answer each question with either "frequently" or "infrequently." Give yourself one point for each time you answer "frequently." If you score a 5 or higher, you've got the right book in your hands.

HOW FREQUENTLY DOES INFORMATION OVERLOAD AFFECT YOU?

1. How often do you sit through a meeting that's more about reporting the numbers than about learning from them?
2. How often do you leave a meeting with more questions than answers?
3. How often do your colleagues spend more time presenting the data than they do discussing the implications?
4. How often do you feel that preexisting beliefs affect the way data is interpreted?
5. Once the results are reported, how often does the conversation end up going down the same old path instead of developing any new insights?
6. How often do you see data cited to confirm a point of view instead of to spark fresh insight?
7. How often do you learn nothing actionable from a data set?
8. How often do you feel you have to make a decision before you've been able to review all the data at hand?
9. How often do you feel that you could make better decisions for the business if you had just a little more time?

DRINKING
FROM THE
FIRE HOSE

The Seven Fire Hose Questions

"Before I refuse to take your questions, I have an opening
statement."

—RONALD REAGAN

Your workday won't be less frenzied after you read *Drinking from the Fire Hose*. And your workweek won't be any less punishing. Nor will this book stop the river of data flooding into today's business world. You won't find the answers to those problems in this book. Or in any other book, for that matter.

What *Drinking from the Fire Hose* has is questions. Questions that will help you recognize the difference between data that *measures* and data that *informs*. Questions that will help you optimize what you do, and what you can do, with the time you have. Questions that will make it easier for you to zero in on the essential information you need to make timely, practical decisions and inspire others to do the same. That's right: No answers, just questions. Questions designed to lead to an orderly process of discovery and action.

Why questions instead of answers? First, because no one knows your business like you do. Second, because we're not interested in forcing your business into our model. We've opened far too many business books that tried to do that. They're all gathering dust on our bookshelves. We were determined instead to write a book that was simple, that included practical advice, and that would deliver immediate value—before our readers finished the first chapter.

In short, we want you to open *this* book over and over again, and not always to the same place. Whenever you feel like a data storm is about to blot out the sun, we want you to turn to the straightforward questions that form the backbone of this book—questions we still ask *ourselves* every day. In other words, don't ask us; ask yourself. But ask the right questions. The questions that will keep you from drowning in a deluge of information, help you find the data you need, and help you and your colleagues make sound decisions based on that information.

As part of that process of discovery, you will understand when to ask for research versus measurement (Figure 4). You'll learn how to divide data into two fundamental groups: data that measures and data that informs.

[FIGURE 4]

**RESEARCH DRIVES BUSINESS ANSWERS,
MEASUREMENT DRIVES TACTICAL IMPROVEMENTS**

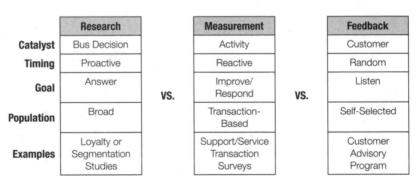

	Research		Measurement		Feedback
Catalyst	Bus Decision		Activity		Customer
Timing	Proactive		Reactive		Random
Goal	Answer	VS.	Improve/ Respond	VS.	Listen
Population	Broad		Transaction- Based		Self-Selected
Examples	Loyalty or Segmentation Studies		Support/Service Transaction Surveys		Customer Advisory Program

Data that measures tracks performance by assessing impact or by tracking the market. Data that informs, on the other hand, builds understanding, tests concepts and strategies, and shapes decisions. Sales data, for example, *measures* recorded behavior, whereas survey data provides information on *likely* behavior.

Within each of these categories you'll use primary data, which is data you generate yourself or can buy from proprietary research companies, such as Nielsen BookScan. Within primary data there might be quantitative (numbers), qualitative (focus groups, comments, blogs), or competitive intelligence. Secondary data is previously published or syndicated data, like that measuring broad industry trends.

In short, we'll show you how businesspeople spend way too much time and money on data that measures, and not enough on data that informs, and to drive that point home we'll introduce the first of the industry experts with whom we spoke while writing this book: Darrell Bricker.

DARRELL BRICKER, CEO of Ipsos Public Affairs, in Toronto, conducts corporate-reputation and social research around the world. Ipsos, the world's second-largest market research firm, with offices in sixty-six countries, offers its clients: advertising research; innovation and brand research; media, content, and technology research; public affairs and corporate-reputation research; customer and employee research; and survey management, data collection, and delivery services.

Prior to joining Ipsos in 1990, Bricker was director of public-opinion research in the office of Canada's prime minister. He holds a Ph.D. in political science from Carleton University, in Ottawa, and a B.A. and M.A. from Wilfrid Laurier University, in Waterloo. He's an active member of the American Association of Public Opinion Research and a frequent media commentator on political, social, and business issues. He's also the author (with John Wright) of *We Know What You're Thinking* (HarperCollins, 2009) and *Canuckology* (HarperCollins, 2010), among others.

According to Bricker:

Every data set—finance, public-opinion research, etc.—always tells a story. The challenge is knowing how to tease that story of tragedy or romance from the data.

The numbers are simply the context. All of it is really about trying to understand the story behind the numbers. There's always a logic to the way people respond to things, even if their response is illogical. So people are always looking for rationality in the things people do, but a lot of times they're just responding on an emotional level. Whether you're working in a political environment or a business environment, or a public sector environment or a private sector environment, there's always a logic, as illogical as it might be, behind how people make their decisions. And the job of a researcher is to figure that out. And then to not only take the data and present it, but explain the logic that's behind it, and help people understand how that group makes their decisions. And that's where the tragedy and the romance comes in . . . that is why people come up with the decisions they do, and whether you like it or not, you've got to deal with it.

We'll return to Bricker and his projectile-like insights on data collection and analysis throughout this book, but for now we'll just say that the Fire Hose Questions are meant to help you find out as quickly as possible whether romance or tragedy lies ahead for you and your business. In particular, the questions are designed to get you to those breakthrough insights faster, and reduce the number of iterations you'll need to complete a presentation or a report that will improve understanding and lead to meaningful change.

As we pointed out in the Foreword, while each Fire Hose Question stands on its own, we've grouped them into three broad categories, according to the role they play in the process of discovery, insight, and decision making. The first group, gathered under the heading "Discovery," contains the questions that help you gather information. The second group, under the heading "Insight," contains the questions that lead to fresh insights, allowing you and others to see complex situations more clearly. The third group, under the heading "Delivery," contains the questions that prepare you for action, help initiate action, and empower others to prepare themselves to do the same.

Again, despite the organization outlined above, the Fire Hose Questions can be used singly or recombined in a variety of ways, depending on your business needs. To use a nautical analogy, the questions can be used in the same way that a competent sailor on a well-outfitted boat uses one sail or a variety of sails, depending on his course and the circumstances he finds himself in. If you're starting a major project, *Drinking from the Fire Hose* can guide you from data collection to analysis to reporting. If you're in midstream, the Fire Hose Questions can help you get to the other side.

In addition, these questions will help you learn to distinguish between the complicated and the complex. In a *New York Times* article on this topic, David Segal refers to the work of Professor Brenda Zimmerman, of the Schulich School of Business, in Ontario.

It's complicated, she says, to send a rocket to the moon—it requires blueprints, math and a lot of carefully calibrated hardware and expertly written software. Raising a child, on the other hand, is complex. It is an enormous challenge, but math and blueprints won't help. Performing hip-replacement surgery, she says, is complicated. It takes well-trained personnel, precision and carefully calibrated equipment. Running a health care system, on the other hand, is complex. It's filled with thousands of parts and players, all of whom must act within a fluid, unpredictable environment. To run a system that is complex, it's not enough to get the right people and the ideal equipment. It takes a set of simple principles that guide and shape the system.[*]

We couldn't have put it any better ourselves, and we wrote the Fire Hose Questions with exactly that idea in mind. Data is *complex*. Analyzing it, gaining useful insights from it, and using it to initiate action is *complicated*.

Finally, while these questions may seem obvious to you, we can assure you that the answers to them are not. And what's more, as straightforward as these questions are, we can assure you that they are often overlooked by many capable businesspeople.

SECTION ONE: DISCOVERY

You'll use the first three Fire Hose Questions to find the data you *need*. And that means limiting the amount of data you gather. So let's start with the one question you should ask yourself, whether you're trying to help your team hit their sales targets, deciding whether you should roll out a new product or service, or looking to increase your market share.

>> What Is the Essential Business Question?

Learning to identify the Essential Question in any inquiry is the most important skill anyone can develop. The right question leads to an orderly, informed process of discovery and, ultimately, to success. The wrong question leaves the core issue unaddressed, buries you and your

*David Segal, "It's Complicated: Making Sense of Complexity," *New York Times,* May 1, 2010.

customers in meaningless data, and often leads to disaster. In this chapter, we'll help you to understand and use this critical question.

Think of it this way. Somewhere in the deep end of the data pool is the information you need. You know it's there. But experience has taught you that it's hard to find, because it's surrounded by random facts and figures, and you can hold your breath underwater for only so long. For that reason, convincing you to consider the Essential Question is one of the most important objectives of this book. Why? Because as the amount of data, the type of data, and the frequency with which data is collected continue to increase, that question is the best way to point a light at the data you need, until it glitters like a coin at the bottom of the data pool. The right question leads to new learning, meaningful information, and, ultimately, action. The wrong question buries you, your team, and your customers under a mountain of meaningless data.

Getting the answer to that question takes time. And the combination of information overload and the ordinary demands of the workday make finding that time more and more difficult. In other words, the problem itself reduces your chances of finding a solution. So how can you break the vicious cycle? With your business's Essential Question as your guide, shift your focus from amassing data—from every available source, with or without a reason—to finding and interpreting only that data you need to answer the Essential Question, and to move your business, or a specific project, forward.

The question can be used in more than one way. When using it to uncover enterprise-wide solutions, or when planning long-term strategy, you'll probably ask it only once a year. The answer you get at the beginning of a project, though, might change as the project goes forward, meaning that it's time to ask it again. Put another way, as conditions and circumstances in the business world change—and they will never stop changing—the answer to your business's Essential Question will change, too.

>> Where Is Your Customer's North Star?

Why do you collect and analyze data? For two main reasons. You collect and analyze data to monitor your company's performance—in absolute terms, against the market's performance, and with respect to your competitors. But just as important, you gather and interpret data to understand your customers' needs, wants, and behavior (again, in absolute terms, relative terms, and competitive terms).

Customer-based data is a recording of sorts, meant to capture the *voice* of your customer—or sometimes the voices of all the customers in the segment. But having recorded those voices, and then mapped those co-ordinates, do you navigate by them? That is, are your strategic decisions, or even your company's day-to-day decisions, based on *customer*-centric criteria or on *company*-centric criteria? In other words, do you follow your customer's North Star or your own?

And even if you do get in the habit of craning your neck to keep an eye on your customer's North Star, it's still easy to get caught up with data that measures what your customers *do* instead of what your customers *want*. Assessment tools like Total Unduplicated Reach and Frequency (TURF) analysis, the van Westendorp Price Sensitivity Meter, or an SKU inventory analysis yield valuable data from an operational standpoint—e.g., in judging the effectiveness of a marketing campaign, the effect of pricing decisions, or the success of inventory controls—but they don't measure customer preferences. Perhaps even more important, they ignore the effect company-centric decisions have on your *customers*. In this sense, keeping an eye on the customer's North Star is a sort of businessperson's Hippocratic Oath: First do no harm.

To understand the effect of a company's decisions on its customers, we employ a simple tool called a Customer Impact Assessment (CIA), a framework you can use to keep the customer's voice within earshot of your decision-making process.

- How could this decision negatively impact the customer?
- How will the customer perceive this change (in price, packaging, advertising, etc.)?
- How will you manage the change—for the customer, not the company?
- How will we track the impact of these changes on customer behavior?

That framework brings to mind another of the expert voices you'll hear in *Drinking from the Fire Hose*—that of Susan Schwartz McDonald.

∞

In addition to—or perhaps in spite of—her impressive credentials, we have always trusted Susan to make her way through the maze of numbers to the human factors that drive customer behavior. Listen to the following story, e-mailed to us after we'd interviewed her for the book, about one iconic brand that took its eyes off its customer's North Star.

SUSAN SCHWARTZ MCDONALD is CEO of National Analysts Worldwide, a market research consultancy that integrates sophisticated methods with specialized industry expertise to guide its clients' most important business decisions. She is also the 2011–12 chair of CASRO, the trade association that represents most major companies in the marketing and opinion-research industry in the United States. Before she and John Berrigan reincorporated the company in 1992, National Analysts was a fully integrated division of Booz Allen Hamilton, where Susan was a vice president. Early in her career, she worked as a writer, contributing articles, essays, and poetry to newspapers and major magazines like the *National Review* and *Harper's*. She is also the co-author, with Alfred Goldman, of an acknowledged standard on qualitative research methods, titled *The Group Depth Interview: Principles and Practice* (Prentice Hall, 1987).

After we spoke about the customer's North Star, I realized that I had omitted a prime example: the New Coke fiasco. To me, the story still seems fresh today, but that could be because of the time I spent at the behest of Coca-Cola's marketing department listening to people keen and wail on the customer service lines down in Atlanta. This infamous blunder is a perfect example of a brand that lost its bearings—or its understanding of how customers find theirs. Because they were losing business to Pepsi, and because Pepsi did a hair better in blind taste tests with kids—which should make you think of the danger of believing the Squiggly Line, or short-term data—Coke concluded that the soda market was all about taste. In fact, taste preference was simply the tangible manifestation of something far deeper—the brand as a personal anchor, and a badge of self-definition. Coke's vitality and contemporary relevance as a brand *was* ebbing, but the company still had an enormous well of cultural history to draw from. Coke was a literal translation of the word "America" to a lot of people. It was a cultural North Star in its own right. What Coca-Cola found was that people didn't want taste from their soft drink; they wanted a personal identity shaped by a sense of belonging. They wanted to buy a lifestyle, not a flavor. So the company's decision to attack its own brand caused a loss of cultural and personal stability in the ranks of its customers.

McDonald's voice, just like Darrell Bricker's, will be familiar to you once you finish this book, especially when we discuss questions like the North Star—that is, questions that bridge the gap between data that describes customer behavior and data that helps decision makers understand and promote customer satisfaction. In short, the North Star question, which should be asked as frequently as the Essential Question, is meant to remind you and your colleagues that if you put your customers second, before long there may be no one left in first place.

>> Should You Believe the Squiggly Line?

Hollywood executives obsess over the opening-weekend box office. Wall Street investors pay more attention to short-term swings in stock price than to earnings potential over the long run. Real estate analysts get hung up on the monthly figures for housing starts. Baseball fans talk about their favorite players' batting averages over the past three weeks. If you do the same thing before making business decisions, you've started to believe the Squiggly Line.

The problem begins when we start looking at small slices of a longer line of data. Too often we focus on the last bit of movement on the line. We're up five points. Or we're down three points. It may be true at the moment, but how relevant are those short-term movements to your long-term objectives? Even more important, do they fall into the standard margin of error—that is, are the changes just noise? In addition, are the near-term microchanges game changers, or far less important than the long tail of your product's or service's life cycle?

Sure, short-term reporting is vital. In order to hit your annual targets, you need to measure progress month by month, week by week, and sometimes even day by day. But what's the point in celebrating a 3 percent hike in last month's sales if your competitor's sales have risen 7 percent? In the same way, why congratulate yourself on increased profitability dependent on "cost take-outs"—that is, reductions in your workforce and facilities costs—that may leave your company unable to supply the market when economic conditions improve? And while price reductions during economic slowdowns may lead to temporarily higher sales numbers, what if, by changing the shopping experience— that is, the brand—you alienate your core customers in the process?*

And what if the Squiggly Line is the result of statistical tricks, either in measurement or presentation? Home prices may be up 10 percent over last year's numbers for the same month but still 25 percent below the peak reached three years earlier. Progress? Certainly. Cause for celebration? Probably not. So keep in mind that it's easy to manipulate a data set, especially by restricting it to the short term.

There are times, however, when the Squiggly Line is an omen of things to come, which brings us to our next section, and our next question.

SECTION TWO: INSIGHT

By reading this book you've already identified yourself as a victim of information overload or, like us, a data addict in recovery. The next three questions, therefore, are meant either to protect you from information you don't need or to help you break the habit of generating it. You can use them to reduce your dependence on data by doing things differently from the way you've always done them, and by reconsidering the ultimate purpose of data collection and analysis. With that in mind, there's no better place to start than with the following question.

---

*These last few sentences demonstrate just how thin the lines are between the Fire Hose Questions. Although the Squiggly Line was the focus of the first question—i.e., Is overreacting to the short-term business cycle and lopping off big parts of your workforce the right move?—it led directly to a North Star question.

>> What Surprised You?

All too often we scan reports looking for confirmation, not information. Or we sit at meetings trying to figure out what management is willing to hear, not what the numbers are telling us. Game-changing information is almost always a surprise, but you'll miss it if you're in the habit of looking for corroboration instead of information. The same thing will happen if you routinely dismiss any number that strays outside the usual range as an "outlier."

Data overload makes potentially valuable surprises even harder to recognize. If you can't keep up with the stream of information blasting out of the Fire Hose every day, how can you zero in on the deviations from the norm that might be real game changers?

Company culture can also be a powerful constraint on the search for surprises. Does upper-level management encourage you to question conventional wisdom? Do you ever see your boss pointing to numbers that *don't* support existing strategies or accepted practices? What about you? Are you constantly alert to surprises in the numbers, and do you encourage those who report to you to follow your lead?

If you keep your eyes open for surprising data, or unforeseen numbers, they can end up breathing life into your go-to-market strategies, making the case for value propositions, or cutting through the chatter to reveal what your customers really think about your brand. Surprises can also make you aware of an opportunity long before your competitors realize it's there. Perhaps even more important, surprises can serve as early warnings, when there's still time to do something about approaching danger (see "What Does the Lighthouse Reveal?" below).

>> What Does the Lighthouse Reveal?

The sweeping beam of the lighthouse reveals not only the rocks along the shore but also the channel that will lead your ship safely to port. What's more, the lighthouse serves as an example itself—that is, as a successfully realized project that will inspire similarly successful efforts.

Any project you undertake, whether it involves introducing a new product or trying to expand existing services, will be accompanied by far more information than you need. Therefore, you need to learn to separate the important signals from the noise, and the useful information from the false, misleading, or irrelevant data. As you sort through those numbers, the most telling information can serve as a lighthouse of sorts, guiding your subsequent efforts and keeping your team on course. This approach also involves recognizing the difference between important goals and *urgent* needs. Returning to a maritime analogy, while it's important to plot your course carefully, taking tides and currents into consideration, it's far more important to stay off the rocks. Data overload, unfortunately, produces so much glare that sometimes it's hard to pick out the lighthouse and to see the rocks you need to avoid.

>> Who Are Your Swing Voters?

The swing voter can make or break your bottom line. Categorizing, segmenting, and targeting your swing voters is the most cost-effective method for driving your company's growth. Yet businesspeople, just like politicians, don't pay enough attention to the middle. All too often, business strategies focus on the extremes—i.e., either extremely satisfied customers or the critics who'll never switch to your brand. Like drivers approaching a traffic light, we really only care about the red or the green, and ignore the yellow.

We see this scenario played out in every presidential election. Seeking their party's nomination, candidates appeal to their political base—that is, the more motivated, highly partisan members of their parties, because those are the voters most likely to participate during the primaries. And in doing so, politicians often end up alienating the vast group of voters in the middle—that is, the "swing voters" without whom they cannot win a general election.

Most customers, just like most voters, fall between the extremes. They occupy the wide middle ground that separates your highly satisfied cohorts and your competitors' highly satisfied cohorts. They are far more likely either to leave your competitors and come to you, or to leave you and go to your competitors, and yet how much data do you see on their preferences, behavior, or tendencies? Identifying these swing voters—i.e., potential customers, or potential defectors—and convincing them to stay on your side of the fence, or better yet to hop across it to give your product a try, often constitutes your company's best, lowest-cost opportunity for growth.

Here too, data overload tends to reinforce the status quo. If most of the data you see focuses either on the highly satisfied or the highly dissatisfied customer, then your swing voter becomes harder and harder to find, understand, and cultivate.

SECTION THREE: DELIVERY

>> The Three W's: What? So What? Now What?

The seventh Fire Hose Question is actually three questions in one—a sort of "buy one, get two free." The "What?" is the right set of numbers. The "So What?" is the insight that your analysis of the numbers produces. The "Now What?" leads to the steps you take as a result of good data collection and analysis.

This three-part approach not only provides you with a simple framework for cutting through information overload; it also allows you to tell a story—the most effective form of communication. A story with a beginning, middle, and end. A story that will make data collection and analysis serve as catalysts for action, not as ends in themselves.

Although we tend to use the Fire Hose Questions one by one, as the occasion calls for them, by thinking in terms of the Three W's, you can divide the questions into groups, each with a distinct purpose and a part to play in the sequence of discovery. The "What?" which includes the Essential Question, the North Star, and the Squiggly Line, contains the questions we use to gather information. The "So What?" which includes the Surprise, the Swing Voter, and the Lighthouse, is designed to develop insights. Finally, the "Now What?" is the question you ask before initiating action. Because that, after all, is what the Fire Hose Questions are all about.

>> Presenting Your Findings

In addition to the seven Fire Hose Questions, *Drinking from the Fire Hose* includes a final, brief lesson on presenting your results. We included it because learning to manage data overload also means never turning the Fire Hose on your colleagues or clients again. But even if you don't use the "Spray and Pray" approach, you'll still need to communicate the

14

small amount of relevant information you gather to point to your conclusions, and present your findings. To do that, you have to know how to effectively communicate those findings.

While we won't go deep into the principles here, the slide shown below is a good example of presenting results. The headline reports the basic information, the numbered points beneath it add additional information, and the arrow charts to the right add effective visual reinforcement. It's a slide, in short, that you don't turn away from—a slide you actually *want* to understand.

[FIGURE 5]

OVERALL LOYALTY HAS SHIFTED TOWARD PRECRISIS LEVELS AND IN FAVOR OF OUR TARGET

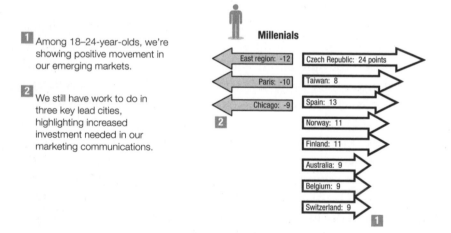

Succinct, crisp, precise reports and presentations are your goal. But exactly how do you do that with numbers? Data-oriented presentations, even when focused only on the information you want to communicate, and the resulting insights can still fail because of poor technique.

The most effective model we have seen is the Three W's—i.e., what, so what, and now what—but the secret lies in maintaining the balance between them. Most presentations present far too much data—that is, they spend too much of the listener's time on the "what" and not nearly enough on the "so what" and the "now what."

>> Minuet or Heavy Metal?

While using the Three W's as a guide for producing and reporting results does mean grouping the Fire Hose Questions according to their underlying purposes, as you turn the pages of this book you'll find that the seven Fire Hose Questions don't have an order of importance.

This is a key point.

As a sign of how seriously we believe this, you might have noticed that we didn't give the questions numbers. The first is no more important than the fourth, and the fourth no more important than the seventh. And depending on the situation, you might ask only one of them, you might pick two or three, or you might ask every one of them. This flexibility is not random; we created it by design. Why? Because looking for your customer's North Star naturally leads to an Essential Question, just like looking for Lighthouse data should make you wonder whether you're looking at a Squiggly Line. What's more, you'll almost certainly want to ask different questions at different points in the product life cycle as more information becomes available, or your plans are completed.

In fact, once we had finally settled on the Fire Hose Questions and begun to put them to work ourselves, we found that we started thinking about them the way a musician thinks about the seven whole notes of the C major scale.* Think about it. The same seven whole notes can give you classical music and rock 'n' roll, show tunes and hip-hop, reggae and country and western. In other words, no single note in the scale is more important than any other, and while musicians from Beethoven to the Beatles have arranged them in completely different ways, the results have been equally successful.

Business, like music, depends on a set of core competencies, but nearly every successful business improvises to some extent. Much like a jazz musician establishes a theme, breaks it down into parts, and then rebuilds something utterly original, the seven Fire Hose Questions can be used to improvise in almost any business situation.

One last thing before we turn, one by one, to the Fire Hose Questions themselves. In the following chapters we'll introduce a variety of

---

*For the purposes of this analogy, we won't include the eighth note in the scale, or the octave, because it's just another C, with the frequency doubled.

case studies. We'll use some of them to show how these questions *might* have been put into action and others to show how they *have* been put into action. Many of those stories feature high-profile brands like IBM, Starbucks, Microsoft, Sears, Kodak, and iRobot. Others highlight startups like Drei Tauben Ltd., an early attempt to match job seekers to jobs, or Trench Fantasy, a fantasy football game that focuses on the offensive and defensive lines instead of the quarterbacks, running backs, and wide receivers who usually get all the attention. Many of the stories we tell, however, were pulled right from the headlines as we wrote this book. Given the publishing cycle, they'll be almost a year old by the time *Drinking from the Fire Hose* hits bookstores, but we'd like to think that these shorter case studies will help get you into the habit of considering the Fire Hose Questions every time you read the news, just like we do.

Now, having given you an idea of what's ahead, let's move from theory to practice and show you how asking the right question, at just the right time, makes managing data overload possible.

SECTION ONE

DISCOVERY

What Is the Essential Business Question?

"For your information, I would like to ask a question."

—SAMUEL GOLDWYN

Every successful business decision depends on the answer to one Essential Question. Without that question, generating data or studying the data you have is pointless. Asking it enables you to focus instead on the data you need. The data that will lead to the one indispensable piece of information you need to move forward.

The answer to the Essential Question, in fact, will unlock a whole set of answers and let you know whether you should go left or right, or stay on course. In other words, when confronting information overload, don't think in terms of data, or research, but in terms of answers. Once you know what you are asking *for*, the dialogue surrounding any undertaking will shift from data to strategy.

CHAPTER LESSONS

1. What is the one vital piece of information you need to move forward?
2. Does the data point to that vital piece of information or conceal it?

Let's say you're rolling out a new product or service. The Essential Question should lead you to the one piece of information you need to make that rollout successful. That question might be: How do we identify our most promising prospects? Once you've chosen the question, the answer might come from any of a variety of sources. It might come from existing sales data. It might come from survey data. Or it might come from the men and women out in the field, who speak to their customers almost every day. So the question doesn't determine the data set; it just pinpoints the relevant information in the data set you decide to examine. Think of that question as a valve, or a filter, on the data hose. It puts you in control. It governs the rate, flow, and direction of the data you collect and manipulate, and even helps determine how you'll be able to deliver it.

Without that precise question, though, you can find yourself poring over data for the entire industry or targeting a potential customer you cannot possibly reach. Or studying market research for similar, not identical, products. There's plenty of data out there—and that's the problem. Without the Essential Question, you're diving into the deep end of the data pool. With the right question, you can grab a bucket and scoop out only the information you need to answer that question.

If you plan to introduce a new feature on an existing product, that question might be: How can we excite our current customers with this new offering, and how can we encourage them to adopt it? Or if you're simply trying to boost sales, that question might be: What effect will pricing have on sales? The question differs, in other words, depending on your business goals—whether you're rolling out a new product, trying to stimulate sales of existing services, or looking to reestablish your customers' trust in your product or service. And by arming yourself with that question, you can defend yourself against data overload.

Figure 6, for instance, graphically illustrates the way longer-term strategic objectives are successively winnowed down until just a few basic decisions, or Essential Questions regarding new business development, remain.

But while the question differs depending on the circumstances and the objective, one truth stays the same: Our ability to come up with the answer is blunted by our addiction to data. In fact, in today's over-measured, overtracked, overreported business world, data is the morphine that numbs the senses of almost every private or public entity. But we can't seem to do without it.

[FIGURE 6]

Business Development requires a portfolio approach to place strategic investments yielding targeted successes

Strategic Objective: Create $1B in net new growth business in 5 years

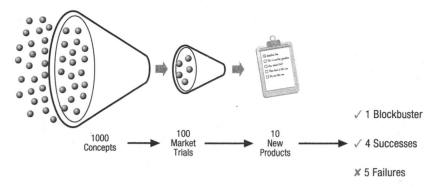

			✓ 1 Blockbuster
1000 Concepts	→ 100 Market Trials	→ 10 New Products	→ ✓ 4 Successes
			✗ 5 Failures

And when there is no data, we cook it up on the spot, because it's expected of us. It's as if no one remembers how to make a point without it.

Which brings us to Scott Penberthy, a friend and colleague from the IT side, who had so many stories to tell on this topic that we had to ask him to stick to three of his favorites.

SCOTT PENBERTHY STARTED programming shortly after the Apple II was released, in 1977. His passion for writing computer games led to a scholarship at MIT, where he earned four degrees in computer science and artificial intelligence. After finishing his Ph.D. in the nineties, Penberthy wrote the initial software for IBM's Web browser, Web application servers, and hosting business. His talents didn't go unnoticed, and before long he was appointed IBM CEO Lou Gerstner's technical assistant.

Satisfied that he'd done all he wanted to in the corporate world, he returned to his programming roots in 2005 and was quickly invited to join a series of successful start-ups (one of which will be featured in a later chapter). He now runs a software company outside New York City that specializes in iPhone, C/C++, and Objective-C applications.

Says Penberthy:

I've heard top executives of companies like IBM ask what you call the "Essential Question," and I've heard it asked at start-ups, too. And it usually doesn't concern complex data . . . that is, it usually isn't overcomplicated technically, which I tend to do personally. It almost comes down to human behavior . . . a visceral pain, or a visceral need.

In other words, Penberthy, a scientist by training and vocation, sees Essential Questions in almost purely human terms. What hurt can be eliminated, and what need met?

To give you an example, when IBM started its hosting business, I'll never forget the way the general manager came out and said, just as if he were speaking to a customer, "Of course you could clean your teeth with dental instruments, but why would you? Why not just get a dentist to do it for you? So, sure, you could host your own infrastructure, but why would you? Why don't you focus on what your real business is and leave hosting to the experts?"

Another good example came after we bought a software company, when our general manager of software was listening to a huge presentation put on by the new company. It took the team more than thirty days to put it together . . . It was very elaborate, with three or four speakers and lots and lots of data, and the GM stopped it about two thirds of the way through and said, "This is all good, guys, you did a really nice job, and I can see that there's a lot of complexity with all you're offering, but I'm a simple guy. I want vanilla, chocolate, and strawberry. So think it over, figure out what the three flavors are, why they taste good, and then come back."

Even at the time, it struck me. Here I am sitting in this austere room, with several of the top leaders of what was then a seventy-billion-dollar company, and I was expecting all kinds of science fiction, and great deep numbers, and I'm sure they were looking at them, too, but the essential business question came down to "What's the simple thing I'm getting?"

Finally, I remember a big presentation on the future of CMOS,[*]

---

[*]Complementary metal-oxide-semiconductor is a technology used to make integrated circuits.

that is, the future of chip design, and when will Moore's Law*
stop, which was a big question back in 1998. So our people did
a big presentation on when Moore's Law would stop, and they
predicted sometime in the early 2000s, and to make their point
they went through all this very complex analysis. At the end they
asked for questions. You could hear a pin drop in the room. And
the chairman looked up at the presenters, thanked them for their
work, and said, "Let me get this straight. If I understand this
right, Moore's Law is about how tiny a chip we can draw with our
pencils. That is, how tiny we can draw that transistor, and the
tinier the chip is, the more computing power we can get." And
the presenters say, "Yeah, that's pretty much it. We're drawing
the same transistor, just smaller and smaller." And then he asked
a very simple question: "Did we ever think of drawing something
different?" And it turns out that's the essence of Moore's Law:
finding ways to redraw the transistor to give you more computing power.

The Essential Question is prevalent in each example Penberthy discussed. In each of the cases, rigorous analysis and data crunching was
performed, yet the key to unlocking the insights was one simple question. The thing to remember is that this problem isn't caused by data
overload; it's caused by research without direction—that is, research
performed without an Essential Question. We'll be hearing more from
Penberthy throughout this book, but for now we want to turn to one
of the most common symptoms of data overload, something we call
"Spray and Pray."

>> Spray and Pray

If your experiences have been anything like ours, you've sat in hundreds of meetings characterized by machine-gun-fire-like bursts of
facts. The colloquial term for this approach is "Spray and Pray." In
other words, the presenter *sprays* every number or factoid he or she
can find onto the pages of a report—or the slides of a PowerPoint

*Intel cofounder Gordon Moore's famous maxim from 1965: "The number of transistors
and resistors on a chip doubles every 18 months." Moore now says he did not initially
specify eighteen months; either way, he eventually lengthened the period to twenty-four
months, the standard still used today.

presentation—and then *prays* that someone, somewhere, will see something that's relevant. (And even if that doesn't happen, everyone around the table is usually so shell-shocked by the time it's all over that they don't know what to say or what to ask.) That, sad as it is to say, is the purpose of the Spray and Pray approach, and it's getting easier to do every day, given the deluge of information being generated.

Twenty years ago, when someone dimmed the lights and shone some hard numbers on the screen, everyone in the room sat up and looked. You might have seen national sales data first, then regional sales data, and if your research guys were really, really good, you might even have seen those numbers broken down by age group or gender. Now, anyone can gather enough data from a quick Internet search to fill an hourlong meeting—whether or not that data is relevant (see Figure 7). Used this way, numbers aren't meant to provide information, but to hide the fact that the presenter doesn't really have anything to say.

We are willing to bet that about ten seconds after you started trying to make sense of this slide, you gave up. So did we. There's clearly too much information—and yet some of the numbers may be valuable. In fact, some of them may even be vital, but how would you know? That is, how would you know where to look, and in what context?

At the end of this book, we'll spend some time discussing methods for boiling information like this down, but for now it's enough to say that the Essential Question is the simplest way to bring an end to the Spray and Pray approach. The next time you see something like this, just ask what, precisely, is the one essential piece of information? You don't need to be confrontational; just ask the presenter *why* you're looking at these numbers. Tell the presenter that you, too, believe the tables contain rich information, but where should you focus? What one thing, in other words, do all those numbers reveal that will move the project forward?

Without an answer to that question, you won't be able pull any useful information out of a data set like this, and if that set is the only source of information, you won't be able to act with any confidence. You won't be able to avoid wasting steps. And whether you're designing a marketing campaign, starting a new business, or attempting to make an existing

[FIGURE 7]

PIPELINE METRICS: DTL BUSINESS SERVICES

3RD QTR: WEEK 1

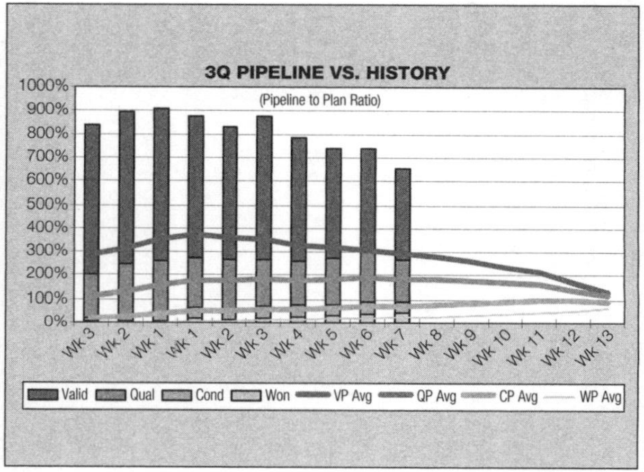

3Q PIPELINE VS. HISTORY (Pipeline to Plan Ratio)

Legend: Valid, Qual, Cond, Won, VP Avg, QP Avg, WP Avg

Continued strong coverage at 118%; down 19 pts WTW

- Acme Paper (19M) dropped out
- Regions below 90% remain: Latin America, Middle East/Africa
- All pipeline steps remain well ahead of historic track
- Qualified pipeline declined
- Conditional pipeline flat WTW
- QTD Attainment improved 6 pts WTW and remains on track
- ✓ Improvements in Americas & Europe

Suggested Focus Areas:
- ☐ Accelerated progression of strong pipeline
- ☐ Execute key deal win plans & milestones
- ☐ Additional focus on progression in weak regions

business more profitable, without an Essential Question you won't be able to confine your search to the data you need, instead of the data that's available. In addition, by asking the Essential Question you'll increase your odds of finding the information you need to make a sound decision, and then use it to convince your colleagues to take action. With that question, you'll also tend to stay away from just one type of data and look for any appropriate source of information.

DATA THAT MEASURES OR DATA THAT INFORMS?

Measuring is easy. Evaluating is hard. Using a metaphor from the kitchen, you can think of the ingredients as data that can be measured, and the recipe as data that informs. Anyone can measure flour, water, and yeast, but without the right information—that is, a recipe that gives you the correct ratio of the various ingredients—the mixture will never become bread, pizza, or cookies.

Take a look at the slide in Year-over-Year change (see Figure 8). DTL, which you will hear about later, was a trailblazing online start-up. Do you see measurements or information?

[FIGURE 8]

DTL ADOPTION AND MARKET PENETRATION: Y-O-Y CHANGE

1. Small businesses are the least aware of DTL. They are also the reluctant to purchase it.
2. Not surprisingly, Millenials are the most aware of DTL and are also the most in favor of purchasing it.
3. Business Decision Makers (BDM), though aware of DTL, are also reluctant to purchase it.

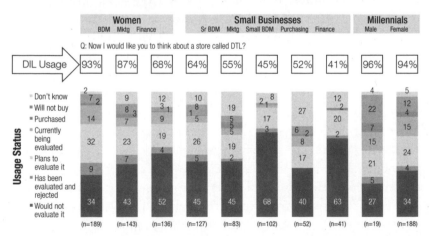

Data that measures gives us the depth, width, and height of something. It consists of dimensions, quantities, and proportions. Data that informs is dependent on perspective. It reveals substance rather than structure. It uncovers preferences, instead of the mere presence of something.

>> If the Shoe Fits

Answering an Essential Question could be a game changer for your business—or sometimes, even for an entire industry. Consider shoes. Most of us would agree that a good fit is the most important thing in a shoe. But if you sell shoes, instead of making them, the Essential Question has changed over time. Until the middle of the twentieth century, shoes were made in a few basic sizes and styles, and the customer had to fit the shoe. Then shoe stores began to carry a vast inventory of styles and sizes, and retailers devoted their time to helping customers find the pair they liked best. But whether style or fit came first, the shoe buyer's only option was the shoe store.

Enter Zappos. Instead of bowing to the prevailing custom, the founders of Zappos asked themselves whether visiting the store was really an *essential* part of buying shoes. There was no lack of information on selling shoes. The sales data existed, of course, from brick-and-mortar locations, and that information, buttressed by conventional wisdom, continued to convince conventional retailers that no one would buy shoes if they couldn't try them on first. Looking at the same data, Zappos believed this wasn't so. Consumers were beginning to buy all sorts of things online, and Zappos's management bet that customers knew their shoe sizes and their favorite brands well enough to buy them without putting them on. Finally, they guessed that the trip to the shoe store wasn't something customers looked forward to but something they did because there was no other choice.

After the Essential Question was answered, other questions followed. And this is natural. As you'll see throughout this book, one Fire Hose Question usually leads to another. In the case of online shoe sales, "What surprised you?" might well have followed the Essential Question. Online retailers, it seems, were pleasantly surprised to find out that many of their customers preferred to buy their clothes from the comfort of their own homes rather than taking a trip to the store. Zappos was clearly thinking about their customer's North Star too, and correctly guessed that the wider selection that an online store could offer would more than make up for the change in traditional shoe-buying habits.

What if the shoes didn't fit? Zappos asked only that the merchandise be returned, at no cost to the customer, in the same condition and in the same packaging in which it arrived. What about the availability of styles and sizes? Zappos, which stored its goods in huge warehouses, with no need for display, was able to carry a much larger inventory than any retail store could. What about service? Zappos didn't underestimate the importance of customer service, but the founders correctly guessed that they could provide it without ever seeing their customers face to face. And they were right. Eleven years after it opened its doors—that is, its virtual doors—60 percent of those who buy shoes from the company are repeat customers. And keep in mind that the company's success depended not on crunching numbers, but on correctly identifying the shoe buyer's Essential Question: Where can I find a large selection of reasonably priced shoes?

Now, to demonstrate that the Fire Hose approach can be used outside the business world, too, let's take a look at a recent, well-documented environmental disaster and apply the Fire Hose Questions to it retroactively.

FIRE HOSE EXERCISE NO. 1: ICELAND'S VOLCANIC ASH CLOUD

Early on the morning of Wednesday, April 14, 2010, Iceland's Eyjafjallajokull volcano erupted, sending a cloud of ash into the air high above the North Atlantic Ocean. The effect of the ash cloud was as hard to predict as the name of the volcano was to pronounce, but within twelve hours, using a computer model, British scientists working for the Met (meteorological) Office predicted that the cloud would shortly enter the atmosphere of the United Kingdom. By the following morning, in a move literally without precedent, the NATS (National Air Traffic Services) decided to shut down all air traffic in British airspace.

Iceland has a total area of less than forty thousand square miles—approximately the same size as Ohio. And there are more than eight hundred miles of open water between it and Scotland, where the ash cloud first darkened European skies. But in an eerie parallel to the collapse of Iceland's banking system, the volcano's distant eruption had an outsize impact on transportation and commerce in the U.K. and Europe. In fact, it perfectly illustrates the problems *predictive* data can cause leaders—whether in business or government—when they're forced to make real-time, real-world decisions. Physicist Haim Harari, quoted in *Wired UK*'s *Edge* blog,* saw an analogy between the ash cloud and the global financial crash of '07 similar to the one we pointed to above. Going further, Harari compared the decisions made once the ash cloud reached Europe to those made by financial regulators during the outbreak of the recent financial crisis.

> The ash crisis and the financial crisis have much in common. Both result from the fact that almost all decision makers do not understand mathematics and science, even in a rudimentary level, while most mathematicians and scientists have no feel for the real life implications of their calculations.
>
> Both camps refuse to admit their failings.
>
> "Financial engineers" created complex mathematical instruments, neglecting to emphasize unavoidable assumptions they had to make. At the same time, senior bankers and regulators did not admit that they had no idea what these papers [i.e., mortgage-backed securities] really meant, and never asked whether there were undisclosed hidden assumptions, lurking behind new quick ways of profiteering.
>
> Theoretical scientific model builders convinced authorities that the ash cloud is here or there, without bothering to measure anything, while no one asked whether the computer model was based on realistic assumptions.
>
> In both cases, decision makers, with good training in standard scientific thinking, would smell trouble immediately, even if they knew nothing about derivatives or volcanoes. The fingerprints of a sophisticated pyramid scheme should be obvious whenever one claims he can always win, and a "killer cloud" that no one can see, affecting an entire continent, based on no actual measurements, should have raised any intelligent pair of eyebrows.

*David Rowan, "Big Thinkers on What the Ash Cloud Means," Wired.co.uk, April 27, 2010, www.wired.co.uk/news/archive/2010-04/27/big-thinkers-on-what-the-ash-cloud-means.

Again, the Essential Question hadn't been answered—What concentration of volcanic ash does it take to damage a jet engine? Instead, "data" was quickly generated—or in this case, "modeled" by computers—and technologists and scientists used it to "project" the spread of the cloud (as well as its density, height, and trajectory). Regulatory agencies, airline executives, and government officials then based their decisions on the results of those projections. What's more, the data concerned the meteorological aspects of the cloud—i.e., its movement in the atmosphere, its concentration, its dispersion, etc.—not its effect on jet engines, or human beings, for that matter. Other than a handful of documented jet aircraft malfunctions, which occurred in completely different circumstances—i.e., jets passing directly over erupting volcanoes—no one had ever designated a level at which ash particulates became a threat to engine function.

By Friday, two days after the eruption, the cloud had reached Europe. And in an area where each nation controlled its own airspace, confusion reigned. No one, as we mentioned above, had reliable information regarding the effect of dispersed volcanic ash plumes on jet engine performance, so decision makers were forced to rely on the results of computer models they did not understand. Before it was all over, tens of thousands of flights had been canceled, causing the worst breakdown in civil aviation since the Second World War. Siim Kallas, the European Union's commissioner for transport, calculated the losses at more than $3 billion.

In the days following the crisis, airline executives, trade organizations, and consumer advocates asked a number of Essential Questions challenging the decisions of aviation authorities—decisions that resulted not only in devastating financial losses but incalculable emotional costs to travelers stranded in airports throughout Europe.

Doing what we can to control for the advantages of hindsight, let's use the Fire Hose Questions to see how these events might have unfolded differently. As we pointed out in the introduction, you can use the questions in any order, either one by one, or in combination. In this case, it seems clear that decision makers couldn't have gone too far wrong by starting with the Essential Question.

What, in other words, was the one vital piece of information aviation authorities needed to confront Iceland's ash cloud of 2010? We're not aeronautical engineers, and don't have *any* data on the subject, but if we'd been in their shoes, we'd like to think the following question would have come to mind: What concentration of volcanic ash is harmful to jet engines?

Keep in mind that no one was walking down the street wearing a mask. That is, no one feared the cloud would cause a health crisis (although authorities warned those with existing respiratory problems to limit their exposure). After all, by the time the plume passed over Scotland, it had drifted more than eight hundred miles across the Atlantic, at least five miles above the earth. And while measurable amounts of ash fell across the U.K. and northwestern Europe, no one seems to have worried about the effect the ash might have on crops already in the ground.* In other words, the ash cloud affected air transportation almost exclusively, and jet engines in particular. But no one even *asked* the Essential Question until hundreds of millions of dollars had been lost and the travel plans of hundreds of thousands of ticket holders interrupted.

Speaking of air travelers, we might also have asked where the customer's North Star was? And while we feel comfortable estimating that ten out of ten passengers would put "arriving safely" at the top of their North Star lists, looking back over the various pronouncements that followed the crisis, we can see virtually no evidence that governments, regulatory agencies, or even airlines assessed the impact the temporary no-fly rule would have on the "customer"—i.e., individual travelers, shipping customers, and airports themselves. What's more, while it's well understood that driving to the airport is far more dangerous than air travel itself, all travel involves a certain level of risk. But since there was no *evidence* the ash cloud substantially increased that risk—at least once it had drifted more than a thousand miles, shedding ash as it went—why was air travel across most of Europe summarily interrupted, and for so many days?

Analogies abound. The hazard posed by flocks of birds in the vicinity of airports, for instance, is well documented. One need only think back to US Airways Flight 1549, successfully ditched by Captain Chesley "Sully" Sullenberger in the Hudson River. But air traffic to

---

*Unlike the radioactive cloud released by the accident at the Chernobyl Nuclear Power Plant in April 1986, which resulted in the preventive destruction of crops and the short-term interruption of milk supplies.

and from airports surrounded by large bird populations has never been restricted as a result.

We'd like to think we might have questioned the computer model's Squiggly Line, too. The computer models used by decision makers were developed for meteorological purposes, not designed to track clouds of volcanic ash. And again, the projections were meaningless if a certain concentration of ash couldn't be said to produce a certain result. And yet projections derived from those models overruled both common sense and decades of aviation experience. Rather than being persuaded by models, someone might have picked up a phone and reached out to pilots with experience flying through dust storms (in the Middle East and North Africa) and volcanic ash (in Alaska, the Pacific Rim, and the west coast of South America).

Finally, this incident, and especially the various governmental responses to it, provided two entertaining answers to the question "What surprised you?"

First, while the U.K.'s Natural Environment Research Council (NERC) sent a propeller-powered reconnaissance flight into the plume to assess ash distribution the day after the eruption—something satellite images could not measure—Northern European authorities did not follow suit until *three days later*. An article published in the *Telegraph*'s April 19 edition found that of "the 40 test flights across Europe, including a British Airways flight on Sunday [April 18], none found any evidence of ash in jet engines, windows, or lubrication systems." According to an article published in the same newspaper a day earlier, even the data gathered on the first propeller-driven test flight the day after the volcano erupted was "inconclusive." To us, this looks like a pitch-perfect example of finding data to support a theory, rather than arriving at a theory as a result of data analysis.

Second, although the ash cloud caused flights to be canceled in virtually every country in Europe, as well as many countries outside the formal boundaries of the union, five days passed before European transportation ministers got around to scheduling a conference call. In the meantime, air travel restrictions were split between a number of uncoordinated fiefdoms, with travelers, businesses, and even military commands left scratching their heads. Nor were public entities the only victims of poor catastrophe-based risk management. As noted in the April 20, 2010, edition of *The Economist*:

Such events are calling standard methods of risk management into question, says Erwann Michel-Kerjan of the Wharton Business School. While not exactly a "black swan" (a volcano erupting is hardly unthinkable, even if it is highly unpredictable), the ash cloud is one of a series of recent catastrophes—natural disasters, terrorism, economic crises, pandemics—that have wrong-footed globalised firms.

While we admit that the answers we've given to the Fire Hose Questions in the above exercise have the advantage of hindsight, you may have noticed that not a single one of them depended on the collection or analysis of data. Again, we're not anti-data. We love numbers. But numbers are a means to an end, not an end in themselves. And when no good numbers exist—or when there are too many—commonsense questions often point the way toward the simplest solutions.

>> Misinformation

One of the other things we stress in data rehab is the ability to recognize *misleading* information when you see it. And that includes data displayed in a misleading fashion, which changes its significance. We'll turn to this in greater depth in a later chapter, but a good, simple example is a chart that uses something other than zero for the *y* axis. By limiting the *y,* or vertical, axis, to a narrower band, the changes along that axis appear to be far more volatile than they really are—that is, than they are in relation to the entire *y* axis.

If, for instance, you track the movements of the Dow Jones Industrial Average (DJIA) over a single day, but frame that activity in a range just below its highest and lowest points—say, between 11,000 and 12,000—you will almost certainly still see movements exaggerated by the extremely short term. If, on the other hand, you put the recent data in perspective, and graph it on a complete *y* axis—that is, extending the range from zero to 12,000—the same daily activity will look far less volatile.

When is this—that is, a misguided focus on a narrow range of data—most likely to happen? When no one has asked a question—an Essential Question—that automatically determines the proper scope of the data.

Another source of misleading information comes from pulling results from surveys meant to measure one thing and using them to explain another. An October 9, 2009, blog post from ReadWrite Enterprise raised this issue in response to the results of a consumer survey of small businesses conducted by a major American bank. Presuming for the moment that the survey itself was statistically representative—i.e., that its five hundred respondents represented an accurate cross section of small businesses in America—the bank reported that the survey's "findings" showed that "social networks are not lead generators" for small businesses. As blogger Alex Williams noted, the results were most likely accurate. That is, for most small businesses, social networks did not yet serve as generators of leads. But looking at the same numbers the bank did, Williams was more interested in the 12 percent of respondents who reported that social networks were either "very helpful or somewhat helpful" in generating leads, rather than the 63 percent who reported they were not. In order to judge the importance of that 12 percent in terms of a trend, though, Williams noted that similar data from the previous year would be necessary. Given, however, that the results were generated by a "much larger questionnaire concerning small businesses and the recession," no such numbers were available. Perhaps the most revealing information regarding the survey, though, was the author's discovery that at the time of the survey, the bank itself—again, one of the largest in the United States—had an extremely limited presence on the country's major social network sites. The results reported by the bank, in other words, might well have been influenced by its own reluctance to use social networks, not an unwillingness on the part of small businesses.

As you can imagine, this sort of data-fueled confusion occurs over and over, but if you keep your eyes open we think you'll recognize it far more quickly than you used to. We'll end with one more topical example. In an article published in the December 16, 2010, *Wall Street Journal*, reporter Andrew Batson questioned the calculus by which the *full value* of iPods "assembled" in China was added to that country's export figures (by both the United States and China).

> How is this possible? The researchers say traditional ways of measuring global trade produce the number but fail to reflect the complexities of global commerce where the design, manufacturing and assembly of products often involve several countries.

"A distorted picture" is the result they say, one that exaggerates trade imbalances between nations.

Given the rising tension between China and the United States as the result of the latter's continuing trade imbalance, and the pressure being applied to China to allow its currency to rise in value against the U.S. dollar, these sorts of misleading statistics are capable of causing harm to more than the bottom line.

Leaving politics aside, let's turn to data generated by retail purchases and bring in Jim Dippold, a colleague of ours who's looked at information overload, and the Essential Question, from the vantage point of the supermarket aisle.

JIM DIPPOLD IS senior vice president of marketing at the Symphony IRI Group. Before coming to IRI, he was one of the founding members of EYC, a privately held information technology and services company that helped retailers implement shopper-driven solutions, both internally and in collaboration with their traditional partners.

His early years in the field were spent at the Nielsen Company. While there—building on his long experience in category management, inventory replenishment, store operations, and visual merchandising—he led the industry into the business of computer-aided-design space management software.

Despite being one of the first in the retail sector to welcome massive amounts of data, Dippold is a firm believer that the "interrogation" of data has to follow an initial question, or a specific goal, and he begins by discussing the topic in terms of pricing and shelf display.

You've got to remember that this question changes according to circumstances. Pricing decisions, for instance, depend on who a company's major competitors are. You'll use one price if Walmart is your competitor, and another price if Whole Foods is your competitor. Just like the size of the products you'll put in place for a store that's located in town, where people live in apartments and don't have a lot of space, is smaller than the size of the products you'll put on the shelves for people who live in the suburbs.

But in order to make it simple for people to be able to answer those kinds of questions, by which I mean the sort of products you choose to display, and the sizes you offer them in, you've got to get the question right before you start analyzing data. And that's tough. You've got to boil all the possibilities down to what exactly it is you're looking for. For what you need to know to make your decision. That allows me to do the analysis the right way, and to know how to present the results so that it will be easy for you to make your decision.

In other words, for data to be valuable, it has to answer an Essential Question.

ONE COMPANY'S SOLUTION

American Express, an early adopter of the Essential Question approach, now asks this question whenever they conduct research or study existing data. Their Global Marketplace Insights team (GMPI), in particular, has implemented a rigorous Essential Question program, driven by Adam Rothschild. In fact, that process guides every initial discussion with GMPI's business partners, and all RFPs (request for proposals) from vendors. It's mandated for every proposal, and thus shapes not only data collection itself but also analysis and reporting (Figure 9).

Include the EQ slide in every deck

[FIGURE 9]

Answer the EQs and provide direction via Implications

Business Question	Answer—What Should You Do?	Food for Thought
Initiative Questions	Conclusions/ Recommendations	Key Findings/Support
How are our marketing programs changing consumers' perceptions to drive demand and grow market share?	• By reaching prospective customers via Four Square location-based promotions you are engaging them at the point of purchase. • Explore increasing text-based marketing and digital channels to match the lifestyle of the millennial target consumer.	• 64% of redeemers are 22 to 29 years old • 27% more favorable after seeing the promo • 19% are aware of the new features • 12% would consider purchasing

As you can see, Rothschild and Bernow pose Essential Questions that have to be answered by *actions* (e.g., go, no-go, create a pilot, etc.). Note also that these questions might be answered by a single study, or could require multiple inputs.

Now, having taken a look at a few Essential Questions in the tech world, online shoe retailer Zappos, and a recent environmental disaster, let's turn to a company that wasn't quite as successful as the shoe retailer, even though its initial prospects may have been brighter.

>> A Promising Start-up Fails to Answer the Essential Question

Thump!

The last one of the three men to take his seat pulled a proposal off the stack he'd just dropped on the conference table, his voice reverberating in the small room: "Now it's time to find out if anyone will really use a bulletin board system to look for a job." With that simple, as yet unanswerable statement hanging in the air, the three men began one of the first attempts to create a system of computerized classified ads. The year was 1992.

They didn't have a lot of capital, but they had data. In fact, they had reams of data.

They had annual advertising expenditures, both retail and classifieds, for every major newspaper in the country. Those figures were further broken down into help-wanted, real estate, and automotive ads. They had national newspaper-advertising expenditures by small, medium, and large businesses. They had readership profiles broken down by race, gender, marital status, education, and age. They had circulation figures. They had point-of-purchase data broken down by home delivery, newsstand, or coin box.

They had market opportunity analyses, competitive landscape evaluations, and market share models. They had studied buyers' and sellers' attitudes, awareness, and usage. They had a SWOT (strengths/weaknesses/opportunities/threats) analysis, and had subjected their numbers to a Five Forces analysis.

They had sales projections, data on market demand, customer segmentation charts, channel strategies, competitive positioning information, a go-to-market strategy, and a well-articulated value proposition. And all the data was synthesized and integrated. It had been poked and probed. The men had, in fact, built a small mountain of what they thought was data that informed, only to find, in the end, that it was data that measured.

That was the start of Drei Tauben Ltd. (DTL)—German for "Three Pigeons." Don't remember the company? Neither does anyone else, but you've probably used a form of the system they pioneered almost twenty years ago. And while the company was just one of the many start-ups of the dot-com era that failed to see the twenty-first century, the nature of its demise reveals a few critical truths about product development and market analysis—or, more precisely, about asking the *wrong* Essential Question.

The concept was simple: an online system of help-wanted ads. Armed with their proposal, which was based on the mountain of data they had gathered and analyzed, the three men began their journey as vendors at a job fair. They were given a standard three-by-six-foot table. To their left was another start-up, called Resumix. Its business plan called for taming the paper beast by scanning résumés and using optical character recognition to convert the text into bits and bytes. We'll bet you've never heard of Resumix either, although it enjoyed the sort of success familiar to many start-ups in the dot-com era. It was bought out by a larger company.

To DTL's right was another start-up. Strangely enough, it was called Monster.com. The men who sat at that table described it as an *online* clearinghouse where companies and job seekers could connect for employment opportunities.

Sandwiched between those two start-ups, the Three Pigeons made their pitch to everyone who walked by. Just like their neighbor to the right, they offered access to help-wanted ads through the use of a phone line and a modem, but they also had something more: a built-in customer base as the result of a creative marketing arrangement with university alumni associations. That arrangement was their answer to the classic push-pull problem all innovative new products face: How do you demonstrate the new product's usefulness, and in so doing generate demand, so that prospective customers don't feel they have to wait until someone else shows some interest in the model?

DTL came up with an exceptionally creative solution. They went to the alumni associations of the nation's leading technology schools and offered the members of those associations free, unlimited access to the bulletin board service—in exchange for ad space in alumni publications. Thus, the associations could offer their alumni an innovative employment service, and DTL could use that alumni base to attract customers. It seemed like a classic win-win—DTL gained broad exposure through its association with well-known academic institutions, and the graduates of those institutions received a valuable service at no cost.

Furthermore, the company's listings targeted technology jobs, believing that both employers and prospective employees in that field would be the first to experiment with new ways of finding and filling jobs. And for two years the company had a string of small, regular successes. DTL was written up in *The Wall Street Journal. Investor's Business Daily* picked up the story. And the company was featured in a book called *Electronic Job Search Revolution*. But shortly before *Inc.* magazine contacted the company to propose a feature story, the three entrepreneurs shut the company down. They had built an early modem-based system from scratch, had signed up eleven universities, had hundreds of ads placed in alumni magazines, and even had a half-dozen paying companies. They had more data than money, though, and when the market didn't materialize as quickly as they thought it would, operational costs finally exhausted their capital. History would prove them right, but before it did, they were history themselves.

How did they go wrong? They had a good product and a well-thought-out business plan. That plan was built on market forecasts, industry reports, and case studies of their competitors—both those already in the business and those that might enter the new online sector. They were faster, better, and cheaper. And they focused on the basics—that is, on the blocking and tackling questions of who, what, when, and why. And they thought to themselves, If we could get just 1 or 2 percent of this huge market, we'll be wildly profitable. But while they had good measurements, they had poor information. Put another way, they failed to ask several Essential Questions.

First, how willing were their customers—both those seeking employment and those seeking employees—to change the way they did business? And if they were willing to try something new, how much time would pass before that change became the new standard? Even more important, DTL didn't ask itself how newspapers—their most important, traditional, entrenched competitors—would react to them, especially since the traditional business model of those competitors was rapidly failing. They thought they would be embraced as a complementary outlet for classified-section content, which in time would generate an additional revenue stream for the newspapers. Instead, they were ignored. As Gerry Crispin, one of the founders, put it, they failed to see that the newspapers with which they partnered were unable to see what they were doing, because *none of them had modems or computers.* Put another way, DTL didn't consider the nature of the business ecosystem they intended to enter, or determine which players would benefit and which players would be threatened by the new model (Figure 10).

[FIGURE 10]

IN THE EARLY 1990S, ONLINE CLASSIFIEDS ARE MISUNDERSTOOD BY NEWSPAPERS AND THREATEN THE PRIMARY DISTRIBUTION MODEL

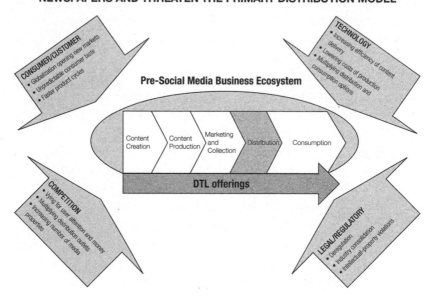

Despite having done their homework, and despite having conceived a viable strategy for their business, they failed to ask themselves Essential Questions about customer behavior—especially regarding the speed with which both end customers and suppliers would adapt to a new, rapidly evolving model of communication and interaction.

As you may have guessed by now, one of us was a principal in the above story, and the other a behind-the-scenes adviser. In other words, one of us has suffered the consequences of failing to ask the Essential

Question, and the other has been kind enough to forget the advice he offered—i.e., that the service be made available "via the Internet," instead of through a proprietary bulletin board system (BBS).*

BBSs were popular mechanisms at the time, but they rapidly disappeared with the advent of the World Wide Web. At the time, DTL's principals thought of the Internet as an outlier and set that system's possibilities to one side, thinking they'd consider them when they had more time—once the company was up and running. That time never came, but the experience wasn't without its reward. The short, exciting history of Drei Tauben Ltd. was the catalyst for this book.

Since then we've both come to understand that no matter how much data you have, or how carefully you've planned your strategy, someone in the room always has to step back and ask: "Is that really true? Is that what our customers really think? Is that what we really need to focus on?" In other words, no matter what sort of data you've gathered, someone has to be able to find the answer to the Essential Question in it.

CHAPTER ONE TAKEAWAYS

1. The Essential Question should be prescriptive. It should be written so that it has to be answered by a business *action* (e.g. target, explore, go, no-go, continue, etc.)

2. Whenever data sets seem to hide more than they reveal, ask yourself the Essential Question: What one vital piece of information is necessary to move forward? The rest of the data may be interesting, and sometimes even important, but focusing on one actionable result is the best way to find your way through the fog of data.

3. The way data is generated, analyzed, or presented often influences the results, to say nothing of your perception of them. Develop basic standards of data collection, analysis, and presentation, and insist that others do the same.

---

*BBSs were early computer systems that allowed users to connect via a phone line and modem.

4. Essential Questions do not have to be complicated. In fact, the simpler question is usually the better question—e.g., What business am I in? What am I providing of value to the customer? Which customers will pay for it?

5. Develop the habit of asking the Essential Question and not only will your insight into business solutions grow, but your personal brand will be that of a trusted adviser, not just a number cruncher.

CHAPTER TWO

Where Is Your Customer's North Star?

"There is no hitching post in the universe."

—ALBERT EINSTEIN

Managing information overload doesn't mean avoiding data. As we said earlier, we're data guys, but, that said, we continually remind ourselves that the kind of data we're looking for tells us what our customer wants. So start meetings by talking about the customer—not about numbers or data. Put the customer's voice front and center in any presentation. As obvious as this seems, and as basic an approach as it is, it is very unusual in today's data-driven business world.

Think about it. By rote, we scrutinize every plan for its impact on revenue. We generate spreadsheets for every major decision, new product introduction, or strategic initiative. We forecast returns and response rates, project growth rates, estimate sales, and study the impact of each of them on the bottom line. And any new initiative that gets over these hurdles is likely to move forward.

But how often do you consider the impact of the plan on the customer?

CHAPTER LESSONS

1. Uncover your customer's needs and wants in your existing data.
2. Confirm that the numbers you're using amplify the customer's voice, not muffle it.

44

   3. Make sure the customer's voice can be heard and that it's lis-
      tened to.

The customer is usually mentioned in the middle of a review, not at the beginning, and rarely at the end. When you ask your team, "Are you sure that's what the customer wants?" don't you usually get an answer like this: "Yes, we've considered the customer's point of view. In fact, we conducted *six* focus groups in *three* different cities, and we used the results as the basis for our plans." Wow. Six groups in three cities. Guess we're ready to go to market.

It takes guts to put the customer's desires first, and constant vigilance to see those desires satisfied. It requires long-term thinking, the readiness to challenge established practices, and the willingness to change your delivery of information. This is true of a request for proposal, a business case, or a presentation. And while making these changes isn't easy, we recommend the simple approach we use to keep the customer first when we're drinking from the Fire Hose—a one-page approach we call the Customer Impact Assessment (CIA). Again, managing data overload doesn't mean avoiding information. Most of the time it means using the data you already have *differently*. It means using that data to locate the customer's North Star, and then using that star to guide every one of your company's initiatives—every strategy, every action, and every communication.

Something's wrong when mediocre service is the norm and customer satisfaction is the exception. Of course, it's easy to believe the opposite is true, given all the energy directed toward loyalty, advocacy, and customer satisfaction. Let's take air travel as an example. Some airlines now make you buy a ticket for your *luggage*. According to the *Los Angeles Times*, "airlines reported the highest quarterly profit margins in years bolstered by revenues from luggage fees and other charges. The profit margins for the country's largest airlines were boosted by increasing revenues that the carriers are collecting in fees charged to passengers to check baggage, change reservations, fly standby and buy food, drinks, pillows, blankets and entertainment, among other charges."* In fact, revenue from ancillary fees, including

*Hugo Martin, "Profit Margins for Airlines Soaring," *Los Angeles Times*, December 20, 2010.

bag fees, reservation change fees, and pet transportation charges, grew nearly 10 percent, to $2.1 billion, compared with the same period in 2009, according to the U.S. Department of Transportation. The revenue from baggage-collection fees alone rose threefold (see Figure 11 below).

As you can see, between 2008 and 2010 customers were charged more than half a billion dollars to take their personal items along when they traveled—on top of the price they paid for their airfare. So while it looks like the airlines are doing well, are they doing so by looking for their customer's North Star or their customer's wallet? The question, then, is whether this is a reasonable, customer-focused redesign of the pricing model—where those who carry more luggage are charged more—or simply a new variation of the same old business game, that is, with more focus on the bottom line than the customer.

Or how about consumer banking? Think of the endless fees you're charged for the *privilege* of putting *your* money in your bank's hands. If you don't keep the minimum balance in your savings account, your bank charges you $15 or $20 a month. And when you overdraw your debit card and your bank charges you $35—sometimes five or six times in the same day—is your bank taking care of you or taking advantage of you? Put another way, is the fee structure set up so the bank takes care of you or so you take care of your bank?

[FIGURE 11]

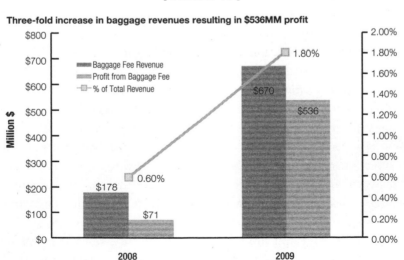

Three-fold increase in baggage revenues resulting in $536MM profit

Don't get us wrong. We're as pro-business as we are pro-data. But we believe that what's good for the customer is good for the business—not the other way around. To us, in fact, it seems that the customer is being moved further and further away from the center of the business universe. And while that's disappointing, it's also somewhat understandable, because building, or maintaining, customer satisfaction is hard work. It requires trade-offs and long-term thinking. Just look at the data. Even companies with good intentions have seen their products, programs, and services slip into mediocrity because they couldn't keep their customers satisfied. A few automobile manufacturers come to mind. Some cell phone manufacturers, too. To say nothing of phone and cable companies, Internet service providers, one or two computer makers, and at least one pharmaceutical company—all of whom seem to have caused more harm than good.

What's worse, the voluminous sales data that's used to track customers' buying behavior—which yields the crudest measure of customer satisfaction—completely ignores customer *dissatisfaction*. RFID (radio-frequency identification) chips allow you to watch your products move from the factory floor to the point of sale, and Universal Product Code (UPC) scanners reveal how quickly your products flow out of the store. But they tell you nothing about your customers' wants—only whether they're buying, and what they're buying, given what's available. And while individual shoppers, in order to benefit from in-store sales, allow stores to build databases that track their buying habits, those records also tell businesses nothing about sales opportunities they might be missing. In other words, this sort of data is great for someone in operations, not someone in marketing.

If you're not living off the grid, the odds are high that you have at least one grocery store customer loyalty card in your wallet. You swipe it every time you go through the supermarket checkout, and you get some instant savings on whatever items the store decides to discount. But have you ever received a custom discount based on your previous transactions? The store has the data. They know what you buy, which brands you use, and how often you shop. Imagine if they e-mailed you a preformatted, custom shopping list, built from your past three months' transactions, organized by aisle to speed up your trip—not designed to make you run the gantlet of impulse buys you've never once put on *your* list. Wouldn't you shop at a store like that more often? But why stop there? Imagine a retailer that went one step further and offered you unique discounts based on the brands you regularly purchase, as well as the complementary items associated with those products. Wouldn't you tell your friends about a store like this? Finally, ask yourself whether you usually end up buying what you want, instead of what's available. Customer loyalty programs could address that issue—if they were guided by the customer's North Star, instead of the cash register.

Given his lengthy experience in the field, it's only right to bring in Jim Dippold to comment on this topic. Dippold, in short, makes it clear that the technology already exists to make tracking the customer's North Star profitable for both the customer and retail businesses—it's just a matter of making the customer, not the cash register, the primary focus of marketing efforts.

> The world is changing. The question used to be "How do I sell more cans of Coca-Cola?" The question now is "How do I meet this customer's needs better, so I can sell them more?" So it's a more holistic approach to the customer. What if, for instance, we identify customers who buy expensive cheeses? Then let's make sure we have related items like good wines, and good crackers, to meet those needs too. At the same time, we might look at another group for whom the kinds of products on the shelves aren't nearly as important as the convenience with which they can put a meal on the table, so let's make sure we meet the needs of those customers, too. As you can see, even though modern technology has made it possible to segment customers, it's still tough from, say, a whole food retailer's point of view, because they've got a lot of different constituencies coming into their stores. Therefore, they have to figure out what each group's needs are, and then communicate individual solutions to each group on a one-on-one basis.
>
> I guess you could say I'm really trying to move grocery stores from a model based on a single circular in the weekend newspaper, to actually being able to personalize circulars to each group, or even each individual.

The point is that you can use sales data to drive sales—for instance, if you stack soda at the end of the aisle, you can move more of it—or to tailor your offerings to your customers. And while the former approach may lead to more immediate results, the latter will lead to more lasting benefits. As Dippold puts it, "If I know that a customer buys dog food once a month, what's the point in sending him a circular for dog food one week after his last purchase?" Again, make the customer, not the cash register, the focus of your marketing efforts.

THE CUSTOMER FIGHTS BACK

WHEN DESIGNING THEIR technologically advanced customer loyalty programs—again, programmed according to their own North Stars—retailers would be wise to consider the possibility that consumers are already beginning to play the same game themselves. In fact, a *Wall Street Journal* article published ten days before Christmas 2010 described price-comparison apps that make it harder for retailers to lure shoppers with loss leaders—again, most of which weren't on customers' original wish lists—and then charge price premiums on the items their customers really want.[*]

"Until recently, retailers could reasonably assume that if they just lured shoppers to stores with enticing specials, the customers could be coaxed into buying more profitable stuff, too.

"Now, marketers must contend with shoppers who can use their smart phones inside stores to check whether the specials are really so special, and if the rest of the merchandise is reasonably priced."

The responses of some retailers to these price-comparing apps reveal just how little they care about following their customers' North Stars. Some merchants now stock items similar, but not identical to, the items they know their customers want. As a result, when customers are in the store they can't use their apps to compare prices, because while the products aren't apples and oranges, they *aren't* the same *kind* of apples, either.

Finally, let's consider loyalty programs that reward customers whose total purchases exceed a certain dollar amount. Are these programs

---

*Miguel Bustillo and Ann Zimmerman, "Phone-Wielding Shoppers Strike Fear into Retailers," *Wall Street Journal*, December 15, 2010.

really designed to benefit the customer, or the business (or airline)? In other words, do these programs offer a reasonable return on customer loyalty? Do you know how much you'll save when you exceed that dollar amount? And whether you ended up with the items you wanted to buy instead of the items they wanted to sell?

Remember, too, that customer satisfaction isn't based solely on price. Companies have many opportunities to navigate by their customers' North Stars (Figure 12).

[FIGURE 12]

10 TYPES OF INNOVATION: IT'S NOT JUST PRODUCTS

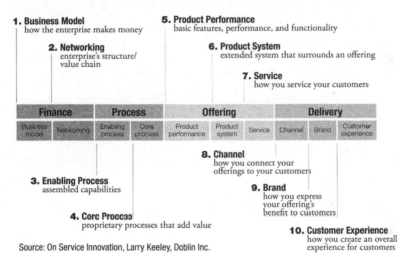

Source: On Service Innovation, Larry Keeley, Doblin Inc.

Judge your own company according to this list. How much time does your organization spend trying to find out where their customers' financial North Star is? Or their product performance star? Or their delivery star? If your company doesn't see each of these processes as opportunities to build customer satisfaction and loyalty, then they've missed something big.

Of course, most companies pay lip service to this idea, using formal market research programs or informal feedback mechanisms. But once again, if there is a concerted effort and a genuine desire to do right by the customer, why doesn't the data lead to some of the offerings we described above, all of which are clearly customer-centric—and all of which would almost certainly lead to a more profitable bottom line, over time. And customers are eager to let you know what they think (see Figure 13).

[FIGURE 13]

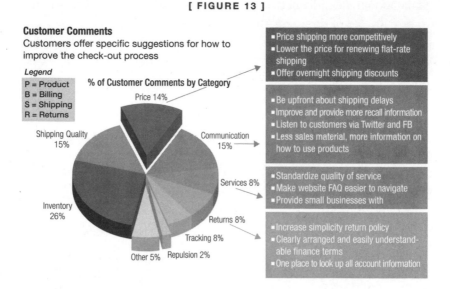

Customer Comments
Customers offer specific suggestions for how to improve the check-out process

Legend
P = Product
B = Billing
S = Shipping
R = Returns

% of Customer Comments by Category

Price 14%
Communication 15%
Services 8%
Returns 8%
Tracking 8%
Repulsion 2%
Other 5%
Inventory 26%
Shipping Quality 15%

- Price shipping more competitively
- Lower the price for renewing flat-rate shipping
- Offer overnight shipping discounts

- Be upfront about shipping delays
- Improve and provide more recall information
- Listen to customers via Twitter and FB
- Less sales material, more information on how to use products

- Standardize quality of service
- Make website FAQ easier to navigate
- Provide small businesses with

- Increase simplicity return policy
- Clearly arranged and easily understandable finance terms
- One place to look up all account information

On that note, let's bring Susan Schwartz McDonald back into the discussion.

I can tell you that [following the customer's North Star] is a battle that I've been personally waging with my clients in the pharmaceutical industry for a couple of decades, and even when I think I might be close to success I'm often disappointed, because people have a way of saying, oh yes, we finally got it, it's not all about us, we're really going to look at the barriers, say, to patient compliance with medications and really try to understand the problem. Then they turn right around and once again use that as a tool to reshape the world from their viewpoint. Sometimes there are things that you can't turn to your commercial advantage, and understanding what you can and cannot impact is really an important realization. And sometimes you have to be careful, not only to be sure that you know where the customer's North Star actually is, but that you don't speak with a voice that's clearly self-interested. The truth is that when most companies talk about seeking genuine customer insight, so they can really see the world from the customer's viewpoint, they still want to use those insights to try to change the customer's essential self, instead of organizing their product offerings by just tapping into the customer's essential self.

SCIENCE VERSUS PSYCHOLOGY

Einstein proved that "there is no hitching post in the universe"—that is, that all the stars, planets, solar systems, and even galaxies move in relation to one another. But from where we stand, theory of relativity or not, the other stars seem to swing across the sky as the earth rotates, while the North Star stays in one place, like a pin on a map.

Customers' North Stars are just as constant, and with all due respect to Einstein, you *can* hitch your company's prospects to them. Just like Polaris has guided navigators for thousands of years, your customer's North Star can guide your manufacturing, marketing, and sales decisions—and that starlight will shine right through the fog of unnecessary data.

Instead, we see far more examples of businesspeople navel-gazing—that is, looking inward, toward their own interests—than we do examples of them "stargazing," or navigating by their customers' North Stars. And it seems that this tendency becomes even more pronounced when they try to use all the data streaming out of the fire hose. In fact, we think this tendency—toward interpreting data only in terms of your business's needs, not your customers' wants—accounts for many of the train wrecks that follow new product launches.

Take smartphones. It seems as if a new one hits the market every month or so. But how many of them were built because manufacturers or service providers checked their customers' North Stars? Instead, it looks to us like most of them are just chasing market share. And it shows in the falling sales of some longtime favorites, because customers can tell from a mile away when someone's baiting a hook for them, instead of serving them what they want.

Today's smartphones—and, more important, the wireless networks they depend on—seem to have every imaginable software module and gadget—short of a handheld latte frother. But are the calls any clearer?

Does your bill reflect the falling costs of digital transmission? Does your carrier proactively notify you if you're approaching a spending limit—say, when you're roaming, and especially if you're overseas—or does it simply let you know via bill shock after you owe a large sum? How about service plans? Does your carrier allow you to customize your voice and data plans, according to your family's usage, or does it force you to pick between five or six plans, none of which precisely matches your needs? Does the triple- or quad-play offer (wireless plus hardwired voice, data/Internet, and video) provide you with the service you want, or do you have to buy everything on the menu just to get the two or three features you're interested in? Can you customize your plan and features to seamlessly bridge and/or differentiate between your work and personal usage? And once you've made your choice, does your carrier follow up with a loyalty plan designed to keep you satisfied over the long term? Again, mobile service providers have the systems available to them and the data they need to offer these sorts of policy, control, and charging options, and yet how many of them offer services that are truly tailored to their customers' wants and needs? And how many work to make sure their subscribers are satisfied with their phone plans, and their service quality, and in doing so avoid the usual loss of subscribers once the plans run out?

Navel-gazing accounts for declines in the sales of previously successful products or services, too. And this shortsightedness isn't confined to small companies with limited research capabilities and inexperienced analysts. It's just as likely to occur in large companies that generate torrents of data—data that seasoned number crunchers wade through every day. Either way, though, most of them continue to throw their darts wide of the mark. In fact, by failing to keep an eye on their customers' North Stars, what they're really doing is failing to face the dartboard.

We've seen this happen over and over again, throughout our careers, especially when a project team begins to obsess over a single issue, or when the team becomes ridiculously self-absorbed when making business decisions. And again, this intense focus on one's own business, products, or services makes it easy for those who generate the data to ignore customers' needs, wants, and preferences. After all, who's looking?

As consumers—and in the end, we're all consumers—we ask ourselves: Why can't they get it right? For example, in the mobile business, the companies can provide subscriber-optimized services that focus on rate plans and features that are provided with price points and controls in the hands of the consumers. By doing so, carriers actually off-load responsibility for usage and behavior to the end customer while increasing customers' satisfaction by giving them the ability to pick and choose the services they want when they want them—mapping to their lifestyle, preferences, and personal choices.

Similarly, how many of us look *forward* to air travel? And we're not talking about the obvious difficulties—i.e., getting to the airport, or parking at the airport, or going through security, or even waiting at the gate for hours after our planes were supposed to take off. We're talking about the experience itself. Traveling by air used to be exhilarating. It used to be energizing. Now, no one looks forward to flying—unless they've got their own plane. In fact, with the exception of newspapers and subscription television services, no major industry has a lower customer satisfaction rating than airlines (see Figure 14).

It's not that customer service has gone the way of the in-flight meal, although it often feels that way; it's that business decisions are made after analyzing data from the perspective of the company instead of the customer. If you're eligible for a mileage award, and manage to redeem it *before* the requirements change, good luck finding a seat on a day *you'd* like to travel. The system is set up so the airline benefits from your patronage, not so your patronage benefits you. And just try changing your ticket at the last minute—not because you feel like inconveniencing the airline, mind you, but because your business plans have changed. Unavoidably. As we all know, you can depend on the cost of the trip going up by 50 percent. They'll sell you the seat, all right, which means they've got space for you on another flight somewhere, too, but they'll make you pay for it. Every time.* And worst of all, you'll fly in the same plane, headed toward the same destination, as the person in the seat next to you—the person who will have paid 50 percent less than you did for the privilege of contributing to the airline's profit.

Amazingly enough, there is even a new "basic class" seat, introduced in 2010, for "semi-standing seats" from Aviointeriors.† Called

---

*With the exception of Southwest Airlines.
†"Can an Airline Seat Get Any Smaller? Yes, It Can," Sky Talk (blog), September 13, 2010, http://blogs.star-telegram.com/sky_talk/2010/09/can-an-airline-seat-get-any-smaller-yes-it-can.html.

[FIGURE 14] AMERICAN CUSTOMER SATISFACTION INDEX 2010

Industry Name	Baseline	95	96	97	98	99	00	01	02	03	04	05	06	07	08	09	10	Previous Year % Change	First Year % Change
Airlines	72	69	69	67	65	63	63	61	66	67	66	66	65	63	62	64	66	3.1	-8.3
Ambulatory Care															81	80	81	1.3	0.0
Apparel	82	81	78	77	79	79	79	79	80	80	82	81	76	79	80	82	83	1.2	1.2
Athletic Shoes	79	79	77	74	74	76	79	76	79	79	79	77	76	79	79	80	80	0.0	1.3
Automobiles & Light Vehicles	79	80	79	79	79	78	80	80	80	80	79	80	81	82	82	84	82	-2.4	3.8
Banks	74	74	72	71	70	68	70	72	74	75	75	75	77	78	75	75	76	1.3	2.7
Breweries	83	81	79	81	82	79	82	80	81	82	79	82	82	83	83	84	82	-2.4	-1.2
Cellular Telephones											69	69	70	70	71	72	76	5.6	10.1
Cigarettes	81	82	77	77	75	76	76	76	76	76	78	79	78	77	78	72	76	5.6	-6.2
Computer Software															75	75	76	1.3	2.7
Credit Unions															84	84	80	-4.8	-4.8
Department & Discount Stores	77	75	74	72	73	72	72	75	74	76	74	75	74	73	74	75	76	1.3	-1.3
Electronics (TV DVD BD)	83	81	81	80	79	83	83	81	81	84	82	81	80	83	83	83	85	2.4	2.4
Energy Utilities	75	74	75	73	73	74	75	69	73	73	72	73	72	73	74	74	74	0.0	-1.3
Express Delivery (Consumer Shipping)	81	81	85	80	78	79	81	78	79	79	81	81	83	81	82	82	83	1.2	2.5
Fixed Line Telephone Service	81	80	79	75	74	73	72	70	71	72	71	70	70	70	73	72	75	4.2	-7.4
Food Manufacturing	84	84	83	81	81	81	81	82	81	81	81	82	83	81	83	83	81	-2.4	-3.6
Full Service Restaurants														81	80	84	81	-3.6	0.0
Gasoline Stations	78	80	77	78	79	76	75	77	76	75	70	69	71	70	74	76	70	-7.9	-10.3
Health & Personal Care Stores												76	78	78	78	78	77	-1.3	1.3
Health Insurance											67	68	72	71	73	75	73	-2.7	7.4
Hospitals	74	74	71	67	72	70	69	68	70	73	76	71	74	77	75	77	73	-5.2	-1.4
Hotels	75	73	72	71	71	72	72	69	71	73	72	73	75	71	74	75	75	0.0	0.0
Internet Brokerage							72	69	73	76	75	76	78	79	74	78	78	0.0	8.3
Internet News & Information									73	74	75	75	73	75	75	74	74	0.0	1.4
Internet Portals & Search Engines							63	65	68	71	72	76	77	75	80	83	77	-7.2	22.2
Internet Retail							78	77	83	84	80	81	83	83	82	83	80	-3.6	2.6
Internet Social Media																	70	N/A	N/A
Internet Travel								78	77	77	76	77	76	75	75	77	78	1.3	1.3
Life Insurance	81	74	75	76	77	76	75	78	79	77	75	75	79	78	78	79	80	1.3	-1.2
Limited Service Restaurants	69	70	66	68	69	69	70	71	71	74	NM**	76	77	77	78	78	75	-3.8	8.7
Major Appliances	85	82	82	82	83	82	85	82	82	81	82	80	81	82	80	81	82	1.2	-3.5
Motion Pictures	77	77	74	71	76	71	68	71	70	71	73	71	73	70	70	74	76	2.7	-1.3
Network Cable TV News	77	76	70	62	65	62	64	62	65	68	66	68	69	67	69	71	74	4.2	-3.9
Newspapers	72	68	69	69	66	69	68	68	63	64	68	63	63	66	64	63	65	3.2	-9.7
Personal Care & Cleaning Products	84	84	80	82	82	81	84	83	81	84	83	83	84	85	85	85	83	-2.4	-1.2
Personal Computers	78	75	73	70	71	72	74	71	71	72	74	74	77	75	74	75	78	4.0	0.0
Pet Food															84	84	83	-1.2	0.0
Property & Casualty Insurance	82	75	77	77	77	79	79	79	77	78	77	78	78	80	81	80	80	0.0	-2.4
Soft Drinks	86	86	86	83	83	84	86	82	85	84	83	83	84	84	83	85	84	-1.2	-2.3
Specialty Retail Stores								73	74	74	75	74	75	75	76	77	78	1.3	6.8
Subscription Television Service								64	61	61	61	61	63	62	64	63	66	4.8	3.1
Supermarkets	76	75	74	73	73	74	73	75	75	74	73	74	75	76	76	76	75	-1.3	-1.3
U.S. Postal Service	61	69	74	69	71	71	72	70	73	72	74	73	71	73	74	74	71	-4.1	16.4
Wireless Telephone Service	61									72	65	63	66	68	68	69	72	4.3	10.8

the SkyRider, it has a twenty-three-inch seat pitch, compared with the minimum thirty-two inches found on ordinary seats. It's designed, according to the manufacturer, to offer passengers deeper discounts *and* provide the airlines with "ultra-high density" seating. Really? Safety issues aside, are we sardines or paying passengers? Put another way, whose star do you think the airlines are headed toward? And while airlines now have a stranglehold on long-distance travel, in the not-too-distant future they may find themselves competing with alternatives such as high-speed train service.

And this sea change in the concept of service, and in the customer's realization that service is no longer important to those who provide it, is not limited to airlines. It's now common in retail businesses, in restaurants, in technology companies, and, as everyone knows, in telephone and cable companies. For that reason, the exceptions—like Southwest Airlines, Apple, Costco, Lexus, and Trader Joe's—truly stand out these days.

Moving up the American Customer Satisfaction Index's (ACSI) ratings, if you skip over the abysmally low federal and local government (including the U.S. Postal Service) customer satisfaction numbers, you come to the providers of wireless telephone services next. Again, using the ACSI's 100-point scale, the average score for cell phone companies is 72. But that's good news, of sorts, for those willing to crane their necks and look for their customer's North Star, because that standard of mediocrity shouldn't be hard to beat—at least not in a crowded marketplace. Using this as our starting point—i.e., that the opportunity to profit from good customer service has never been greater—the question becomes how companies can exploit that opportunity. In other words, how can managers convince their people to move from navel-gazing to stargazing?

Sprint/Nextel CEO Dan Hesse and chief service officer Bob L. Johnson seem to have found a way. According to the December 17, 2010, *Wall Street Journal:*[*]

> Dan Hesse joined as chief executive in late 2007, right as the company was reaching its low point. He said he had three priorities: improving customer service, fixing the damage to the brand and generating cash.

---

[*]Shayndi Raice, "Sprint Tackles Subscriber Losses," *Wall Street Journal*, December 17, 2010.

"The company wasn't meeting some of its financial goals, and so they do what companies do, which is cut expenses, but one of the expenses that was cut was care," Mr. Hesse said.

In addition to cutting back on the costs of customer care—again, before Hesse's arrival—Sprint had also encouraged its customer service agents to act as salespersons—in essence, to use the problems that prompted their customers to call as an opportunity to talk customers into extending their contracts or adding services. Finally, in addition to the brand confusion that resulted from Sprint's purchase of Nextel—a company as well known for its "push to talk" service as it was for cell service—the merger also led to a precipitous decline in customer satisfaction ratings. From 2005, the year of the merger, to 2008, Hesse's first full year on the job, the company's customer-sat numbers fell from an already low 63 to an abysmal 56. Sprint's reputation for poor customer service was well deserved. Someone we know recalls a customer service representative asking him, after he had been put on hold for almost half an hour, "Where were you when you couldn't receive calls?" How, exactly, would he have been able to answer that question? After waiting to be asked that question, it took our friend another half an hour to get to someone who could close his account. That's right, he had to wait to talk to the customer *service* rep to close his account.

A confusing array of calling plans didn't help, and, in fact, Hesse began by greatly reducing the number of those plans and by introducing the industry's first unlimited-calling-*and*-data plan.* And then he put his chief service officer to work on improving customer service. Johnson found that Sprint's call centers had been designed to satisfy the company's cost metrics, not customers. In fact, the longer a customer service rep spent with customers, the worse his or her rating was. To turn things around, Johnson made solving customers' problems—by the end of their first call—the reps' first priority. Their second priority was making customers feel that the company cared. Finally, he changed the bonus structure to reward customer satisfaction ratings, not sales numbers (in this case, contract extensions).

---

*Unlimited-usage plans have actually become an issue for carriers, given oversubscribed networks and excessive bandwidth use, which affects both the quality of service and the carriers' profitability.

How did Hesse and Johnson do it? First, by asking what their customers wanted; and second, by asking themselves how they could deliver it. In other words, they started by looking for their customers' North Star, and once they found it, they asked themselves the Essential Question: How could Sprint/Nextel navigate by that star, and change course?* Of course it's probably just a coincidence, but from 2008 to 2010 the company's customer-sat ratings shot up from 56 to 70.

JUMP UP AND DOWN AND POUND THE TABLE

In the spirit of this book, our North Star question is deceptively simple—but that doesn't mean getting an answer will be. So be prepared for backlash. Asking for the coordinates of the customer's North Star may not be enough—you may have to demand them. To demand real answers, not just a wave of the data wand. To insist that your people start thinking differently and produce numbers that reveal what customers want, not what the company wants. To demand, in short, that your colleagues *start* by looking for the customer's guiding light.

Where will they find it? Again, its coordinates are probably right there in the existing data. That is, the relevant data. They're there in the market research. They're there in the phone interviews and the surveys and the online forums. The numbers—by which we mean, of course, the right numbers—will give you the latitude and the longitude. Find those numbers and you'll feel as if your customers are sitting in the observatory with you, pointing right at their star. Use the wrong numbers and it's as if your customers are locked outside, banging on the door and screaming like traders in a commodities pit but unable to get your attention. And be sure to ask if someone has gotten details *directly* from a customer—that is, unfiltered, raw, and honest. What's more, even when they have the right data, decision makers often can barely hear the voice of the customer—because it's all but buried under reams of unintelligible data, or hidden behind pointless presentations, or obscured with innumerable charts. Navigating by your customer's North Star, though, will always keep you and your

---

*As you flip through these pages, you'll see that one of the Seven Questions generally leads to another, no matter which question you start with.

team on course, especially when someone tries to turn the fire hose on you. And so, even if it means pounding the table, you've got to demand a change in approach. If you don't, to take the example of most airlines, you'll make a dentist's chair more appealing than a seat on an airplane.

>> Webroot

According to the October 21, 2010, *New York Times,* the results of a recent online survey convinced the head of marketing at the security software firm Webroot to pitch his company's products in simpler terms.[*] Why? Because while those security software users who responded to an online survey were most concerned about protecting children from online predators—a result the company anticipated—Webroot's marketing department was surprised to learn that buyers across the segment also wanted simpler explanations of the benefits such software offers. Seen from the company's perspective, cataloging the specific, often complex functions of its software made sense, especially since the survey also revealed that security software users were unaware of the frequency with which attempts were made to hack into their computers. The customers saw it differently, and as a result Webroot's marketing department redesigned its ad campaign from the customer's perspective, stressing the software's general features and business benefits, not the highly technical means employed to achieve them.

And although we'll wait until later in this book to consider Webroot's story more closely, their marketing department might have come to a similar conclusion by asking another Fire Hose Question, or even two. The discovery that its customers preferred ads that explained the benefits of the company's software in plain English was a good example of the sort of information that results from asking, "What surprised you?" And in much the same way, had the company asked itself "Who are your swing voters?" they would have discovered that a great many *potential* customers simply didn't realize how often cybercriminals attempt to compromise their computer's security, and how at risk their personal information is.

*Andrew Adam Newman, "A Campaign About Computer Security, Couched in Plain English," *New York Times*, October 21, 2010.

This news wasn't newsworthy to Susan Schwartz McDonald.

It's interesting that they were surprised, because one of the things you learn in a lot of high-tech industries is that even . . . relatively sophisticated customers, like physicians, for example, have a limited patience for knowing how things work. It's not that they're stupid, it's not because they're busy; it's because they have a fundamentally higher aspiration, and a higher mandate . . . to achieve results.

>> Starbucks

When Howard Schultz opened the first Starbucks coffeehouse in 1982,[*] he wasn't just selling something you could drink from a cup; he was selling an experience. In other words, as strange as it seems, Schultz wasn't going into the coffee business. Starbucks, instead, was going to be a "third place," a place somewhere between home and work. In other words, he opened his doors under the North Star of customers who were looking for a weird mixture of European café, the water cooler at work, their living rooms, the street corner, and their offices.

Sure, he was selling a premium cup of coffee, but his early customers were buying the experience of standing in line there, too. It was hip, like no place your father took you. And you could order premium coffee and other beverages just the way you wanted them, with every minor detail to your taste and each cup delivered with a smile. The brand offered more than a cup of coffee; during your typically hectic workday, it offered a moment of luxury, and the sensation that you were being pampered. And while a cup of coffee may have been your excuse for going there, being part of something else was as important as the coffee, whether or not you stayed to drink it.

American sociologist Ray Oldenburg coined the phrase "the third place" back in the early 1970s. In a modern world dominated by two isolated spaces—home and work—Oldenburg believed that public

---

[*]The first Starbucks sold coffee beans, not coffee. Schultz was brought on as head of retailing and marketing about ten years later, and after failing to convince the owners that they should be selling coffee, too, he left the company to start his own chain, Il Giornale. A year later he bought Starbucks and began to create the chain as we know it today.

meeting places like restaurants, bookstores, bars, and even post offices served a critical societal function. More than just places where people went to buy stamps, lunch, or a beer, they were communal areas you could retreat to at any time of the day. Neither at home nor at work, you could unwind for a moment, drink a cup of coffee, look over a report without interruptions, or even talk to strangers. Schultz successfully created that atmosphere at one Starbucks after another, even though the company was opening a store a day in the late 1990s. The atmosphere is so powerful a draw that business travelers in foreign countries and airports clearly identify the overseas Starbucks as a connection with home. They don't just buy a cup of coffee there, but step into a third place in a foreign land that makes them feel as if they're still on U.S. soil—almost like visiting a U.S. embassy.

By the turn of the century, though, the experience that Starbucks offered made it a victim of its success. The rapid expansion had reduced the chain's hip factor and threatened to turn its neighborhood stores into generic coffee distributors, not much different from gas stations, dairy marts, or fast food outlets. Starbucks also began using its retail space to sell a variety of products unrelated to their core business—like books and music—while adding an array of (by all accounts) mediocre food that slowed down lines and made customers feel like cattle in a chute.

As brand consultant Jim Barnes observed in his *CustomerThink* blog in 2008:

> While it is still a place to meet friends for many customers, others in downtown business districts now see Starbucks as a place to grab a quick cup of coffee to take back to the office. There is no stopping to chat or sitting to read a newspaper. In fact, in many Starbucks locations in the basements of office towers, there is nowhere to sit. Others now see Starbucks as a drive-thru—a concept historically associated with Dairy Queen and McDonald's. Ordering a Caramel Macchiato from the window of your car just doesn't seem to have the same cachet.
>
> The Starbucks experience is just not the same when it involves picking up a coffee from a drive-thru window. Where is the "third placedness" in that?

By 2007, twenty years after he bought the bean-roasting business that would start America's love affair with premium coffee, and six years after he had relinquished his title as CEO, Howard Schultz agreed. In his now famous "epiphany" memo, written to his successor at the company's helm, Jim Donald, Schultz acknowledged that in order to achieve scale, Starbucks' management had made "a series of decisions that, in retrospect, have led to the watering down of the Starbucks experience, and, what some might call the commoditization of our brand." When Schultz returned as CEO a year later, he initiated a series of changes to return the customer's voice and experience to Starbucks. Since 2008, Schultz and his president for global development, Arthur Rubinfeld, have made major changes, including smaller espresso machines that do not isolate customers from employees, less cluttered and environmentally sensitive store design, longer bars with more cashier terminals to shorten lines, and community tables that might cause customers to bump into someone they didn't know while plugging in their laptops. Finally, in the summer of 2010, Schultz announced the availability of free Wi-Fi in all Starbucks locations.

As chairman, and then again as CEO, Schultz certainly had a massive amount of sales and financial data at his disposal. He knew the number of stores, the average number of customers in them, the sales trends of particular products, the number of employees, the stock price, and the return on investment. And he surely consulted those numbers on a routine basis. But his reawakened interest in his customers' North Star led to the changes that reinvigorated the brand. And once he'd identified his customers' North Star, it seems he asked himself an Essential Question: How could Starbucks maintain market share when competitors were either offering decent coffee at a lower price, or doing a better job creating a "third place" experience? It seems he also asked himself the *customer's* Essential Question: Why pay more for coffee at Starbucks if it's become a fast food store experience that's too crowded or poorly designed to be a third place? From our perspective, that question would lead back to the data, and in particular the swing voter—i.e., how do I keep my present customers coming through the door, and how do I convince new customers to try the Starbucks experience instead of our competitor's? But more on that in Chapter Five.

>> Can Your Customers Point to Their Own North Star?

We realize that customers at times may not know what they want. Put another way, it's hard to do research on innovation—that is, on products and services that don't yet exist. No customer ever asked for a *single-button* mobile phone like iPhone. Just in case you thought finding your customer's North Star was as simple as waiting until nightfall, grabbing a cheap telescope, and then mapping the constellations over your customers' heads, think again. If you were to try, you'd notice that some of your customers were just milling around. Why? Because occasionally even *they* don't know where their North Stars are.

Let's bring Susan Schwartz McDonald in again for her take on the Starbucks story.

The real question is, did people know they needed that third place, in the first place? Or maybe the public knew once, but forgot. Keep in mind that in the eighteenth century the coffee shops of London offered an equivalent experience.* That is, people knew way back then that the place itself had a role to play. In the twentieth century, Starbucks just re-created [the third place] . . . They kind of rediscovered the need and caused people to acknowledge it. So looking for the customer's North Star sometimes means hanging a star up for them, one they didn't really know they looked to.

Food shopping, too, has always been an extremely social experience . . . and so there are lots and lots of things that Starbucks could have tapped into. But by creating that environment, it actually took into account a variety of behaviors, manifested in various ways, like the desire to be with strangers, or to be doing public things privately, in a publicly welcoming place, where you sort of have both anonymity and social presence. I think Starbucks' story is really a wonderful case of give and take, or a dialogue of sorts, between customers and marketers. So in an ideal world, it's more than just sensing, or learning, what our cus-

*In fact, the first coffeehouse in London was opened in 1650, and those that followed were often placed near centers of commercial activity, where they served as informal meeting grounds.

tomer's North Star is; it's taking that [information] and then applying it to a new way of thinking. And then maybe turning their noses by only five degrees, and showing them a different little constellation.

>> Customer Impact Assessment

If you have difficulty discerning the customer's North Star, you can apply a simple tool *we* use to make sure the customer's voice is heard: the customer impact assessment (CIA). The CIA is a short list of questions that incorporate the customer's perspective into all major decisions. Therefore, when any major business decision is proposed, we recommend insisting that the proposal include a customer impact section, including the answers to the following four questions:

1. How could this change negatively impact the customer?
2. How will the customer perceive this change?
3. How are you going to manage this change for the customer?
4. How are we going to track the impact of this change, and how precisely are we going to measure its progress?

By adopting this process for every major business decision, not only will you hear the customer's voice and find his or her North Star, but your use of the analysis will accelerate cultural change inside your company. The four questions form a bridge between the results (the data everyone uses) and the question that leads to policy and action: What do we do differently tomorrow? Imagine what would happen if senior managers used these tools to hold up decision making, forcing everyone involved to first consider the impact the decision would have on the customer. Sure, it would take a little more time up front, but then again it might save you time over the long run.

Still, while the CIA will give you much better coordinates on your customers' actual wants and needs, and their reaction to products, it's important to remember that sometimes not even your own customers have all the answers, so thoughtful probing on change management and expectations is a necessity. Remember, sales data alone will tell you

64

nothing about the battle raging in the mind of a customer confronted by an excess of choice. You need only read Malcolm Gladwell's article—or see his TED Talk*—about psychophysicist Howard Moskowitz's search for the ultimate spaghetti sauce to realize that sometimes the customer's word is as unreliable as the data. In short, through the use of extensive food trials, Moskowitz discovered that in attempting to satisfy every customer's taste at the same time, food manufacturers usually ended up satisfying none of them. His solution? Offer a variety of products—in this case, spaghetti sauces—intended to satisfy a number of *individual* buyers, instead of every buyer. That's right, your multiple choices on the supermarket shelves are due to a marketing breakthrough that led to a focus on individual customers' desires.

A wide variety of choices, however, don't always result in customer satisfaction. In fact, Barry Schwartz, in *The Paradox of Choice*, provides plentiful evidence that too many choices often leave buyers dissatisfied. Think of a child in front of a candy counter, or a teenage girl trying to choose the shade of lipstick that's just right for her—depending, of course, on what she's wearing that day, or what color she's dyed her hair.

At this point we'd like to introduce Jim Hilt, another valued contributor to *Drinking from the Fire Hose* and a friend and colleague who has built a career around meeting customers' retail needs.

JIM HILT IS a former divisional vice president and general manager for Online Services for Sears Holding Corporation and also served as "chief life manager" for Manage My Life. While at Sears, Hilt was responsible for all product management, user experience and design, and front-end development for all Sears Holdings online properties. Jim's career also includes a series of early-stage entrepreneurial ventures within larger companies. He also held roles in business development, technology, and marketing at SAP and IBM.

I think the Essential Question and the North Star question are somewhat the same. I think that if you can answer that funda-

---

*Malcolm Gladwell, "Malcolm Gladwell on Spaghetti Sauce," TED.com, www.ted.com/talks/malcolm_gladwell_on_spaghetti_sauce.html.

mental question—that is, what is it that the customer needs?—then you'll be able to constantly reorient your approach if you veer off-track.

Having said that, though, it's really important to remember that it may not be possible for you to be part of the solution. That is, understanding the customer's North Star might actually lead to a decision to *not* pursue a sales opportunity. If the customer wants milk, for instance, and what I sell is bread, my figuring out how to better position bread isn't going to help that customer meet their needs. So while they may occasionally grab half a loaf, I'm not really following their North Star, and so I'm probably not going to be successful.

But keep in mind that the customers' needs can change, and so the best part about approaching business this way is that if you keep asking the North Star question you're more likely to end up pursuing the right strategy, or making the change in direction you need to, at the right time.

To summarize, traditional data and analysis explains what customers do. Stock-keeping unit (SKU) data tracks the arrival of goods at the loading dock, their movement to the shelf, and their sale at the cash register. Total Unduplicated Reach and Frequency (TURF) analysis can reveal the number of potential users reached by a marketing campaign, the frequency with which they use a certain product, or even the factors—like price or placement—that motivate them to buy it. But both view sales from the company's perspective, not the customer's.

Therefore, plotting the customer's North Star via the CIA will give you three powerful levers to pull:

1. The credibility the customer's point of view will give your decisions, and the persuasive voice they'll be in the corner office.
2. A powerful presentation tool; when you bring the voice of the customer to the conference room, every manager's ears will perk up.
3. A companywide point of view, with the customer front and center.

Try it on your own team. Embed it into your performance evaluations, your midyear account reviews, your marketing and product development plans, and your long-term strategies. In short, make it a part of every major decision and every review you perform. By insisting on answers to these questions before making *any* decision that affects your customers, you can begin to create a culture that is customer-centric instead of company-centric.

CHAPTER TWO TAKEAWAYS

1. Ask yourself whether you're navel-gazing or navigating by your customer's North Star.
2. Find out whether your customers themselves know what they want by asking them the four key Customer Impact Assessment (CIA) questions.
3. Develop a customer impact assessment for your business.

CHAPTER THREE

Should You Believe the Squiggly Line?

"In any given year . . . you will start to notice patterns and clusters. By December the temptation will be nearly overwhelming to generalize from this data, to turn coincidences into trends and trends into matters of world-historical significance. The ad hoc, arbitrary, week-in-week-out sampling of stories and pictures must add up to something, right?"

—A. O. SCOTT[*]

U sing short-term data to make long-range plans is like putting Coke bottle glasses on to look for something on the horizon—they're great for magnifying the little numbers but don't allow you to see anything down the road. We call this overreliance on short-term data the Squiggly Line syndrome. If you make the time frame small enough, the data almost always appears as a squiggly line. And whether you're looking at sales figures, fashion trends, or even the availability of raw materials, the numbers are almost always less volatile over the long term.

Because success in today's business world depends on your ability to deliver immediate results, everyone's hungry for the latest numbers. There is, however, a way to work within this reality, or within what has become the normal rhythm of business. And sticking to our pragmatic approach, we're not going to try to change that reality, just provide you with tips and tricks to help you work smarter and more successfully.

*A. O. Scott, "The Cinematic State of Things," *New York Times*, Sunday, December 19, 2010.

CHAPTER LESSONS

1. Gain perspective by stepping further away from the data.
2. Bring broader thinking to the short-term nature of business.

As for us, even after having worked in the business world for more than twenty years each, we're still surprised at the way people zero in on 2-to-4-percentage-point changes—even if they *are* significant—when assessing macro issues. How can small movements like those be celebrated as *real* improvements, or used as a siren call for change? While they may be statistically significant, are they meaningful? Is the trend sustainable? Even more important, are they reason enough to get you to shift your course—that is, to overrule the Essential Questions at the root of your investigation?

We all know what the answer is. The answer is no. And we know it instinctively. Even those who depend on the Squiggly Line know it. That sort of myopic approach, with its focus on the Squiggly Line, is not just misleading—it robs you and your business of the equilibrium on which long-term success depends. The cure, we're happy to tell you, is simple. The most effective way to discuss results is to consider just three factors: the absolute score, the competitive score, and the score over time. And by triangulating these three easily measured data points, you can gain almost all the perspective you'll need, and ensure that you don't get hung up on the Squiggly Line (see Figure 15).

[FIGURE 15]

ESSENTIAL QUESTION
How are our marketing programs changing consumers' perceptions to drive demand and grow market share?

Measure the absolute position of the product

Assess the product's or company's position relative to competitors'

Track the product's movement of position over time

Your absolute position is your baseline. That means today's numbers. They could be total sales or market share—take your pick. Your competitive score, instead, is comparative. How are we doing relative to our competitors? Finally, how are we, and our competitors, doing over time?

Jim Dippold, speaking once again of the grocery business, thinks that the important thing is dividing the data sets between those you use to make tactical decisions and those you use to make long-term strategic decisions.

> The answer always depends on which question you're trying to solve. This business [grocery stores] looks at its sales week by week to see whether or not it's going to make its numbers, and tactically, those numbers will show you things that you can act on. But if you're doing long-range planning, you obviously want a different data set. If my long-term growth strategy is to get customers who started doing their grocery shopping at Walmart to come back to my store, then taking a snapshot of one week's sales isn't going to help me draw up that strategy. But as far as short-term decisions go—you know, about what products to put on the shelves, and where, and at what price—the data *can't* be too short-term. So not only will I look at the weekly numbers, I'll look at the daily numbers too.

When making long-term decisions, in other words, demand long-term numbers. Weekly sales numbers rise and fall. Quarterly sales numbers indicate trends. Annual sales numbers confirm, or contradict, potential trends. So if you're gathering information before making big bets for the business, or to inform strategic plans about your team priorities, ignore the squiggly lines. Longitudinal data has value. Short-term movements, while interesting, are often misleading.

Darrell Bricker, speaking as a social scientist (with the accent on *science*), doesn't automatically disqualify squiggly lines, either. The question, according to him, is whether those lines are meaningful, and how you make that judgment.

> There are many explanations for a short-term change in the data, or a squiggly line, and you shouldn't stop at the first one. From

a data perspective, for instance, or a research perspective, part of it may be methodologically derived. The real question is: When is change *real* change? I had something like this happen to me just a couple days ago. I was going into a presentation, and somebody brought me some data that showed the change year over year, and I said, that just doesn't make sense. Why would that number of people go from there to there? And where did they go? Because I can't find them anywhere in these numbers.

Are you telling me that Godzilla came down here in the middle of the night and rearranged things? And I didn't hear about it? And you didn't hear about it? And our client didn't hear about it? There's got to be something wrong. And the person who gave me this was a well-trained, smart researcher.

It turned out they changed the way they asked the question. But if you look at enough data over time, you'll know when something looks real and when it doesn't. And it's based on experience. In other words, I think the answer to "Should I trust the Squiggly Line?" is: Trust your gut. If it doesn't make sense, if it looks like that change happened and there's no reason for it, don't just assume, well, maybe it changed. You have to ask why. And you have to start with "Did I measure it correctly?"

Reliable, repeatable measurements, in fact, are Bricker's main defense against any sort of misleading data.

One of the things that drives me bananas about the market research business, and even the business that I'm in [public affairs and corporate-reputation research], is that people forget about the fundamentals. They're the fundamentals because they work, but today researchers are absolutely infatuated with new methodologies, and are always looking at ways of changing things around merely because it's new rather than because it helps to reveal what the truth is.

It's so easy to manipulate numbers now. When I started, it used to be really hard. If you just fire up your PC or your laptop, or maybe even your iPad now, you can run a cross-tab, or a multiple-regression equation, or a log-linear analysis, or whatever, that used to take days and days. And because you can do it really easily now, you get a lot of garbage in and garbage out, or something like a monkey with a machine gun.

Bricker is highlighting a key point: It is not about the data readily available, but the ability to look at the data to see what no one else has seen.

THE HYPE CYCLE

Sometimes the Squiggly Line isn't the result of poor methodology, or shortened time frames. Sometimes it's just part of a normal, recurring cycle. Entrepreneurs, product managers, and venture capitalists, for example, refer to the "hype cycle," first coined by the Gartner Group in 1995, whenever they assess new products or services. That cycle is a great example of the way data lines can become "squiggly" at certain times, even if they don't remain that way over the long term (see Figure 16).

[FIGURE 16]
HYPE CYCLE

Note the squiggly microdata in the "Peak of Inflated Expectations," which fall between the "Technology Trigger" and the "Trough of Disillusionment." And pay attention to the way the line trends across the

"Slope of Enlightenment" and the "Plateau of Productivity," too. And while this graph represents the hype cycle of a "typical" new product or innovative service, if you superimpose your own data on top of it, you can get a sense of where your product or service is in the timeline, and then make some informed guesses about the future—again, looking past the squiggly parts of the line to the longer-term trends.

These are not mere theoretical constructs. Almost two years ago, in fact, in a 2009 article for TechCrunch, Robert Moore of RJMetrics saw Twitter's growth already passing the "Peak of Inflated Expectations" (see Figure 17).

[FIGURE 17]

Robert Moore of RJ Metrics used Twitter API (application programming interface) and publicly available data to go under the hood of Twitter to investigate DTL current and future growth, and wrote up his findings in TechCrunch [http://techcrunch.com/2009/10/05/twitter-data-analysis-aninvestors-perspective/].

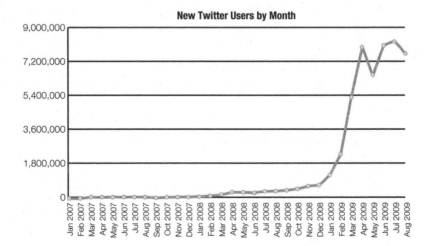

Furthermore, anticipating the "Trough of Disillusionment," Moore noted the following:

- More than 75 percent of Twitter users have ten or fewer followers.
- 38 percent of Twitter users have never sent a single tweet.
- More than 75 percent of Twitter users have sent fewer than ten tweets.

- Only 25 percent of registered Twitter users tweet in any given month.

What Moore found, in fact, was a group of "power tweeters" who generate most of the activity. Therefore, marketing and public relations executives who are charmed by the number of Twitter users, or the volume of tweets—which continue to skyrocket, according to Twitter's own blog—may see things differently after viewing Moore's findings. However, as of 2011 Twitter had an estimated 94 million users and 1.6 billion visits monthly in the United States, according to Quantcast (www.quantcast.com). If you began to use Twitter in hopes of joining a "community," what does it mean if nearly 40 percent of that community minimally participates?

Consider the following chart (see Figure 18). This is an actual example of a line chart that was the basis for a seven-point competitive-strategy planning session. Based on the most recent annual measurement, a great deal of activity and focus was generated off of this one chart. While it was a starting place, the squiggly lines were treated as a launch pad for a longer-term plan. It does not show longitudinal data, but rather a point in time measurement.

[FIGURE 18]

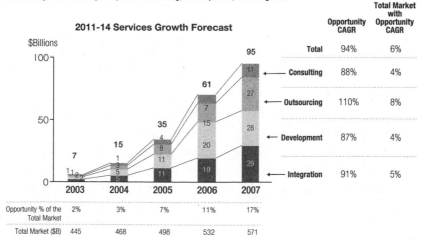

Our market is expected to significantly outpace broader segment growth in each service segment with major impact to consulting, development, and integration

74

APPLYING THE LESSON

1. Watch out for discussions that focus on "recent trends" and short-term projections.
2. Even if changes are statistically significant, remember to ask yourself, "Are they meaningful?"
3. Always ask yourself whether the short-term change—or the Squiggly Line—is sustainable.
4. Insist on precise definitions for terms like "directional improvement."
5. Revisit the Essential Question that led to the research.
6. Interrogate the charts and graphics:
    a. Is the population large enough, or are the findings based on a limited sample?
    b. Do side-by-side charts use the same scale?
    c. Is the change real, as defined by rigorous testing and accepted models, or is it just noise in the foreground?

Short-term attempts to cut costs also produce some of the most outrageously misleading squiggly lines you'll ever see, and the years 2008 to 2010 provided some particularly wicked examples. As a result of aggressive layoffs, corporate profits in the fourth quarter of 2009 surged approximately 30 percent above those in the fourth quarter of 2008 (*after* being adjusted for inflation, depreciation, and inventory profit).* At the same time, productivity increased by 3.5 percent, compared with only 1.0 percent a year earlier.

Now *that's* a pretty squiggly line. But if you look back six or seven years, you'll find a somewhat similar increase immediately after the recession of 2001, when productivity rose from 2.9 percent to 4.6 percent. Go back another ten years, immediately after another recession, and you'll find that productivity in non-farm businesses rose by 1.5 percent in 1991 and by 4.0 percent in 1992.†

So while U.S. corporations shed more than two and a half million

---

*Sara Murray, "U.S. Corporate Profits Kept Climbing at End of 2009," *Wall Street Journal*, March 27, 2010.
†U.S. Bureau of Labor Statistics.

employees in 2008, and productivity and profitability surged, the historic data shows us that those increases are likely to be very short-lived. So the numbers are real, and meaningful, but history shows that they're not likely to last.

What's more, once the business cycle turns up again, and record profits and productivity increases disappear, many firms will find that by cutting costs they've weakened their operations and research staffs, to say nothing of the hiring and training costs they'll incur when they have to rebuild their labor forces and management staffs.*

It's bad enough that you spend hours of every workweek flipping through the pages of reports, clicking on PowerPoint presentations, or scrolling down Excel files. It's even worse when the information you're being asked to consider was gathered over such a short time frame, or across such a restricted region, that the numbers reveal almost nothing meaningful about long-term trends.

Sure, if you're in the movie business, a film's opening-weekend box office will tell you a lot about its chances of making its money back. But given the way the movie business is changing, it's now just as important to look at revenue from DVD sales, online streaming rights, and broadcast rights. You can't ignore merchandizing or gaming revenue, either. So while a movie might sell a boatload of tickets over its opening weekend, and then see the number drop off, secondary sources of revenue might still ensure that it recoups its investment over a two-to-three-year horizon. If, on the other hand, you're launching a new software product, the number of units you sell over the first weekend has virtually no meaning. The same is true of automobile sales. If you're in the real estate business, the same is usually true of monthly new-home sales—especially if they're compared with the previous year's numbers (when prices just happened to drop faster than they did for wrapping paper the day after Christmas). In other words, if last year's prices fell 30 percent below the ten-year average, and this month's numbers are up 10 percent (compared with the same month one year ago), then new-house sales are still well

---

*This sort of overly aggressive belt tightening shouldn't be confused with the "lean manufacturing" concept for operations. Lean manufacturing principles, which include "continuous improvement" and "respect for people," are meant to be part of an enduring approach to doing business, regardless of the business cycle.

below their long-term average. And keep in mind that you'll get a different squiggly line if you confuse houses for which contracts have been signed with actual sales—that is, contracts that have gone to closing. So while looking at the housing market that way might make things look better in the short term, it generally leads to significant reevaluations later.

To take yet another example, in an entirely different environment, if you've invested your retirement money for the long term, and split it evenly between bonds, domestic equities, and foreign equities, what effect should weekly fluctuations in the markets have on your allocations? Absolutely none, of course. Those numbers are part of a squiggly line you would do well to ignore. Instead, you should concentrate on rebalancing your portfolio every six months—and then *only if* changing values caused one part of your holdings to rise above 33 percent of the total.

Or let's look at the long-term price of petroleum. Those of us who have had driving licenses since the mid-seventies have gotten used to pretty severe fluctuations in the price of gasoline. And yet a quick glance at long-term petroleum prices—adjusted for inflation—shows price spikes to be relatively infrequent occurrences—at least over the long term (see Figure 19).

If we look only at the past ten years—from 2000 to 2010—we see enormous fluctuations in price. If we track prices over the ten years from 1990 to 2000, we still see a great deal of short-term movement, but within a far, far smaller range. Between 1975 and 1985, we come across another period of remarkably volatile prices. But if we look at prices over the past 140 years—again, adjusted for inflation—we see a remarkably stable price level, with only three major exceptions, of similar amount and duration.

Of course, some Squiggly Lines do lead to lasting changes, and if we see similar fluctuations in the price of oil from 2010 to 2020, then we might reasonably begin to think that a new trend and threshold had been established—that of a permanently Squiggly Line where oil prices were concerned.

At this point we'd like to introduce another longtime friend and colleague—Eric Koivisto, CEO of the fantasy football site Trench-Fantasy.

[FIGURE 19]

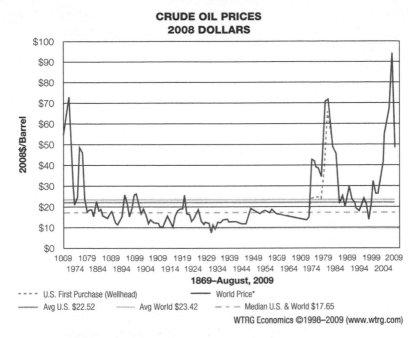

CRUDE OIL PRICES
2008 DOLLARS

WTRG Economics ©1998–2009 (www.wtrg.com)

IN CREATING TRENCHFANTASY.COM, Koivisto combined his wide-ranging experience with start-ups, his management of *Fortune* 500 global brands, and his passion for pro football.*

Prior to founding TrenchFantasy, Mr. Koivisto worked with the Seattle venture capital firm Ignition. While there, he was VP of brand management at Marketrange, a developer of subscription-based community platforms like PerfectMatch.com, and VP of marketing and business development at Avogadro, which developed platform software technology for an IP-based wireless messaging solution now in wide use. Finally, years before the entrepreneurial endeavors listed above, Eric enjoyed a seven-year career at Microsoft, where he oversaw worldwide advertising and managed advertising for the Business Solutions Group.

*Full disclosure: One of this book's co-authors, Paul Magnone, is also a principal in the business. Koivisto and Christopher Frank also worked together at Microsoft in the nineties.

Koivisto's take on the Squiggly Line was different from anyone else's. He started by pointing to those times someone should be paying attention to blips on the screen and, just as important, who ought to be doing it.

> Someone should be looking at that Squiggly Line, but not everybody. That Squiggly Line for us, on any given day at TrenchFantasy, is a raft of customer complaints or data handling hiccups. So someone needs to look at that Squiggly Line, deal with it, and straighten it out. But the CEO, or the business development guy, or the product guy, shouldn't be the ones doing it . . . They shouldn't even be looking within the parameters that line represents.
>
> I think another one of the hard things to determine is the context around that Squiggly Line. Is it just a shortened time horizon that's producing the change? Or is it actually other data? For instance, let's say you see awareness of your brand dropping. But did you look at that drop in the context of sales? If both awareness and sales are dropping, you've got a problem. But if sales are up and awareness is down, then maybe you've got a sampling issue with your research.
>
> So the answer is, for the most part, no, most people in your business shouldn't be looking at the Squiggly Line. But when someone has to, the challenge is in what you analyze, because the squiggle isn't always caused by a shortened time frame.

We'll return to this point later, and ask Susan Schwartz McDonald to comment on it as well, but for now it's enough to say that there are times when you should believe the Squiggly Line—that is, when the squiggle *wasn't* the result of a shortened time frame, or a shortened *y* axis.

BASEBALL STATISTICS

Baseball statistics may offer the best pure example of the meaninglessness—or the entertainment value—of short-term data. In the early weeks of the 1941 Major League Baseball season, for example, Joe DiMaggio went to the plate twenty times without getting a hit. His batting average (BA) dropped to .184. When he finally picked up a hit on May 15, however, he went on to hit in the next fifty-five games, establishing one of baseball's most untouchable records, the fifty-six-game hitting streak. And his batting average at the end of the year—.357—was the second-highest of his career.

Of course, a player with a high BA doesn't necessarily win more games for his team. Consider, for instance, a player with a .300 batting average, a .320 on-base percentage (OBP),* and 40 runs batted in (RBI) for the year. Then compare that player with another who has a .280 average, a .360 OBP, and 60 runs batted in for the year. Clearly the first player (whose BA is .300) is a "better" hitter than the second player (whose BA is .280). But the second player does more of what wins baseball games—that is, causing runs to score. This could be true for a number of reasons, including the number of home runs he hit—30 HR would alone account for half of his run total—the batting averages of those who hit behind him, the number of bases he stole, or the number of walks that put him on first base.

Our notion of the relative worth of the two players might change again if we check the number of hits each had with runners in scoring position (RISP), which is calculated by dividing *hits* with runners on second or third base by *at-bats* with runners on second or third. This statistic corrects for the natural tendency for those in the middle of the lineup to drive in more runs, because managers usually put players with higher OBPs at the top of the lineup, giving the batters behind them greater opportunities for runs batted in (RBI).

Note, however, that despite the various stats we've reviewed, we still haven't been able to say which of our two players *won* more games for his team. To determine that, you could track what is called win probability added (WPA), or calculate what are called win shares. WPA attempts to measure the degree to which an individual player's performance exceeds the average performance of other players in the same situations (for example, with the batter's team down by one run

*OBP is an extremely complicated but very important statistic, calculated by adding hits + bases on balls (walks) + hit-by-pitches, and then dividing by at-bats + bases on balls (walks) + hit-by-pitches + sacrifice flies. Players with high OBP typically bat at the top of the order, because they are more likely to get on base and be driven in for runs.

in the bottom of the eighth, with runners on second and third). Such scenarios, however, can be varied to the degree that they occur only a few times a season. We could, for instance, have stipulated that the hitter was right-handed, the pitcher left-handed, and the game played at night in a domed stadium.

Win shares (for which no acronym appears to be in common use) requires an even more complicated calculation. In short, three win shares are apportioned for each team win, so that a team winning one hundred games in a season would divide three hundred win shares among its players. Those shares are then divided with a slight advantage—52 percent to 48 percent—for defensive players, in order to allow pitchers to collect more shares. Among defensive players, pitchers are awarded approximately twice as many win shares as fielders. Offensive win shares, instead, are apportioned between the hitters responsible for creating runs (which could mean they scored the runs or caused them to be scored). We'll conclude this discussion by noting that some critics of win shares want to see loss shares computed, too.

If this quick look at baseball statistics has your head spinning, then our job is done. In sports, just like in business, data overload can quickly leave everyone wondering what's what. The key to making good use of baseball stats, in other words, is being able to look beyond BA and OBP. If over the thirty most recent games our .300 hitter has batted .350 (presuming ninety-nine trips to the plate), his squiggly line will make the second player all but invisible.* However, if the second player consistently drives in runs throughout the entire season, at critical moments in games with runners in scoring position and with two outs (i.e., with little margin for error), then the second player is the one you want at bat during the playoff run. And this "value" can be reflected in many of the newer statistics we discussed above, as well as others like OPS (OBP plus runs scored) and value over replacement player (VORP).

Finally, if a third player hits close to his .240 lifetime average throughout the entire season but has a .450 season average and .800 OBP against lefty pitching, then a manager is likely to use that player

---

*Of course, it's one thing if those 30 games occur in April and May and another entirely if they occur in September and October.

late in the game, pinch-hitting against a new lefty reliever no one on the team has faced before. In this case, while player three's BA remains remarkably consistent over time, his squiggly line with respect to lefty pitching has real meaning in certain game situations.

So whether you're in the dugout or in the corner office, if you use short-term data to guide your long-term business decisions, your win/loss record is going to be somewhat erratic. This doesn't mean that quarterly sales numbers don't matter. They do, and so do monthly and weekly numbers. But there's no reason to get excited about a 3 percent bump in sales over the space of four weeks if the average month-to-month movement, either up or down, is 5 percent. Nor does the 3 percent increase look good if the sector as a whole saw sales increases nearer 7 percent. The point is that while you need to collect data on a regular basis, short-term data should rarely drive decision making. It might, however, serve as a signal that more lasting change is ahead, a topic we'll turn to in the chapter on "What Surprised You?"

U.S. carmakers provide another example. Over the past fifteen years—unquestionably a Squiggly Line in the history of automobile sales—their profits have depended almost entirely on sales of sport utility vehicles (SUV) and trucks. That was partly due to the cost of Corporate Average Fuel Economy (CAFE) regulations, which were not applied to "light trucks" like SUVs and minivans, and thus made the smaller, more fuel-efficient cars that had to meet those regulations less profitable. But as profitable as SUVs were—U.S. carmakers' profits per SUV unit averaged around $10,000—they were both more expensive to buy and more expensive to operate than standard cars. In other words, they were company-centric products, not customer-centric.* As a result, when the Great Recession of 2007 coincided with a spike in oil prices, the market for them collapsed, as did the fortunes of U.S. carmakers. Of the Big Three—GM, Ford, and Chrysler—only Ford was able to remain in busi-

---

*As you move through these pages, you should begin to see, without any prompting from us, opportunities to ask the questions we've covered in earlier chapters. GM's dependence on SUV sales, for instance, was not only a failure to see past the Squiggly Line but a failure to navigate by the customer's North Star. And when the economy collapsed, fuel prices skyrocketed, the credit markets froze, and the demand for SUVs disappeared almost overnight, GM couldn't adjust quickly enough to avoid massive losses.

ness without government assistance and the federal oversight that accompanied it. Why was Ford able to do this? Because CEO Alan Mulally didn't believe in the Squiggly Line of SUV sales. As a result, in 2006, he borrowed more than $23 billion—in essence, mortgaging the entire company—and thus had the cash on hand to stay in business when the credit markets seized up in 2007 and 2008.

FLAT LINES THAT START TO SQUIGGLE

Of course, there are times when the Squiggly Line should serve as a warning, especially when it's superimposed on a relatively flat, long-term line like, say, the rate of inflation in the United States. From 1985 to 2010, the annual rate of inflation has remained remarkably steady, averaging around 3 percent. (For those of you planning to retire, though, keep in mind that even a 3 percent increase in prices, year after year, means that costs *double* every twenty-five years. Put another way, if you need $100,000 a year to live the life you want to today, and inflation rises *only* 3 percent per year, in 2036 you'll need $200,000 a year to maintain the same lifestyle.)

But what if we look at inflation in the United States over the past century? We see a really squiggly line, not a flat one. In fact, we see only two relatively flat sections in that hundred-year line: the one we discussed above, from 1985 to 2010, and the one that ran from the mid-fifties to the mid-seventies. Yes, that was two decades of relatively stable prices, but look at the volatility that followed them. From 1963 to 1973, the average rate of inflation was just under 4 percent. By 1973, however, the rate had climbed to just over 6 percent. The following year it exceeded 11 percent. That's right, *the rate of inflation nearly doubled over a single year.*

For that reason, at least toward the end of a year like 2010, it's a good idea to look at more than one line to try and predict what's coming. Yes, inflation continues to run *below* the Fed's target number, but at the same time a broad basket of commodities and services—for example, gold, shipping costs, cotton, college tuition, and prescription drugs—have reached all-time highs. What's more, the averages for certain broad categories, like energy and food, hide significant differences in the costs of individual goods.* Put another way, you can find squiggly lines inside what look like relatively flat lines.

While energy costs (as a group) have risen almost 6 percent in 2010, gasoline prices have risen more than 9 percent. Natural gas prices, on the other hand, have fallen by more than 35 percent in the past year. We see similar variations in the price of food. While food prices (as a group) rose only 0.6 percent from October 2009 to October 2010, protein sources like meats, poultry, fish, and eggs rose by nearly 6 percent (or ten times as much as food prices in general). Fruits and vegetables, on the other hand, barely registered an increase. This is especially interesting given that both produce and proteins—or meats, poultry, and fish—are among the most important generators of profit for larger grocery stores.

So don't allow yourself to be fooled by the Squiggly Line, but keep in mind that, sooner or later, if history teaches us anything, flat lines will begin to go squiggly.

BRAND DILUTION

Another common error associated with paying too much attention to the Squiggly Line is brand dilution. As the economy collapsed in 2008 and 2009, luxury industry analysts were stunned to see Bergdorf Goodman, Saks, and Barney's alter their advertising and messaging in an attempt to attract more cost-conscious consumers. And while they may have succeeded in boosting sales by attracting shoppers who would not normally have thought of shopping at their stores, they also risked alienating their core customers, who were unaccustomed to mobs in the fitting rooms. What's more, as the recession begins to ease, those same core customers may be reluctant to pay the sort of price premiums they did three or four years ago. The point is that making long-term strategic moves—like targeting different buyer segments— because of short-term sales trends can negatively impact the brand over the long run.

*Conor Dougherty, "U.S. Inflation Virtually Flat," *Wall Street Journal,* November 18, 2010.

This, in turn, leads us to think about possible shifts in the North Stars of the customers of premium brands. Was the Great Recession of 2007–09 powerful enough to change the habits of specific buyer segments, or will they revert to the mean once the economy picks up speed again? If, instead, a longer-lasting shift has occurred, will it be the same for core customers as it will for newer, more price-sensitive customers? Premium brands are obviously asking themselves the same questions, and are experimenting with lower-priced product lines for large department store chains (e.g., Vera Wang for Kmart) and television shopping (e.g., the *Isaac Mizrahi Hour,* or the *Judith Ripka Hour* at QVC). In this case, the Squiggly Line may point toward a different, and more profitable, future.

BRAND HEALTH

Squiggly lines often show up when you track brand health—that is, the image your customers have of your company. Much has been written on this topic, so we'll restrict our conversation to the way the Squiggly Line syndrome can affect the measurement of your brand's health.

The Awareness, Attitudes, and Usage model (AAU) explains the relationship between, and the movement along, the three factors it tracks. In its simplest terms, awareness of the brand can lead to changes in attitudes, which ultimately lead customers to use, or buy from, the brand.

>> Awareness

Obviously, a customer has to be aware of your company's products or services before they'll consider paying for them. So one of the most important goals of a brand-building program is keeping your company "top of mind" with the consumer.

>> Attitude

The degree to which brand awareness translates into active consideration, and ultimately a purchase, depends on how positive an image of your company the customer has. In other words, buyers may be aware of your brand, but that awareness has to be combined with a positive, relevant image of your brand before they'll consider buying from you. Once your product is included in the "consideration set," a variety of drivers can contribute to a customer's ultimate preference for the brand, which could lead to an initial purchase and eventually steady usage. To understand those drivers, it's important to remember that every customer has a specific set of needs the product must satisfy. The ability of the brand and the product to meet these needs is the key to market success and customer loyalty. If your company's image is closely associated with the drivers of choice, there is a higher probability that your product will be included in that buyer's consideration set—or the set of products and services the customer will consider buying. (The more positive the image the potential customer has of your company, the higher the "consideration rate.") Likewise, if your product is more closely associated with a customer's specific drivers of choice, there is a higher probability that your company will be the brand purchased (which can also be described as an increase in the conversion rate—i.e., the degree to which customers abandon other brands to use yours).

>> Usage

Once a buyer has purchased your product, you'll typically move on to measuring loyalty, or the strength of the customer's desire to continue purchasing from your company, as well as the enthusiasm and frequency with which he or she recommends your brand to others. It is, therefore, important to understand loyalty and satisfaction performance.

These three metrics (AAU) are typically looked at over time.

Of course the frequency with which these measurements are taken will affect their accuracy, something Susan Schwartz McDonald turned to during our interview.

It's like weighing yourself five times a day. A critical task for anyone who's doing research and interpreting data is to make a sensible decision about meaningful measurement intervals, be-cause, for instance, we know it doesn't make sense to look at the

Dow Jones just one week a year. Typically our clients will ask, "How long should I track?" and our answer is almost always that they should track less often than their compulsive instincts encourage them to do.

Finally, when speaking to us about a related issue, Eric Koivisto noted the importance of matching the length of the marketing campaign to the time most customers need to make a decision.

First you've got to ask yourself, What sort of influence model is at work during the purchase process? And also what length of time does the purchase process cover? Those really are the marketing questions, and they'll let you understand what sort of expectations you should have with any sort of marketing and communications campaign or sales efforts that you direct at the market. If the purchase process is 12 months, say, for an enterprise IT solution, well, you better have a campaign that spans 12 months. But if you're selling Windows PCs, a consumer can walk into a store and buy it tomorrow, so you could actually have three-month campaigns. And it's not only about the purchase. When you're putting a marketing campaign together, you have to acknowledge the length of time it takes customers to decide to purchase your product, how much time it takes to install it, and then how soon afterward you can try to measure that customer's satisfaction.

In sum, data overload often leads us to attach too much importance to short-term data. If you want to drink from the Fire Hose, you've got to do so sparingly, and to do that you've got to learn how to look past the Squiggly Line—at least whenever you're making longer-term decisions.

CHAPTER THREE TAKEAWAYS

1. Learn to identify long-term trends that coincide with your company's long-term interests.
2. Always triangulate results using absolute position, changes over time, and comparative measures—like year-to-year gains or losses—carefully, and always compare short-term data to long-term trends.
3. Focus on changes in competitive gaps.
4. Be aware of the "hype factor" and its tendency to inflate initial results, while failing to sustain products and services over the long term.

SECTION TWO

INSIGHT

What Surprised You?

"Society is always taken by surprise at any new example of common sense."

— RALPH WALDO EMERSON

Surprises are wake-up calls to your brain. Surprises are bias killers. Asking "What surprised you?" will spur new discussion, uncover fresh learning, and lead to new insights. People want answers. The secret to uncovering these answers is to apply a prism to the data streaming across your desk. Just as a prism separates light into parts, the question "What surprised you?" separates meaningless data from relevant numbers. The reason is simple: The question exposes outliers in the data, draws connections between seemingly unrelated conclusions, and opens different avenues of discussion with your colleagues.

As Szent-Györgyi put it, "research is to see what everybody else has seen, and to think what nobody else has thought." Most of the time we don't collect data to learn something new; we collect data to confirm what we already know, what we would *like* to be true, or, worse yet, what we believe *everyone else* wants to hear. For all those reasons, really valuable data is often ignored, because everyone's looking past it in an attempt to see what he or she wants to see—whether or not it's actually there in the numbers.

CHAPTER LESSONS

1. Take a hard look at the numbers on the page, not the numbers you *expected* to see.
2. Use your intuition to spot mistakes and your natural skepticism to look for surprises.
3. Don't dismiss every number you can't explain as an outlier.

Think about what happens, instead, when the results *don't* fit people's expectations. Rather than asking themselves if the results might be accurate, they debate the way the data was collected, analyzed, or presented. They challenge the findings, question the approach, and object to your conclusions. Of course, this same sort of scrutiny usually doesn't occur when the results are aligned with everyone's expectations, or indicate the success of a program. In short, if the data is positive, the program is brilliant; if the numbers are negative, there must be a problem with the way the data was collected. For that reason we need to get in the habit of looking for things we don't expect or, put another way, to ask ourselves what, if anything, surprises us.

But surprises are hard to spot when you're busy managing data overload. It's a whole lot safer just to keep a tight grip on the Fire Hose, even if the majority of the numbers blow right past you before you can even get a look at them. It's physics, not a conspiracy—just one more unanticipated consequence of data overload. In order to keep the Fire Hose from whipping right and left, we just try to stay on our feet and do everything we can to keep the data stream pointed in one direction. And after a while we get used to treating any data that sprays too far to one side or the other as an outlier, or a mistake. As H. L. Mencken said, "There is always a well-known solution to every human problem—neat, plausible, and wrong."

In short, almost no one's looking for surprises, or is inclined to go against conventional wisdom, and as a result we end up missing a lot of great opportunities for new insights. As we pointed out in Chapter Two, Webroot's newly redesigned 2010 ad campaign—which focused on the *benefits* of its security software rather than a technical description of its products—is a perfect example of the way a company can put a surprise to work. And keep in mind that the source of that surprise was a simple statement in a customer survey: "I wish security software brands would just explain things in plain English so I could really understand what I'm protected against." Webroot's marketing department didn't expect a strong customer reaction to this statement, which was almost filler in their questionnaire. Instead, it turned out to be a customer favorite, winning third place behind customers wanting to protect their children from online predators, and the degree to which they underestimated the threat of cybercrime. And that surprised Webroot's marketing department.

PHOTOBUCKET

Founded in 2003, Photobucket is an image-and-video-hosting service used by a number of high-profile Web sites like eBay, MySpace, and Facebook, in addition to blogs and Internet forums too numerous to count. The service offers free storage up to 1GB and, for a fee, storage up to 100GB (to noncommercial users).

By 2006, according to *TechCrunch*, a group-edited blog covering tech start-ups, Photobucket was serving 63 percent of all media links on MySpace (compared with 8 percent for Flickr). In 2007, Photobucket founders Alex Welch and Darren Crystal sold the company to Fox Interactive Media, owner of MySpace. Two years later, News Corp., Fox Interactive's parent, merged the service with Seattle imaging start-up Ontela (retaining the Photobucket name). Despite the company's phenomenal success, the former vice president of engineering at Photobucket remembers how close the start-up came to stalling in its trial stage. That man's name? Scott Penberthy.

Photobucket was founded by a network guy, a guy who worked in the back office. He wanted to build another Flickr, you know, a beautiful site for editing and sharing images. As the story goes, he comes home after building his site, looks at his credit card, and he's got a bill for $700. This is in 2003. And what's happening is that people were uploading pictures on his site, and because he left his back door open they were linking his pictures to eBay, which at the time limited the number of pictures you could post, because it was so expensive to serve up images at that scale because of the cost of the bandwidth. And if you remember, 2003 was the year *Sports Illustrated* first tried to protect its images, because people were stealing them and putting them on other sites, which meant *SI* had to pay for the bandwidth. So a lot of people considered it a big problem.

So the engineer was really depressed and told his wife, "Look, I built this site and all they're doing is uploading images and not even sharing them with their friends, they're just linking them to eBay. I feel like I built some stupid Netbucket in the sky. No one's really using my site, they're just using me to host their images."

But his wife saw that the price of bandwidth was dropping precipitously, and she put two and two together and said, "Look, if the price of bandwidth goes to zero, and it's going that way, pretty soon it's going to be really cheap. What if we built a business just for hosting the images?"

"I don't know," her husband said. "Here I built this whole elaborate site, and all they're using it for is hosting their stupid images," and his wife said, "Are you kidding? There's something here." So they were going to call it Netbucket, but they did a search and found out that Netbucket was taken, and that's when she came up with the name Photobucket.

So he puts the site up, which had a one-page script, and he had a thousand users the first week. A few months later he mortgaged his house to pay for the bandwidth. He was still in his twenties. And a month or so after that, his former boss quit *his* job to work on the project, and before long he was mortgaging *his* house to pay for some more routers.

A lot of people don't know that Photobucket even exists, but almost everyone has used the service without knowing it. And that's because the engineer's wife was right: The price of bandwidth did drop, and Figure 20 demonstrates the decay of billed revenue per minute over a thirty-year period.

[FIGURE 20]

BILLED REVENUES PER MINUTE AND PER CALL

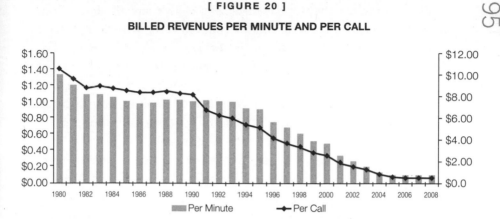

Source: "Trends in Telephone Service," Industry Analysis and Technology Division, Wireline Competition Bureau, FCC, September 2010

Darrell Bricker, who's made a career of looking for surprises, says it all comes down to continually challenging your assumptions.

> You have to be prepared to challenge your assumptions all the time. New things are always emerging, because the world is always changing, and sometimes these things represent a new trend and you have to pay attention to them. But in order to decide whether you should pay attention, you have to have the discipline to do one thing, and the humility to do another. The discipline involves actually following through on all the scientific principles we talked about earlier, because sometimes surprising results are just mistakes. But when you find something that's truly revealing, that's really different than what you expected, and that thing forces you to think, you have to have the humility not to dismiss it. You have to be prepared to admit you were wrong, because the scientific method is about admitting that you're wrong, that things might not be the way they seemed.

Of course, surprises aren't always ignored. Sometimes it's not that you brush them off; sometimes you just miss them. It's not that they clashed with your assumptions or hurt your pride. You just didn't see them, even though they might have been right there all along. You might have stared at them for months, or even years, without ever seeing them. Or you might have noticed them but decided to address them later, and then when that *later* comes it turns out to be just a little *too* late. Finally, they might be things you've got to turn a few rocks over to find. Once you develop the habit of looking for surprises, especially after you first catch the glint of gold in a panful of gravel, you'll be more likely to make it part of your routine.

Even if you're looking, it's still hard work. Especially when you're so busy you can't find fifteen free minutes to clear your head. What's more, when reports, conference calls, and meetings fill every waking hour, you tend to develop a mechanical approach to doing business. It's the only way you can keep going. Under conditions like these, it's extremely difficult to set aside preconceived notions, to open new doors, or to find new vantage points. In other words, the willingness to be surprised is often one of the first victims of the frenzied workday and the never-ending torrent of data that flows into it.

IBM GRID COMPUTING: PAUL MAGNONE

One morning about ten years ago, when I was still at IBM, senior management pulled me out of a business development training session I was running and told me to forget about what I had been doing up to that point—they had something new for me. What they wanted was an in-depth report on the emerging field of virtualization and grid computing. In short, the management team wanted to know what parts of the emerging business, if any, were commercially viable. And if there appeared to be any potential beyond hardware sales, they wanted to know *how* the company should enter the field.

So I started by assembling an investigative team of technologists, consultants, market researchers, salespersons, and operations managers. Virtualization, or the aggregation of computing resources that are then made accessible to all, had already established a presence in the technical and academic community, where it was focused on physics and mathematical simulators. My Essential Question was pretty obvious: Did business needs exist in other industries for what was still a somewhat theoretical approach? And if the answer to that question was yes, then I had to find out whether the business community was ready to adopt the technology and if there could be a systems integration or consulting revenue opportunity for IBM.

For the next four months, part of my team and I gathered information on the approach, trying to forecast its likely direction and its potential for expansion. At the same time, I sent the sales team out into the field, where they met with somewhere around seventy-five prospective customers over 120 days. At first, armed with what little we could tell them about a technology that wasn't really operational— at least not in the business sense of the word—they just tried to gauge interest. Meanwhile, though, in the backs of their minds, they were already picking out a few likely candidates for the customer pilot programs we planned to run. Once they came in from the field, we correlated the feedback they got from their potential customers with the technological and operational data and the marketing research, and produced the report that management had asked for.

Our initial findings weren't surprising, but then again, they hardly ever are. And that's the point. We all go looking for what we want to find, not for what's really there. Which brings me to one of the things Chris and I talk about all the time, something that goes on at almost every meeting we're ever in. Typically, there you are, stuck in the conference room, and every question anyone asks comes with a ready-made answer. And even though everyone at the meeting knows this is going on, no one wants to rewrite the script. There's no fact-finding going on, no free exchange of ideas, and no real information being passed along. It's more like a table-wide conspiracy to provide only the numbers that support what everyone there knows the boss wants to hear. There are never *any* surprises. But we were determined to have a different type of meeting and a better outcome.

At any rate, as I said earlier, smaller markets for data virtualization and grid computing already existed in certain applied sciences—and in the pharmaceutical and life sciences industries—and so IBM's technological expertise, along with its global sales and support capabilities, made the company a natural player in the game. The surprises we discovered in the course of our review, however, made the real case for the company's involvement.

To begin with, our market research guys found a huge untapped opportunity in the financial sector, especially in analytics acceleration for quantitative analysts, or "quants"—number crunchers who needed vast pools of computing power to execute the calculations necessary for financial modeling and derivatives pricing. Financial firms also needed extra computing resources to optimize support for the "end-of-the-day book closing" they had to do to meet government regulations. Car manufacturers could use the grid techniques for engineering and design purposes, to say nothing of simulated crash tests and cross-team coordination. Even more promising, we found a market for petroleum firms that needed more computing power for seismic analysis calculation to draw oil reserves more efficiently, and energy companies that could use the technology to calculate weather patterns more accurately and save on the costs associated with firing up auxiliary power plants to meet spikes in demand.

The real surprise of our report, then, was that, contrary to prevailing wisdom, the largest markets for virtualization weren't in the academic and research sectors but in mainstream industries like finance, manufacturing, and energy. Once we knew that, we were able to align ourselves pretty quickly with an existing IBM division, in a complementary space for sales and services, which greatly speeded up the launch of our new consulting offerings and drove the customer pipeline.

And because of what we found, we were also surprised to find that we needed application developers and business process consultants—in addition to the hardware system designers we already knew we'd need. This was a real transformation for customers in both process efficiency and cost savings, given the change that virtualization would bring to the IT infrastructure, applications, and processes in place at the time.

The surprises didn't stop there.

Building on our work, IBM subsequently founded the World Community Grid (WCG), a public computing grid available to public and nonprofit organizations—which might otherwise be unable to pay for the high cost of the necessary computer infrastructure—to use in tackling humanitarian problems around the globe. Our team provided the initial staff to launch and support WCG operations. IBM sent a handful of us out into the wild, looking for surprises in emerging business opportunities, and ended up building not only a whole new set of service offerings but a computer infrastructure—and application expertise—for an evolving list of humanitarian problems.

As Chuck Salter wrote in the May 1, 2010, edition of *Fast Company:*

IBM's World Community Grid (WCG) [is] an unprecedented effort to deploy ordinary people's idle computers to create a free, open-source lab for researchers around the globe. Massive computational research is broken down into discrete problems and distributed across a vast network. Since the tech giant launched the nearly $2-million-a-year project in November 2004, more than half a million people in 218 countries have volunteered some 1.5 million laptops and desktops. In raw computing power, the grid is comparable to a top-10 supercomputer. The average PC would take more than 328,000 years to complete the grid's calculations so far.[*]

>> Surprising Market Opportunities

While the team Magnone put together to investigate opportunities in grid computing was surprised to find large markets no one had yet considered for that emerging technology, some companies are surprised to find the same sorts of opportunities within existing markets for better-established technologies. We recently came across an excellent example of such a discovery, made by a company in the predictive modeling industry: Adaptive Technologies Inc.

ATi, founded in 2001 by physicists Chris Stephens and Henri Waelbroeck, offers a variety of software products and services, ranging from customer value management to direct marketing solutions. The sophistication of its products, though, and the infrastructure they require, limited ATi's market to companies with annual revenues of billions of dollars. Then, almost by accident, chief strategy officer Dave McLurg came across a midsize company[†] that showed interest in ATi's products.

[*]Chuck Salter, "How IBM's World Community Grid Is Helping Cure AIDs, Cancer, and World Hunger," *Fast Company,* May 1, 2010.
[†]ATi defines companies with annual revenues between $100 million and $2 billion as "midsize."

AS CHIEF STRATEGY officer, Dave McLurg is responsible for a wide range of company initiatives and programs, including sales, marketing, strategic relationships, client relations, joint ventures, capital development, and brand management. A seasoned entrepreneur, McLurg has led a variety of organizations providing proprietary technology and advanced analytics, across industries as diverse as data intelligence, health care, retail, hospitality, and financial services.

McLurg is a graduate of London's Westervelt College but gives equal credit to the dozens of executive courses he's taken over the past thirty years in leadership, strategic planning, branding, sales, marketing, analytics, supply chain management, total quality management, and behavioral science.

According to McLurg, the market for midsize organizations had been there all along, but the company mistakenly believed that the cost and the platform requirements limited the market to *Fortune* 500 companies.

ATi has been providing predictive modeling solutions for major corporations for more than ten years, and although the field is now growing rapidly, the company was well ahead of the curve when they opened their doors. Most of what they did in the beginning was large enterprise work, like providing the algorithm switch engine for a large block-trading company on Wall Street, and modeling work for the U.S. military.

In fact, the company's early growth followed the typical pattern of the "law of the diffusion of innovation." You know when you're talking about implementing this kind of complex technology there's a very small group, say 2 or 3 percent, who are your innovators. After that come the early adopters, and then what's called the "early majority." Again, at the beginning of any complicated or leading-edge technology, only a small percentage of the potential market adapts to it quickly, and predictive modeling is still in that stage.

So, as I said, ATi was well ahead of the curve when they came up with this ten years ago, and the market still hasn't quite caught up. In the meantime, the business world has moved from the information age to the information-accumulation stage, which raised the issue of information relevance. So now the issue is, we have all this data, and how do we begin to use it? How do we make it relevant, given whatever it is we're trying to do? And so we began to look at the marketplace, and a lot of these innovators were the large corporations that understood the power of data and the importance of driving their operations through data.

The company that surprised McLurg, and got him thinking about a midsize market for his company's technology and services, was interested in Adaptive Technologies' direct marketing product, SMART DM. And at that point there was another surprise in store for McLurg.

At an enterprise level, all our customers wanted everything customized, you know, specific to them, because every one of those businesses was different, and their problems were somewhat unique. With the midsize market, instead, we found they didn't like the word *customized*, because they associated it with being expensive. So not only did we have to redesign the product; we had to change our messaging.

Despite being smaller than ATi's typical prospects, the company was already spending a lot of money, spread out over multiple sources, mostly in an effort to generate leads for new revenue. So the question they put to McLurg was this: How could they go through all that information and make sure they were optimizing their resources, and successfully leveraging their spending? And again, given the sophistication of predictive modeling, they wanted to come up with a solution they could afford, and one their present infrastructure could support.

Having seen the opportunity, McLurg commissioned market research to gauge the size of the market, and the general uses that midsize companies might have for predictive modeling. At the same time he spoke to people inside ATi, from salespeople to marketers and technologists, to see what they thought about the redesign. Finally, once they began to get results from focus groups they'd set up, McLurg helped them use that information to inform the product redesign.

Once my eyes had been opened to the opportunity, ATi's leaders had the vision, and the technological expertise, to take their *Fortune* 50 solution and create a version of our direct marketing product that a midsize business could afford to buy, could afford to support, and could afford to run within their budget.

Again, ATi would never have seen this particular forest for the trees had McLurg not been open to the possibility of a surprise—in this case, the existence of a market that didn't fit the customer profile Adaptive Technologies had used up until then.

Even though I have multiple business interests, and lead several businesses, I consider myself to be a sales guy, and I don't believe anything happens until a sale is made. Peter Drucker was one of my mentors, and he said that the purpose of a business is to find and keep customers. So I'm focused every day on trying to come up with a better way to do that, and so I always try to listen as carefully and as naively as I can.

Next we'd like to turn to another of our own experiences, one that occurred when Chris was working at Microsoft.

MICROSOFT ROSS: CHRISTOPHER FRANK

I had the same kind of epiphany Paul did earlier in my career. I was working at Microsoft at the time, and it just kind of came to me at the conclusion of a quarterly review of customer satisfaction data. The data had been collected from thousands of customers, via a twenty-minute online survey designed to assess the overall health of the relationship customers had with the brand. The respondents included decision makers in multiple roles and functions across finance, marketing, and IT. Using a battery of questions, the survey was meant to identify the various aspects that shaped the overall customer experience.

Our senior execs began by looking at the data in absolute terms: In general, were customers satisfied or dissatisfied with Microsoft's products? Were they satisfied with the customer service? With Microsoft's product support? Did satisfaction vary by age, gender, or nationality? Were there any hot spots? That is, were there any subsets of data—again, by age, gender, nationality, or region—that varied greatly from the general results? Finally, how did Microsoft's customer satisfaction data stack up against that of its competitors' in the software business?

I'd already gone through a number of these quarterly sessions, none of them particularly revealing, when someone, just as this particular meeting was being wrapped up, asked me whether there were any data points I couldn't explain. Yes, I said, without really thinking—there were. I'd come across a handful of sales districts that had seen double-digit growth in customer satisfaction, but they were spread all over the map. I meant that literally; there was no logical demographic profile connecting the seven distinct areas across the country. And even though the growth in customer satisfaction was meteoric in these regions, it wasn't consistent with the other results. And so my team and I naturally dismissed the numbers as outliers—that is, as data points that were statistically significant but for which no explanation could be found.

We think Darrell Bricker's thoughts on the subject—again from the perspective of a social scientist, rather than a market researcher—are revealing.

Good research is not really about looking for confirmation; it's about disproving the null hypothesis. Open up any basic introduction to social science research and that's what it'll say.

What he means is that everyone should work at attempting to prove the extent to which something is *not* so. And only the degree to which they *fail* to do that gives the proposition they're investigating any validity. But the opposite, according to Bricker, is typical of the limited mind-set of the ordinary market researcher.

It's kind of bass-ackwards, if you think about it, because we spend so much time trying to get to the point, and focusing on exactly what we're trying to understand, we forget that the way that you get there is by *disproving* all the other stuff. And a big part of that is being willing to go with a hunch. Like I said earlier, the important thing is to retain the humility to understand that you don't understand everything. Research should be a very humiliating process.

For instance, I do a lot of media commentary, because we do a lot of research on things that are happening now in the news, and I always go in there thinking I know just what I'm going to find—and I'm humiliated by the data *all the time*. I should have the best gut, or the best intuition, of anybody in the field, and yet mine is often the worst. Because no matter how long you've been at it, you're still a product of your own prejudices, right?

To return, then, to Microsoft, the issue for Chris was whether or not the surprises in the data were significant or just outliers.

So these particular outliers, from the quarterly customer satisfaction review, were a perfect example of the data leaving the market researcher—who just happened to be me—dumbfounded. But with this I was asked back to find the reason behind the outliers, if there was one. And what my team and I found surprised everyone.

Unbeknownst to most senior managers, Microsoft had instituted a pilot program called the Rapid Onsite Support Service, or ROSS, to beef up support for certain enterprise accounts. When we overlaid a map of the ROSS pilot areas on the customer satisfaction data, the correlation was almost perfect. As it turned out, there was a very good reason for those atypical results, but we'd never have known it if we had dismissed them as the outliers they appeared to be.

Once upper-level management saw what was going on, the ROSS initiative was quickly incorporated into Microsoft's Software Assurance program. Subsequent data confirmed its value. Sure, the program would almost certainly have found its way into the company's support offerings sooner or later, but who knows how long it might have taken. Instead, because of one simple question—Are there any data points you can't explain?—the value of the pilot program was recognized early on, and put to work as part of the company's basic support package.

FIRE HOSE EXERCISE NO. 2: THE ROOMBA

Now we're going to take a look at a relatively young company that's nearly in a class by itself: iRobot. Founded in 1990 by MIT roboticists

Colin Angle, Helen Greiner, and Rodney Brooks, the company initially concentrated on military/industrial applications of robotic technology, like space exploration robots, minesweeping robots, and tactical mobile robots (which were used both in theaters of war and to search amid the rubble of the Twin Towers after 9/11).

Then, in 2002, the company took a chance and entered the fledgling domestic-robotics market with a product that might just as well have dropped down from outer space. But from the moment a heavily disguised Roomba sucked Dave Chapelle's pants off in a Pepsi commercial, a star was born. We spoke to Nancy Dussault-Smith, vice president of marketing communications at iRobot, to learn a little more about the history of the Roomba, and to put a couple of the Fire Hose Questions to the test.

NANCY DUSSAULT SMITH is VP of marketing communications for iRobot Corporation. She spearheaded the first successful product launch of a home robot in America, introducing the iRobot Roomba Vacuum-Cleaning Robot to the world in 2002. Ms. Smith currently oversees all of the public relations and branding efforts at iRobot, from promoting acceptance of military robotics to tweeting with mommy bloggers about home products. She was a National Merit Scholar and holds a B.S./B.A. in marketing and advertising from Merrimack College.

Smith began by telling us that the Roomba, despite our guess to the contrary, was not an outgrowth of the industrial/military work for which the company was known. The development of the first robotic floor vacuum was, instead, a conscious move, if not a priority.

A couple of our engineers said we have an idea, and they went to Colin [Angle], our CEO, and told him, "I think we should make a robot that cleans your house. You know, that vacuums the floors." So Colin gave them a very small sum of money, I think it was around twenty thousand dollars, told them they could use a couple of other engineers, and said, "Okay, let's see what you can come up with." Before long they had come back with some pretty interesting prototypes, and that really opened Colin's eyes. And once he'd seen a few examples of the kind of thing they could make, he had the foresight to say, Yeah, there's a market out there for this. Of course, it was really in keeping with his philosophy, that is, the whole reason he started iRobot, which was to build practical robots. In fact, our central message is "Real Robots for the Real World," which is perfectly consistent with Colin's mission, which evolved over time with the other founders, to bring robots out of science fiction and bring them into people's homes. And it turned out that vacuuming floors was a great practical application of that mission.

According to Smith, there were a lot of surprises along the way. For one, the company had never built a product for retail sale, and that required a new attention to cost controls during production.

The first thing we had to learn was how important a nickel was, or even a penny was. When you're building military robots, or you have a DARPA* contract, or you have a certain amount of money to prove a concept, it's not that money's no object, but it's not the same as trying to serve a mass market. With an industrial project, the customer might say, "Let's put this in, and this in, and this in, and if it adds ten dollars of cost, it adds ten dollars of cost." It's not a big deal, especially when the price is as high as it is for industrial robots. When you're mass-producing a robot, though, that's going to be sold in retail, saving a nickel is extremely important, and that surprised our team. So cost reduction was something we had to learn very early on, so that we could get it to the point where it was affordable for most people.

Smith said that another big surprise was the design disconnect between the company's engineers and potential customers. Again, keep in mind that nothing remotely like the Roomba had ever been offered for sale. In its way, it was as new and different as the first Kodak cam-

*DARPA, the Defense Advanced Research Projects Agency, is the research-and-development office for the U.S. Department of Defense. Its mission is to maintain the technological superiority of the U.S. military and prevent technological surprise from harming our national security. It also creates technological surprises for U.S. adversaries.

era—about which we'll have more to say later—or the Sony Walkman. There simply had been nothing like it before, and so the public had no idea what it *should* look like. That said, potential customers did have an idea of what it *would* look like.

> The point is that we were going into a completely new industry, with a completely new product, that nobody had ever seen, or even thought about. So when we went into focus groups we'd ask, "Okay, what does a robot vacuum look like?" and everyone would draw a picture of a humanoid robot pushing a vacuum. You know, like something out of *The Jetsons*. In other words, nothing like the small, disk-like thing we were making. We knew, of course, that everyone thought humanoid robots would look like us, just made of metal. Everybody had seen them in movies, and TV shows, to say nothing of the Tin Man in *The Wizard of Oz*. But obviously that's not the best way, or the most economical way, to build a robot vacuum. Anyway, when we'd show people in the focus groups a picture of the Roomba, and ask them what they thought it was, most people thought it was a scale. So even though they'd never seen one, they had to take a leap of faith with regard to its form.

It was only after iRobot launched the Roomba, however, that the real surprises began to pop up, one after the other. First, the company's marketing research revealed the astonishing fact that 67 percent of the people who bought Roombas *named* them, as if they were pets or members of the family. Second, those same initial post-purchase surveys revealed that a surprisingly large number of people who bought it had some sort of disability.

> We had never thought of it as an enabling device, so we were shocked to see how many people bought one because they were *unable* to vacuum. We just didn't see that one coming. People with different levels of mobility were buying them, people who had impaired vision were buying them, and, probably most surprising of all, the elderly were buying them, who you wouldn't normally think of if you were trying to come up with a profile

of the "early adopters" for robots. It turned out that seniors who wanted to remain in their homes but couldn't do the cleaning themselves immediately saw the benefits. So it wasn't just a cool gadget to have; it satisfied a real need for them. In fact, serving the elderly is now a huge topic for robotics, and I could talk to you for hours about it, especially because of our aging population and the cost of assisted living, to say nothing of the psychological value of personal independence, and it just turned out that the Roomba was the kind of robot that could help make that happen.

With global demographics skewing toward the elderly—to a degree never before seen in human history—Smith and iRobot believe that vacuum and floor-cleaning robots are just the first step. Robots could be used to remind people to take their medications. They could be designed to carry heavy groceries, or simply to help the elderly stand up. And while larger robots would, of course, cost far, far more than the Roomba, one need only consider the cost of hospitalization and rehabilitation after a fall to see the market potential.

Still, Smith pointed out that sending the right message to that segment of the market was particularly challenging. While the elderly welcomed the Roomba, because it met a real need, the company's surveys also revealed a fine line between their desire for help and their desire for independence. Pride, too, played a part—after taking care of themselves, and their families, for six or seven decades, seniors didn't want to be told they *couldn't* do something. The desire for privacy, however, may favor robotics—that is, a robotic helping hand in and out of the shower may be preferable to a human hand. Whatever form the "elder robots" take, Smith acknowledged that iRobot and a lot of other companies are focusing on that area. In fact, iRobot already has a health care unit to explore the possibilities.

Again, the point is that iRobot's marketers were better able to serve this part of the market—by looking for its North Star—because they didn't just look at sales figures for their domestic robot line, they continually found surprises in the customer survey data, and those surprises led them to new market opportunities.

And in fact, once the Roomba had opened the door to the domestic market, the company quickly expanded its product line, offering pool-

cleaning robots, and even gutter-cleaning robots. As a result, the domestic market now accounts for approximately half of the company's
revenue.

> This was a real surprise, because the domestic technology was
> all new. It wasn't just recycled from industrial projects, al-
> though some of the algorithms we were using for military
> search robots did give us some valuable insights about the
> Roomba's design. If you think about it, when robots go out to
> search for land mines, they have to cover an entire area effec-
> tively, an area with lots of obstacles. So working around trees
> and boulders is really the same thing as cleaning a living room,
> where there are couches and chairs and, if you have kids, things
> left all over the place.
>
> Of course, a domestic sale is very different from an industrial
> sale. The robots that go out in battlegrounds are very expensive.
> They're six figures, and so every unit doesn't get one. They only
> go to the EOD* squads and to the police and to the SWAT teams,
> and so there's a limit to the number of people who can use them.
> Still, they're doing a great job.

Since we had Smith on the line, we figured we might as well run a
few of the other Fire Hose Questions past her, to see if they applied to
iRobot's strategic decision making.

> Again, our primary message is "Real Robots for the Real World."
> But since we're a business, we have to ask ourselves how much it
> will cost to make a certain robot, and how much will people pay
> for it. Especially because almost everything we build has never
> been seen before, so a potential buyer doesn't have a cost-benefit
> number in their head. So if we go out and do too much market
> research, we can get into analysis paralysis like everybody else,
> because people have no idea how much the things we sell should
> cost. That's why we always start by asking, Is this product solv-
> ing a real problem—that is, will it give people a benefit they can
> see, at a reasonable price, given the job it's doing?

*Explosive ordnance disposal.

Here, once again, we see the interconnectivity of the Fire Hose Questions. iRobot begins by asking the Essential Question, which leads to surprising consumer survey data and a better understanding of their domestic customers' North Stars.

> And if it hits those criteria, then we move forward. If it doesn't, then we have to look at one of those two areas. If the price is a problem, we ask ourselves if there was any "feature creep" in the project—i.e., adding too many features—which is always an issue for us, and I'm sure it's an issue with other people in other industries as well. Our engineers always want to pile more and more features on our robots, and our customers too, so we have to ask ourselves if they're helping the product to do its main job, or just cool additions.

Even though nothing like the Roomba had ever been seen before, everyone knew what vacuum cleaners cost, and so iRobot had some idea of what people might pay for its robot vacuum. But there was no benchmark for the Looj, iRobot's gutter-cleaning robot. There was literally nothing to compare it with, except the cost of a good ladder—or the time and money it would cost you if you fell off that ladder while you were cleaning your gutters. On the other hand, iRobot's Scooba, the floor-washing robot, had to compete with mops and buckets that together cost only $10. And since the Scooba costs thirty times that, a lot of people were clearly going to ask themselves if they needed to spend $300 on something that does what a mop and bucket do. The point is this: You can do all the advanced studies in the world to try and find out what the general public will pay for something, but until you have a product out there, a product that people can really touch and smell and see, price can be very hard to judge. Still, if you've got infants crawling around on the floor and then putting their hands in their mouth, you may be able to convince a certain segment of the market that the cost is reasonable. It's all about getting the message out, letting people see what the product does, and then convincing them to pay for it.

According to Smith, that message is entirely different when the military is the customer.

It's different with the military robots. They go out into war zones, find bombs, and render them safe. How do you put a price tag on that? So when we're talking about minesweeping robots, and people say, "Wow, they cost $130,000," we say that's a bargain. To date, it's estimated that they've saved tens of thousands of lives. And you have to think of the casualties outside of the military, too, the collateral damage. How do you put a price tag on that?

Finally, we talked to Smith about another innovative iRobot product line: maritime robots.

We've got robots out in the ocean doing amazing things. I'll give you a stat that blew me away the first time I heard it. After the [BP] oil spill, the government sent out research vessels to see how much oil was in the water, and what it was doing there, and where it was, and where it was going. Our people told me you could put seven of our sea gliders out there and operate them for three years, sending information back every single day, for what it cost for the research vessel to be out for one week.

In short, iRobot's marketing department isn't just occasionally surprised by the data they collect—they're out there every day actively hunting for surprises. As we said at the beginning of this book, once you begin to ask the Fire Hose Questions, and see their benefits, they'll quickly become part of your day-to-day approach and will prove to be very contagious, too.

DO YOU HAVE THE TIME TO BE SURPRISED?

Finally, we want to cover the issue of time. Specifically, the amount of time you need to allow yourself to be surprised. Because it won't happen if you're busy every minute of the day. The U.S. Bureau of Labor Statistics' (BLS) American Time Use Survey (ATUS) for 2008 revealed that the average American aged 25 to 54 who lived in a household with children under 18 slept 7.6 hours every night. (See Figure 21.) Working and "work-related activities" consumed another 8.8 hours. Eating and drinking, household activities, caring for others, and all "other" activities averaged about an hour apiece, leaving a little more than two and a half hours for leisure and sports, most of which, it turned out, was devoted to watching television. (Perhaps most of the respondents were watching sports on television, and that accounts for sports and leisure being lumped together.)

[FIGURE 21]

TIME USE ON AN AVERAGE WORKDAY FOR EMPLOYED PERSONS AGES 25 TO 54 WITH CHILDREN

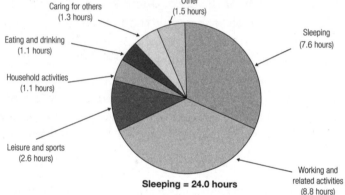

NOTE: Data include employed persons on days they worked, ages 25–54, who lived in households with children under 18. Data include non-holiday weekdays and are annual averages for 2009.
Source: Bureau of Labor Statistics

We'll bet that this "average" time use chart doesn't look anything like your average day, because it doesn't look anything like ours, either. Even when we manage to take an entire weekend off, which happens only slightly more often than the Mets win a World Series, work or work-related activities tend to account for *a lot more than* half of our weekdays. Set aside six and a half hours for sleep, an hour for getting dressed and ready for work, and an hour each for eating and drinking, household activities, caring for our children and parents, and "other" activities, and 24 hours are barely enough to satisfy our responsibilities, with no "leisure" involved.

What's worse, today's hyperconnectivity, which allows us to work on our way to work, robs us of the time we used to be able to devote to reading the paper, shooting the breeze with whoever was sitting next to us on the train, or just shutting our eyes and letting our thoughts drift. The point is that we need to create a little space, and give ourselves the opportunity to be surprised. While it may seem a luxury, it is in fact a necessity. World leaders do it, business leaders do it, parents are encouraged to do it, and if you're serious about improving your work/life balance—and about learning how to drink from the Fire Hose—then you need to do it, too. Being surprised, and being open to surprises, means putting aside a little time every day to look for the unexpected. And that just won't happen if you're always rushing to catch up with you calendar.

CHAPTER FOUR TAKEAWAYS

1. Don't fall into the trap of gathering data to support existing conclusions.
2. Anomalies in the data are more likely to reveal opportunities than numbers that conform to expectations.
3. Create time to consider the possibility of surprises.

CHAPTER FIVE

What Does the Lighthouse Reveal?

"A weather report is somewhat irrelevant to a ship on the bottom of the ocean."

—CORY WILLIAMSON

Modern businesses are ships steaming through vast oceans of data. Some of that data describes rocks near the shore. Like growth in a competitor's market. Or a decline in sales in a key region. Or rising supply costs. Other data streams portray dangers that can be thought of as currents or tides. Like imminent changes in industry regulations. Or other firms that submit competitive bids. The cost of finance is a good example. Copycat products from new start-ups are another. And the political environment, which changes just like the weather, is one more.

So, as you navigate through the facts and figures, you need to know which numbers symbolize the rocks in your path. And to do that, you have to learn to separate the useful information from the irrelevant data. That sort of information confers real power. It enables you to deploy your resources with maximum efficiency. It saves you time. It enables you to focus on the meaningful issues and ignore the rest with a high degree of confidence.

People often turn to research to find this information. But research won't provide it. In fact, research *shouldn't* provide it. Effective analysis is not intended to provide answers. It's only there to narrow your choices to the core set of issues that, combined with your business acumen, will result in the best decision.

In this chapter we'll show you how to apply the Lighthouse approach to routine data, whether or not you know anything about modeling, forecasting, or regression analysis. True to our Fire Hose principles, this is really about asking the right question at the right time, and making the dialogue a catalyst for uncovering the dangers between us and our objectives.

CHAPTER LESSONS

1. Define the criteria that are meaningful to your business.
2. Identify the data to illuminate new learning.
3. Develop strategy that's defensible and can scale.

At some point in almost any business project, you'll be confronted with *far* more data than you need. The data you want, however, should lead to clear, actionable information, with no ambiguity. It is what we call Lighthouse data—that is, the sort of critical information that will keep your business out of danger. And once you have that information, your job is to develop a robust, informed response to the dangers it reveals. Then, when that's done, you've got to put beacons in place to be sure everyone in the business stays clear of the trouble.

By learning how to spot this Lighthouse information, you'll enable your team to focus their attention on day-to-day operations and move your business forward without *unnecessary* risk.

Approached in this manner, selective data collection and perceptive analysis will enable you to map and size the obstacles in your way in the same way a lighthouse shines its light on the rocks along the shore—before you come to them. That, in turn, leads to more effective decision making.

You can also think of Lighthouse data as the answer to the following question: What's going on that I should be worried about? Looked at in this way, the question is the mirror image of the one we asked in Chapter One: What one vital, indispensable piece of information do I need to move the project or the company forward? The answer to that Essential Question puts the project on course; answers to the Lighthouse question let you know when you have to change your bearings.

FOLLOWING THE BEAM

In any hundred scraps of information, ninety-five will be of little consequence. In fact, you're lucky if you find four or five that are really critical. These four or five are what we call Lighthouse data. After that it's up to you, but your Lighthouse insights will enable you to use your business acumen to keep your projects on course. Without the insights gained from those four or five pieces of information, you'll be forced to depend on intuition and instinct. And with unfiltered data streaming past you, it's easy to miss something—until it's too late. That said, data is still only a supporting character in any business. Information and insights won't make decisions for you, but they will orient the conversation and help you establish guardrails.

The trick, then, lies in not confusing any of the ninety-odd factors with the truly critical information needed to successfully go to market. Then, by continually tracking the data that really matters—the Lighthouse data—an effective leader can set a course and stay on it. Or, looked at from a different angle, a hundred different factors may bear on the course a business owner sets to bring forward a new initiative. These may include the market direction, the depth or complexity of the business solution, the unknown delivery challenges for your new investment, surprising economic shifts that prevent a viable business case, the presence of other competition, and the visibility of other strategic or tactical market factors that hinder progress.

This sort of data provides navigational guidance, rather than a warning (see Figure 22).

Used this way, "What Does the Lighthouse Reveal?" is the Fire Hose Question you'll use to identify the four or five dials you need to identify to keep your business humming and allow it to grow. The question, then, is what kind of data, numbers, or information do you need to keep out of trouble? Real trouble. According to Susan Schwartz McDonald, gathering this Lighthouse data is a fixed part of the market researcher's job.

That's kind of standard fare for market research . . . and your eyes should open wide when you start to see people doing things that they didn't use to do. And I think that the marketplace is full of those shifts, like the shift from brick-and-mortar retail to the

[FIGURE 22]

DEFINING WHERE TO FOCUS

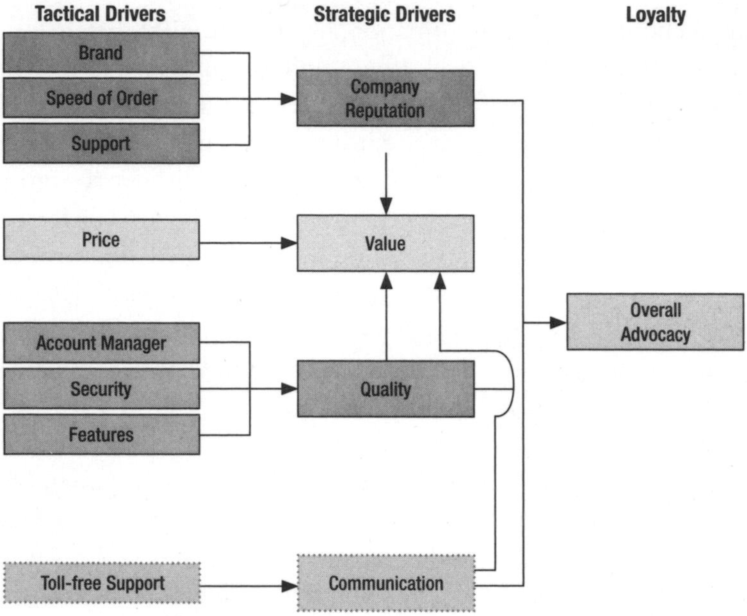

Tactical Drivers	Strategic Drivers	Loyalty

Brand
Speed of Order
Support
Company Reputation
Price
Value
Account Manager
Security
Features
Quality
Overall Advocacy
Toll-free Support
Communication

Web. So you do that all the time by tracking what people are doing and looking for changes in those behaviors, and partly what you hunt for when you do those things is news in the environment that makes you nervous.

BEACONS

The age of information has given us newer, more immediate means of warning and guidance. The Ushahidi platform, for instance, pioneered by Ory Okolloh and Erik Hersman, is an example of the power of multiple beacons, especially when collected, mapped, and then disseminated with the help of modern technology. In just a few words, the Ushahidi platform is a social-media tool that "crowdsources" information, mapping data delivered via SMS, e-mail, or the Web, or spreading it along a timeline. The word *ushahidi* means "testimony" in Swahili, and the program was created in the violent aftermath of the 2008 elections in Kenya. Fed by eyewitness reports and digital photographs from more than 45,000 users around the country, the platform created a map of post-election violence, allowing peacemakers to focus their attention on the worst outbreaks. It also allowed Kenyans to document human rights abuses and to avoid the violence themselves.

Once the viability of the approach had been confirmed, it was held up as a shining-lighthouse example—primarily by the nonprofit TED, best known for the lectures it sponsors and distributes via the Web—and quickly adapted for use around the world. One particularly powerful recent adaptation is the Louisiana Bucket Brigade, which created a version of the platform to track the BP oil spill in the Gulf of Mexico.

Incorporated in 2000 by executive director Anne Rolfes, the Louisiana Bucket Brigade originally focused on refinery-based pollution, using a collection "bucket" approach pioneered by California attorney Edward Masry (whose assistant, Erin Brockovich, is now familiar to many). These buckets were distributed to communities near refineries and chemical plants—in so-called fence-line locations instead of miles from the source of the pollution—allowing residents to monitor local air quality and, when necessary, to challenge official data issued by the plants and/or regulatory bodies.

Then, on April 20, 2010, ten years after the Brigade was formed, a gas leak on the Deepwater Horizon offshore drilling rig led to an explosion that took the lives of eleven men. Overnight, the direction of the organization changed. After the rig burned uncontrollably for a day and a half, it sank into the waters of the Gulf, and soon thereafter oil began to appear above the leaking wellhead, five thousand feet below on the ocean floor. Frustrated by the agonizingly slow, poorly coordinated responses on the part of BP and the U.S. government, the Brigade created its own version of the Ushahidi platform, putting out a call for "citizen journalists" to map the oil spill itself and to compile lists of out-of-work fishermen, endangered wildlife, and public health problems associated with the spill. And that mission continues, long after the crowd moved on to the next disaster.

Today's technological advances enable us to go beyond gathering Lighthouse data from multiple sources. Rather, the tools provide a means for two-way dialogue in real time. This listening platform can be a powerful tool for businesses to shed light on the barriers they need to avoid, and bridges they're able to cross, as it has been for the Louisiana Bucket Brigade. Lighthouse data, in fact, is available from a variety of sources, but just like a sailor seeking to avoid danger, you have to be looking for it to see it.

TRIANGULATION

The usefulness of Lighthouse data often depends on its comparison with other data. Much like basic geometry or calculus, the metrics have real meaning only when they're mapped. One might, for instance, employ a sales metric, but without comparing those results with, say, absolute position (against a baseline) and change over time (from a relevant date or market position), or against competitive gaps in form or function, the data will have little meaning.

For Darrell Bricker, in fact, that sort of methodology is the only foundation on which meaningful insights can be constructed. It also makes appearing on camera a lot less intimidating.

This is a big one for guys who do media commentary, like me. Some people get very intimidated about going on television and doing interviews about political topics. But you don't have to be smart. You can be the dumbest stump out there. But because you're the only one with any facts, you're the smartest guy in the room.

It's literally like painting by the numbers. If, as a researcher, you follow the rules drawn up by the people whose shoulders we stand upon, rules that were worked out over the ages, if you just do that, you'll come up with the right information set to guide the answer. And as I said before, as long as you follow the principle of parsimony, where the simplest answer's the best one, you should be able to put it up on one slide. It's not a eureka moment; it's good research, because you followed this mundane process of research passed down to us by our forefathers in science.

So good Lighthouse data, like all relevant data, is yielded by fundamentally sound techniques of collection and analysis—not through wild guesses or after-the-fact attempts to find numbers that will support preordained conclusions. What's more, Lighthouse data usually *doesn't* stand on its own, but alerts us to danger through its relation to other data or information. Again, a 5 percent drop in national sales may be the result of a general economic slowdown. But if your competitors showed gains of 10 percent over the same period, you're in trouble.

NEW LIGHTHOUSES

While the reliability of data gathered on social-media sites is often difficult to gauge, the broad range of contributors and the absence of a central authority—both of which make the data more difficult to manipulate—as well as the real-time immediacy of the reports all combine to create a powerful new sort of digital beacon. Earlier in these pages, for instance, we noted the skyrocketing demand for bandwidth used to post and view video online (while acknowledging the difficulty of determining the real value of such "data"). However, a recent *Wall Street Journal* article[*] titled "How to Sell on YouTube, Without Showing a Video," focused on the use some entrepreneurs have made of the comments sections of video posts—that is, comments made by unsolicited customers—to promote their products. The line between joining such discussions and simple self-promotion is very narrow, however, and online communities can turn against products or services as quickly as they began to support them. Put another way, these forums can play a part in your marketing efforts *and* serve as a lookout for signs of danger—especially if they are first used as listening platforms, and then to drive a dialogue between a company and its customers. And by joining discussions instead of initiating them, marketing departments can learn a great deal about their customers' likes and dislikes, while demonstrating that they are actually *listening*. They can also discover new, previously unimagined uses of their products by trolling online forums.

In a similar vein, *The New York Times* recently reported on the quickness with which technologically savvy users had modified Microsoft's Kinect gaming device, using it in ways the company had never imagined.[†] And while, according to author Jenna Wortham, Microsoft initially threatened some sort of sanctions, "cooler" heads quickly prevailed as the company recognized the value of the buzz generated by the modified systems. Across all of the examples, intelligent companies learned, through Lighthouse techniques, what had formerly

*Dennis Nishi, "How to Sell on YouTube, Without Showing a Video," *Wall Street Journal,* November 15, 2010.
†Jenna Wortham, "With Kinect Controller, Hackers Take Liberties," *New York Times,* November 21, 2010.

been hidden about customer's desires, habits, and practices. The information streams are available to all companies today; the mark of a dynamic company is that it's the one with the courage and agility to act quickly with this new information.

Similar adaptations were made to iRobot's Roomba as soon as it entered the market—including, of course, the Pepsi commercial that made the vacuum famous (even though the Roomba was heavily disguised). But far from discouraging the practice, Ms. Wortham reports, iRobot went so far as to offer a product, the iRobot Create, that's *made to be adapted* by robotic enthusiasts—a Roomba made for tinkerers that doesn't even vacuum the floor.

Again, the actual "value" of such online buzz is difficult to measure, but its steadily increasing influence can't be denied. *The Wall Street Journal*'s review of the best and worst ad campaigns of 2010* was notable not so much for its picks but for some of the metrics used to describe the more successful ads. In short, with total ad expenditures in 2010 still far below their prerecession peak, marketers continue to try to leverage social media and Short Message Service technology to supercharge their traditional campaigns. And keeping an eye out for data that indicates any sort of backlash can keep companies off the rocks just as surely as a lighthouse can. While success is described in terms of total YouTube views, celebrity appeal surveys, Facebook fan pages, and mobile phone app downloads, failure is measured by critical comments on social media pages or ad campaigns that become fodder for late-night monologues.

That said, techniques that have worked over the past half-century shouldn't be discarded offhand, especially because traditional data analysis, when performed by an experienced industry expert, can still be a very powerful tool. The following story, from Susan Schwartz McDonald's early years in market research, is a fascinating example.

This concerns one of the seminal experiences I had when I was first beginning in the business and had clients in the brewing industry. One of my clients was Schlitz. Schlitz was one of the premium brands, and at the time Miller was just beginning to come out of relative obscurity. It was almost a pedantic brand. You know, guys

*Suzanne Vranica, "Hits and Misses from Madison Avenue," *Wall Street Journal,* December 23, 2010.

who wore Mister Rogers sweaters drank it, but those guys wearing sweaters really started coming out of the gate, and so there was a fundamental power shift beginning to occur in the industry as upstarts like Coors and Miller started to give the big, complacent brands like Bud and Schlitz a run for their money. Schlitz, in particular, was floundering for a couple of "North Star" reasons. First, they let the accountants start running the company, and they knew nothing about the customer. Second, they dumped one of the best campaigns in the history of the industry—and J. Walter Thompson, the agency that created it—for something pugnacious, something that actually seemed to antagonize customers.

The first campaign featured aerial shots of sailboats cutting through glittering water, and proclaimed: "You only live once in this life . . ." It was a fabulous, iconic way to evoke escape and personal effectiveness at the same time, and it caused the same sort of emotional response the Budweiser Clydesdales do at Christmas. Yes, they're very different emotional timbres, but both are very powerful, very resonant.

The campaign that followed it featured a big, muscular, threatening goon who stared down the camera, pointed a menacing finger, and asked: "You gonna take away my Schlitz?" That ad, instead, took a love affair between man, brand, and lifestyle and turned it into a form of pugilism that customers felt was directed at them. Really unfortunate. I've never seen a brand plummet so fast. Other brands were busy seducing away their customers with powerful, positive imagery, and Schlitz simply forgot the chief rule of the game—that the relationship between customers and brands is a romance, not hand-to-hand combat.

They also tried to set a new strategic course, using a segmentation study to go after some high-volume opportunities. It wasn't any sort of tracking study, but it did include data on the customer's image of the brand, and while I was rooting around in there, I noticed something that puzzled me, even though it wasn't statistically significant. And it was this.

We knew that beer drinkers couldn't tell one beer from another in a blind taste test, and yet they would swear that they could. To understand this it helps to know that very few products are viewed with such bright "halos" above them—seen only by their loyal consumers, of course—as the products of the brewing industry are. So one of the ways you *know* that someone is a loyal user is that they give their brand higher ratings on just about everything you measure—i.e., taste, quality, etc. But, oddly enough, in this particular data set I saw that Schlitz drinkers were not giving Schlitz a higher rating than Miller. Things had just started to flip a bit. The shifts were tiny, but I saw right away that the halo was gone. Anyway, I looked at this and I thought, Well, this is something I have to report, even though it wasn't my main mission.

The information, in fact, was crucial. But unfortunately, it came too late. In twelve months Schlitz was dead. Off the market.

So the data I'd caught, which you'd call the Lighthouse data, wasn't statistically significant, but it was a *reversal* in a structural pattern that had always been there. And that reversal, however small, was a very powerful indicator to me. And it taught me a lesson, even though I was kind of doing it reflexively: It taught me to always look kind of carefully at how so-called committed users are looking at their brands versus other brands, and especially for cases where there is some sort of subtle shift in the relative charitableness of people to brands other than their own.

This story, in fact, illustrates an especially subtle combination of several of the Fire Hose Questions: Lighthouse data that showed rocks ahead for Schlitz, North Star data that showed certain customers beginning to follow a new polestar, and the way once-die-hard customers can become swing voters over time, and thus fair game for your brand. And as McDonald notes above, the significance of good Lighthouse data is usually revealed by comparison, or triangulation, with other data, whether new or historical. And finally, that data doesn't necessarily have to be *statistically* significant, just indicative of a shift in baseline behavior that rarely moves over the long term. But when it does, you'd better send a sailor to the bow and tell him to keep a sharp eye out.

RAPID ITERATION

Insights are born out of rapid iteration. Just as lighthouses can be used along a journey, synthesizing data through rapid iteration enables you to continually reassess your position and make course corrections along the way. Once you try this approach, we're willing to bet that you'll begin to see presentations that articulate hard and fast plans in a new light. The idea may be counterintuitive at first—that is, that flexibility should be built into any long-term strategy—but in today's fast-paced business world, with data pouring in from a variety of sources, you would be wise to give yourself a little room to react should you come across any Lighthouse data (see Figure 23).

[FIGURE 23]

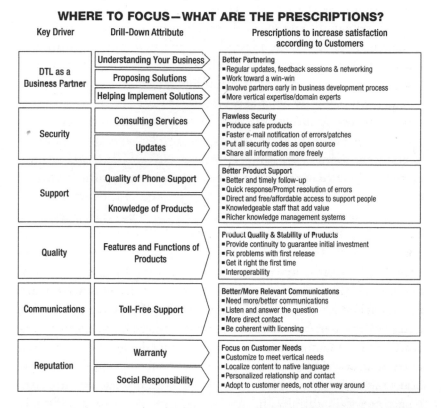

WHERE TO FOCUS—WHAT ARE THE PRESCRIPTIONS?

Key Driver	Drill-Down Attribute	Prescriptions to increase satisfaction according to Customers
DTL as a Business Partner	Understanding Your Business / Proposing Solutions / Helping Implement Solutions	**Better Partnering** ■ Regular updates, feedback sessions & networking ■ Work toward a win-win ■ Involve partners early in business development process ■ More vertical expertise/domain experts
Security	Consulting Services / Updates	**Flawless Security** ■ Produce safe products ■ Faster e-mail notification of errors/patches ■ Put all security codes as open source ■ Share all information more freely
Support	Quality of Phone Support / Knowledge of Products	**Better Product Support** ■ Better and timely follow-up ■ Quick response/Prompt resolution of errors ■ Direct and free/affordable access to support people ■ Knowledgeable staff that add value ■ Richer knowledge management systems
Quality	Features and Functions of Products	**Product Quality & Stability of Products** ■ Provide continuity to guarantee initial investment ■ Fix problems with first release ■ Get it right the first time ■ Interoperability
Communications	Toll-Free Support	**Better/More Relevant Communications** ■ Need more/better communications ■ Listen and answer the question ■ More direct contact ■ Be coherent with licensing
Reputation	Warranty / Social Responsibility	**Focus on Customer Needs** ■ Customize to meet vertical needs ■ Localize content to native language ■ Personalized relationship and contact ■ Adopt to customer needs, not other way around

Every plan should have a barriers-and-bridges section containing a series of Plan B's, or alternate courses, if a significant change in market conditions takes place. But keep in mind that not all Plan B's are responses to negative situations. Chris recalls a meeting at Microsoft, for instance, where a request was made for a major initiative. It involved a significant investment, a variety of resources, redeployment of teams, *and* new capabilities. After the team had crunched the numbers, they built a robust business case. They had charts, data, forecasts, and benchmarks. That basic information was supplemented with reams of research and input from senior members from across the various business units. All of it was poked, prodded, and dissected. They knew where the big rocks were in the road, and they had plans and talking points for each one. Completely buttoned up—and fired up—they went into the pitch meeting and made their request.

They were ready for everything. Well, almost everything. There was one question, it turned out, that they couldn't answer. In fact, they hadn't even considered the following Lighthouse question:

What happens if you're wildly successful?

That may not seem like a Lighthouse question, but in its own way it's as important as asking yourself what you'll do if things don't work out. So you should ask yourself just how you're going to fulfill demand and meet customer expectations if your plan is not just successful but *wildly* successful. This, of course, is the sort of problem every businessperson would be happy to have, but it's a problem nonetheless. While your competitors may envy you as customers line up to purchase your products, if your manufacturing arm can't meet demand, or you can't train your support staff quickly enough to handle the higher volume of calls, your "success" will create a legion of disappointed customers.

Think about what happened to AT&T when it began offering the iPhone. While sales skyrocketed, and the buzz was almost deafening, its network was quickly overwhelmed by its new customers' thirst for broadband access. And the call plans AT&T offered—at least initially—weren't calibrated to the amount of broadband used by each customer. As an unintended result, those customers who didn't do as much Internet surfing on their phones were in effect subsidizing the heavy users. This was, in fact, a precursor to additional business challenges now thought of as fair-usage and net-neutrality regulations. So, by not planning for wild success, AT&T not only shot themselves in the foot, they actually created demand for the iPhone on another carrier.

When making plans, therefore, you've got to give yourself room to react to Lighthouse data—whether it's good news or bad news.

Jim Dippold had a similar take on the danger of success.

A really good example of this occurred when I first got into the retail business, long before I moved into analytics, and we put Advil on the shelf for the first time. I was in charge of the "over-the-counter" category, and it took me almost three or four months to understand the way Advil had taken off in the marketplace, because that information was lost in all the other data. And at the time, I didn't have an alert system to say, "Hey, when a product is exceeding sales forecasts by such a large factor, tell me." Of course, I was in charge of something like seven thousand items, and I hadn't yet learned to ask the question "Are there products among them that are experiencing far greater sales than we expected?" So we certainly sacrificed some sales as a result, and we also missed the opportunity to use the item's popularity to leverage other promotions.

WAR AND DATA OVERLOAD

A ship's captain who fails to see a lighthouse can lose his life—and take his crew and cargo down with him. But a businessperson's failure to look for Lighthouse data can cause real harm, too, and you only have to glance toward Detroit to see the evidence. Once a central column in the structure of American economic power, the U.S. auto industry came dangerously close to toppling to the ground only a few years ago. As impossible as it is to believe, no one in power at any of the major companies realized how precarious their positions were, and only Ford took steps to protect itself in the event of a market downturn. And the collateral damage—that is, to all segments of the industry, and most of those who work in them—is still mounting.

But even the loss of a livelihood, of a health insurance plan, or of a house can't compare with the loss of a life, and mounting evidence suggests that our high-tech military is suffering from a data overload problem of its own, with deadly implications.

Writing for *The New York Times* in January 2011, Thom Shanker and Matt Richtel noted that the problem already exists and may be getting worse.*

> When military investigators looked into an attack by American helicopters last February that left 23 Afghan civilians dead, they found that the operator of a Predator drone had failed to pass along crucial information about the makeup of a gathering crowd of villagers.
>
> But air force and army officials now say there was also an underlying cause for that mistake: information overload.

Shanker and Richtel go on to report that data overload now plagues the military in precisely the same way it does the business world, and our personal lives. But the consequences, clearly, are far more dangerous.

> Across the military, the data flow has surged; since the attacks of 9/11, the amount of intelligence gathered by remotely piloted drones and other surveillance technologies has risen 1,600 percent. On the ground, troops increasingly use hand-held devices to communicate, get directions and set bombing coordinates. And the screens in jets can be so packed with data that some pilots call them "drool buckets" because, they say, they can get lost staring into them.

The military, according to the article, isn't ignoring the problem, but has to serve two masters.

> Data is among the most potent weapons of the 21st century. Unprecedented amounts of raw information help the military determine what targets to hit and what to avoid. And drone-based sensors have given rise to a new class of wired warriors who must filter the information sea. But sometimes they are drowning.
>
> Research shows that the kind of intense multitasking required in such situations can make it hard to tell good information from bad. The military faces a balancing act: how to help soldiers exploit masses of data without succumbing to overload.

*Thom Shanker and Matt Richtel, "In New Military, Data Overload Can Be Deadly," *New York Times*, January 17, 2011.

Shanker and Richtel go on to report that the military has requested the assistance of prominent cognitive scientists to combat the problem. Using high-tech sensors, some of those scientists have been able to view the brain's activity at the moment excessive information effectively disables it. And while neither the scientists nor the military expect to be able to rewire the human brain, additional research may reveal the natural limits of our brain's ability to synthesize information—a level they can take care not to exceed. It may also lead to training regimens that would enable soldiers to focus on specific data streams when overload threatens their ability to make sound decisions. And it may be possible to adapt programs of that sort to civilian—and business—use.

The point, once again, is that information overload can prevent us from recognizing critically important data—that is, Lighthouse data—and by cloaking such information allow us to sail into danger without knowing it.

CHANGING COURSE

Returning to the world of retail, we asked Jim Hilt about the data he collects to avoid the rocks, and we were surprised to hear what he had to say.

I actually think that it's less about being able to get to that sort of data, because I think we can get to it, and so trying to stay within this metaphor, I think it comes down to how you set your course knowing what you have to avoid, or might take advantage of, in terms of what lies along the way. So I don't see a problem with finding what you call "Lighthouse data"; I think it's about execution. In fact, I really don't believe that most people are buried under so much data that they can't figure out how to get to the most important pieces. I think the problem, not with the companies I've worked for, but in general, is that people don't know how to execute on that "Lighthouse" information even when they have it.

In fact, I think some people use information overload, and the need to sort through so much data, as an excuse. I think they use it as a rearview mirror excuse to explain why things went wrong, or why they made the wrong choices, or why they failed during a process. And I'm not saying this to be harsh, because I don't think failure is necessarily a bad thing—a lot of times it leads to important insights. But in general it's very easy to point to all the information you had to go through as an excuse for your inability to find the important pieces. Again, I think you can get to the information you need, and you can pick out the important data, and so it's a matter of whether or not you can execute against it, or whether you *choose* to execute against it. And there's nothing wrong with that—that is, making a choice that doesn't work out.

You know, I think about it every day when we make product feature choices—that is, decisions about what we're going to build and what we're not going to build. We do that based on real data in the marketplace, and what customers are talking about, and what they want, and in the end it isn't clear to me that an occasional failure or an inability to do something, or even a success that you can't correlate to the data, was really about having so much data that I couldn't find out what was important.

And while I certainly wouldn't say that I have every piece of data I need, I think the point is that we're too worried about the amount of information, and getting to the pieces we think are important, and sometimes it isn't about getting more, or even getting the so-called right pieces, but asking yourself what you have, and what you're going to do with what you have.

While we believe that data overload is a real problem, and that it's getting worse, we do agree with Hilt that in the end it's all about execution. Whether you're looking for your customer's North Star, or keeping a lookout for rocks near the shore, the information you gather is always just a means to an end: moving your business forward. ·

APPLYING THE LESSON

1. Ask yourself what things might go wrong.
2. Design a Plan B for every one of them.
3. Define leading and lagging indicators to track.
4. Focus on three data points for each of those indicators: current (baseline) position; competitive gap: and change over time for the key attributes (generated from question 3 above).

5. Ask a battery of questions when trying to pinpoint your focus:
Does this data guide our products or services to market? Does
it showcase a first-of-a-kind transaction with a new customer
that illustrates a hidden but emerging market? Is the market
big enough to justify the time, expense, and risk involved with
setting up a new product line?

You should begin by focusing your attention on the central business issue you need to resolve—by asking the Essential Question—and then use the answer to help you find the numbers you need. Put another way, you need to find the light that will show you the way, or will alert you to any dangers that lie between where you are and where you're going. And simply doing that will enable you to avoid data that's irrelevant, data that will distract you, or data that will lead you astray.

As business guides, Lighthouses often come into view in pretty much the same way they do for sailors—along the way, rather than at the beginning of a journey. Whether inspired by a random comment from a customer or a sudden insight, new business ideas constantly pop up, and when they do, you'll want to look for the next Lighthouse along the shore, which is usually pointed to by market research. That data won't make decisions for you, though, so you could say that the beam from this first Lighthouse is somewhat weak. All it will do is narrow the range of information you'll consult as you move forward, something we'll turn to below when we discuss the process by which business development proceeds. However, though the signal might be weak at first, business leaders actively listening for indicators will see this first signal as a first step toward the new goal.

For existing products or services, management typically depends on another series of Lighthouses, which can be loosely grouped together as key performance indicators, or KPIs, which can serve either as guides or as warnings. These, of course, will differ according to the division employing them—i.e., manufacturing, marketing, operations, sales, etc. Furthermore, such indicators can be used to measure both quantitative and qualitative factors, like sales and customer satisfaction. And while some KPIs are used only to monitor results, which management may be unable to affect, others, called "actionable" indicators, identify areas in which a company can take action.

In business development, approaching emerging market segments or new geographic territories with existing product lines is all about finding Lighthouses. The first goal is to succeed with a series of initial customer wins that can be promoted as Lighthouse examples—both to attract more customers and to teach your team how to conduct business in the new market. The sales or marketing field teams in the individual regions then see the Lighthouse example as a template for success, complete with indicators of what should—and should not—be done. Even more important, those early successes can convince other sales leaders that "if it can be done there, I can do it here."

CHAPTER FIVE TAKEAWAYS

1. Identify your Lighthouse by asking Essential Questions.
2. Decide whether your Lighthouse will guide, warn, or serve as an example.
3. Keep your eyes open for unconventional Lighthouses.

CHAPTER SIX

Who Are Your Swing Voters?

"No company should ever take for granted that managing customers for loyalty is the same as managing them for profits . . . in managing these true friends [highly loyal customers], the greatest trap is overkill."

— REINARTZ AND KUMAR,
HARVARD BUSINESS REVIEW

Successful businesses are able to generate an additional dollar of revenue without incurring a corresponding dollar of marketing cost. This simple but powerful maxim is the key to driving profitable growth. In this chapter, we'll show you how to accomplish this by tapping into existing purchasers of your products or services. These customers already use your products or services, but they're not committed to you. Ripping a page from the political playbook, we've labeled this group Swing Voters, because they can quickly swing from being very satisfied to being dissatisfied—or vice versa. They might buy from you today and from a competitor tomorrow. Think of them as your "silent majority." And as such, they have the power to dramatically change your growth curve. Find these customers, and discover what they want, and you'll gain a new perspective on your business, your marketing efforts, your potential sales, and, ultimately, your bottom line. By categorizing, segmenting, profiling, and targeting them in distinctive ways, you can drive faster growth, increase their desire to do business with your company, and accelerate positive word of mouth (see Figure 24).

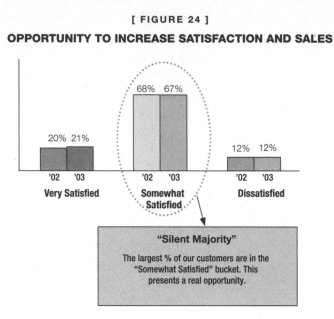

[FIGURE 24]

OPPORTUNITY TO INCREASE SATISFACTION AND SALES

"Silent Majority"

The largest % of our customers are in the "Somewhat Satisfied" bucket. This presents a real opportunity.

CHAPTER LESSONS

1. Categorize your customers as favorable, neutral, or unfavorable.
2. Segment your neutral customers into leaners, neutrals, or defectors.
3. Profile each customer segment so you can engage it.
4. Target each segment with a dedicated message.
5. Reassess your customer categories and segments.

In this chapter we'll take you through the five-step process listed above so you can use it to teach your team how to categorize, segment, profile, target, and reassess your silent majority of potential customers. That is, we'll show you how to collect actionable data on the Swing Voter and use it to your advantage. You'll learn how to identify this cohort and how to engage its various parts. You'll develop insights that will allow you to counteract negative perceptions about your products and services in the short term, and build trust and confidence over the long term. And every swing voter you tip to your side will be better educated and more likely to remain with you. And when these customers do have concerns, your customer service, marketing, sales, product management, and engineering departments will be better coordinated to address them. What's more, the approach detailed here will work for any business, no matter how big it is or where it is—that is, in a brick-and-mortar building or in a virtual store online. And it will work either with information you already have or with information you can easily secure.

Before taking the first of the five steps, however, it is important to understand the concept of customer loyalty, and to find out what it really means and what it doesn't.

Pause and consider the extent to which your strategies, tactics, and resources are targeted toward the extremes. By that we mean either your most satisfied customers or those customers least likely to buy what you have for sale. Milking a cash cow is a sound strategy, and one you don't need to read a book to understand. The reality, however, is that the majority of those customers that might become "highly satisfied" are found between the extremes, and that is where the greatest potential for low-cost growth lies. Their concerns are less numerous and pronounced. These swing customers are on the fence. Depending on what you do or don't do, they could tip either toward your company or away from it.

Do your plans, therefore, deliver the subtle signals that could convert a fence sitter to a truly loyal customer? By "signals" we mean a campaign that bears multiple messages, given that your swing voters, just like your prospects—or your employees, suppliers, and vendors—don't all have the same opinions or want the same things. So in the same way that political campaigns have learned to microtarget specific groups of swing voters, you can improve your bottom line by tailoring your message—and your products and services—to groups of swing customers. That means you have to know how to identify and target them.

Given that the phrase "swing voter" was coined in the political sphere, we turned to Darrell Bricker for his opinion.

The first thing you've got to admit is that they *exist*. There has to be an admission that they exist. Because once you've done that, you can take your cleaver out and chop off two big groups in the population—you know, those who will definitely vote for you and those who never will and that you shouldn't bother worrying about. And it's the same whether they're voters or consumers. Still, people in politics and people in business spend an unbelievable amount of time talking about them, even though both groups are equally committed to their positions and are hardly ever going to change their opinions.

The other thing I hear all the time, and it really drives me crazy, is that we only need to focus on our *existing* consumers. Because by saying that you only need to focus on your consumers, you've as much as admitted that the market can't grow. You can't just say "We're going to focus on our core voters." Because guess what? That's all you'll ever have.

So swing voters are the ones that are either likely to abandon you or to come to you, based on what you say to them. And you can define these voters or buyers demographically, geographically, and psychographically. And finally, even though you do need to focus an undue amount of attention on the swing voters, you have to at least understand all the other populations, too.

Paying attention to the Swing Voter is consistent with one of the core principles of this book: maximizing your existing data. More often than not, you won't need to collect more data; you'll just need to pay attention to *less* of the data you've already got at hand. In other words, a concentrated subset of your existing data. But even if you do already have actionable data on your swing customers, you might not have accurately profiled them or correctly calculated what they can do for your business.

SWING VOTER

The term "swing voter" refers to individuals whose vote can "swing" from one party to the other over a series of elections. The Gallup organization, in 1937, was the first to identify and poll the swing voter. Gallup's method for defining and measuring the swing voter quickly influenced the worlds of market and political research. Over the decades that followed, pollsters, consultants, and marketers developed a more nuanced understanding of the swing voter and began to apply a range of tools and techniques to persuade or activate these individuals. To do so, they divided swing voters into three major groups, groups that have as much significance in business as they do in politics.

The first are the "leaners," those who do not express a clear preference when first asked but when probed more deeply will express a "leaning" preference for one candidate—or product, or service—as opposed to another. They are on the edge of becoming very satisfied, becoming advocates, or being loyal.

The second are the "undecideds," or the most neutral respondents. In politics, they have no pronounced preference for any candidate; in business they have no brand loyalty.

Those in the third group are marked by "reservations" they have about the candidate, or product, in question. They clearly aren't advocates, but they aren't critics, either. Yet they're not undecided, and they're not leaning. They are on the edge of becoming very dissatisfied.

Since World War II, hundreds of pollsters and social scientists have sifted through data and studied elections to refine their own approach to tracking subgroups of swing voters and projecting how they will behave. We've followed the hockey moms, NASCAR dads, baby boomers, Gen Xers, silver surfers, and Walmart grandmas; we've watched the focus groups on CNN; we've noted the swing voters in school-board elections, local politics, and referenda. Astonishingly enough, though, most businessmen—and in particular marketing experts—have ignored this field and its implications for competitive strategy.

PHANTOM LOYALTY

Trader Joe's, the innovative food-store chain, doesn't accept coupons, advertise weekly sales, or track its customers' buying behavior with loyalty cards. Instead it features healthy specialty foods sold at competitive prices. It can't undersell Walmart or ShopRite. It didn't even install price scanners until 2001. It doesn't track customer purchases for marketing purposes. But Trader Joe's customer satisfaction and service ratings are among the highest in the business world, time and time again.

Trader Joe's isn't the only company that ignores fashionable company-driven strategies like long-term contracts, cancellation fees, loyalty cards, and annual memberships. Apple, Brooks Brothers, Kenmore, Southwest Airlines, Virgin Mobile, and many other highly profitable companies continue to inspire customer loyalty without programmatic gimmicks, and their success underscores the problems with some of these programs. Customer reward programs, for instance, increase customer satisfaction only if those programs offer benefits your competitor's programs don't. If the benefits are similar, and the shopping experience is comparable, then your customers will most likely join several customer reward programs. From their perspective, why not? You're not offering them anything special.

Contracts, fees, and promotions raise other issues. If your business is already doing what it should to ensure that its customers are satisfied, why does it need to lock them in? Why don't they stay of their own accord? In fact, why aren't they fighting their way in? Why aren't they refusing other offers? And as for fees, what exactly is the thinking behind asking—or insisting—that your customers pay to do business with *you*? What small percentage of your profit margin would you have to sacrifice to eliminate those fees, and aren't the chances pretty good that the sacrifice would be mitigated by an increase in customer satisfaction? And if that's not so, and the fees are a necessary part of doing business, is the reason for them clear to your customers, and are they set at reasonable levels? Why are promotions offered to new customers while long-term, loyal customers are asked to pay higher rates?

Trader Joe's and other innovative brands know that at least part of the answer lies in engaging *all* manner of customers—which include, naturally, their Swing Voters—in ways that speak to each customer's particular relationship with the brand. In fact, the company is obsessed with making sure that its customers aren't just satisfied but *highly* satisfied, and that as different as their tastes are, they're all having a great experience.

GOOD ENOUGH MEETS NEW AND IMPROVED!

We're well versed in today's wide variety of customer loyalty strategies. We've spent more than fifteen years leading global loyalty and satisfaction measurement programs. We're on the front lines, accountable for talking with customers, crunching satisfaction and Net Promoter[*] numbers, and discussing customer experience and loyalty strategies. We are steeped in the rabid fan, the company advocate, the delighted customer, and the secure customer. We know about moments of truth and the difference between experiences and expectation. And this list of customer loyalty models grows with every new book and article that is published. But they all revolve around one central, seldom questioned tenet: To drive growth, you care for and feed your most satisfied customers. According to this sort of conventional logic, a highly satisfied customer is the foundation of any successful business.

We see it differently. Yes, we believe in building customer loyalty, but focusing an inordinate amount of attention on your most loyal customers can draw you into a trap, no matter how well intentioned your efforts. By this we don't mean that you should focus exclusively on your swing customers, either, because you've got to maintain your base. But the simple, often ignored truth is that swing buyers offer the greatest potential *return* on your marketing and product development investments. And done the right way, creating loyal customers out of this swing audience will improve sales *without* damaging your highly satisfied customers' perceptions of your brand.

Think about it this way. If your business is thriving because of your customers' loyalty, that means you're capitalizing on that loyalty based only on what you're offering them today. That means you're *betting* that they will like the next product you introduce. So you're putting all your chips on one number. Looked at in this way, when you develop a new product or service, you're competing with yourself for your existing customer's wallet share. The better approach is to capitalize on your sunk costs with a proven product your customers have embraced, and expand your revenue streams with new offerings—offerings targeted to both existing customers *and* to your most likely swing prospects. Because even if that new product is really innovative, there's no telling how many of your loyal customers will want it, or believe they need it, regardless of their loyalty to your business or the quality or

*Net Promoter is both a loyalty metric and a discipline for using customer feedback to fuel profitable growth in your business. Developed by Satmetrix, Bain & Company, and Fred Reichheld, the concept was first popularized through Reichheld's book *The Ultimate Question*. www.netpromoter.com/np/index.jsp.

utility of the product itself. Simply stated, you could become a victim of your own success.

In other words, what your customers are buying today may be all they want. They may not *need* the "new and improved" product, the innovative new feature, or the premium version. And if *they* don't, how can you grow your business? Without new revenue streams, parts of which will almost certainly flow from your Swing Voters, your sales may be capped by satisfied customers who just don't need the next upgrade. And this could result in a period of revenue drought until the next product refresh is truly in demand by customers. Can your company survive while it awaits that new revenue? In fact, many businesses collapse under the expense of continual innovation, especially when the bulk of innovation costs are incurred to maintain their small but profitable customer base. What's more, a satisfied customer is not *necessarily* a loyal one. Satisfaction is based on past transactions. Satisfaction at its core is the difference between experience and expectation. Loyalty is a *relationship*. The correlation between customer satisfaction and customer loyalty isn't a straight line; it's more like an S curve with a flat section in the middle, and that's where your swing customers live. Encouraging them to strengthen their *relationship* with your brand means initiating deeper conversations with these customers and in so doing acquiring a better understanding of how they perceive your communications, products, brand, and services.

If yours is a commodity, consumer product, or retail firm—such as fast food, laundry detergent, Trader Joe's, Virgin Mobile, or a restaurant chain—your customers make frequent and regular purchases on a sustained basis. The loyalty trap lies in continually and exclusively delivering new targeted products, or product-line extensions, intended for your heavy repeat purchasers, in an attempt to keep them coming back. But firms that adopt this approach and succeed in strengthening the breadth and depth of their loyal customers' relationship with their brands will eventually see the wallets of those same customers begin to empty. No matter how loyal they are, committed customers are part of a finite set with limited dollars. Think about the Tide to Go stick competing with Tide detergent. Or Listerine PocketPaks competing with Listerine mouthwash. While these have been shrewd, successful extensions of the original product lines, where does the brand go from there? You already have Tide at home and Tide when you're on the run. And each time you add another twist, the innovation curve becomes steeper, that next dollar of revenue costs more to realize, and the investment needed in R&D increases.

If, on the other hand, your company is a high-ticket business such as BMW (automobiles), Kenmore (appliances), Brooks Brothers (men's clothing), or Apple (computers, smart phones), the predicament differs in kind, but the result is often the same. The pattern is familiar to anyone in branding and marketing. The high-ticket customer develops a connection to the brand, and the brand in turn becomes a *badge*. By wearing the badge publicly, these same customers encourage friends, colleagues, and loved ones to wear it themselves. Over time, as this process repeats itself, the company slowly develops a profile for their long-term loyal customers (think Prius for large-ticket items, or IKEA for affordable home solutions). Once that profile is established, the company builds new products and shapes its messaging to suit what quickly becomes a *legacy* model of their brand-loyal customer. And as soon as this occurs, companies walk right into the loyalty trap. By focusing on a single, targeted demographic portrait and tailoring their brand to fit it as precisely as possible, companies ignore the far, far larger group of swing customers who might respond to a slightly different appeal. And it's harder for those companies to reach out to new segments without diluting what they stand for—also known as their brand "promise."

Consider this pattern in light of what you know about your own business. Begin by considering all the customers who have purchased products and/or services from you. Clearly they're aware of your company's existence, so your marketing department's first job is done. These customers continue to buy a certain set of your products, and they continue to use some of your services. If, however, they are neither advocates for your products, like Apple's iPhone users, nor critics of them, like those who favor Google's mobile platform, Android, you have failed to engage them. They are customers, but they remain independent. And so at virtually any time, either you or your competitors could offer them something that compels them to act differently. The question is: Have you ever stopped to ask why? Have you ever asked yourself why the loss of some of your customers is only one, limited-time, "free shipping" promotion away?

Often, when so many customers remain indifferent, your business is overinvested in your highly satisfied and committed customers, leaving the large group in the middle unserved. When these customers are on the fence about your product or service, they could easily tip toward, or away, from your products and services. The concerns of this majority, however, are less pronounced, and therefore a lot harder to decipher. Still, based on the size of the cohort, their wallets can make or break your firm. And despite the continual efforts you make to improve your customers' overall product experience, a large number of them remain neutral in their opinions.

LEANERS, UNDECIDEDS, AND AT RISK: AN OPPORTUNITY FOR SUSTAINABLE, LOW-COST GROWTH

We're going to give you some data you can rely on. According to most industry sources, the share of "very satisfied" customers ranges from 15 to 35 percent of the market. "Dissatisfied" customers, on the other hand, average only 10 percent. "Undecided" (true neutral) customers, therefore, account for 55 to 75 percent of all customers. This follows a fairly standard distribution, seen countless times over the years.

Now, let's assume that very satisfied customers will spend 100 percent of what they have in their wallets for your product or service. Furthermore, just for purposes of illustration, let's say that this group amounts to 25 percent of your total addressable market. So here's the problem. The extent to which you concentrate on maintaining this base of rabid fans is also the extent to which you're missing out on a far more significant opportunity—the chance to convince a large number of swing customers to become loyal customers.

This is fertile ground and should be looked at like a new green-field space or competitive win-back territory. Its inhabitants are ripe for the plucking. And planting new seeds in this particularly fertile ground can result in astonishing growth. Furthermore, it won't require a significant change in your messaging—that is, it won't require a change that will alienate your base. The rarely tapped Swing Voters, in fact, often respond to messages that require only a slight modification of the same messages you use to maintain your base. To successfully modify that central message, though, you need to identify the two or three factors that are unique to neutral customers. Why? The levers you need to pull to shift neutrals' perceptions to a more positive place are different from those that are important to a satisfied customer. And if you succeed in categorizing, profiling, and targeting these customers and in isolating and addressing their specific issues—that is, the factors for which they have given you low marks on satisfaction—you can increase their loyalty. You'll not only increase your revenue—again, after having deducted the attendant marketing costs—but you'll also have the chance to create a new group of loyal, long-term customers.

FIVE STEPS FOR SWINGING THE VOTE YOUR WAY

Our approach is as simple as the problem is complex: five simple steps designed to identify, reach, influence, and impact this population (see Figure 25). Below you'll learn how to engage the swing consumer, how to rapidly respond to market situations, and how to shift your strategies. You'll learn how to isolate different types of swing consumers, size their potential, and identify their motivators. The results will likely mean higher sales, and higher engagement. You'll be able to generate more loyalty and positive word of mouth about your products and practices.

[FIGURE 25]
5 STEPS TO FIND YOUR SWING VOTER

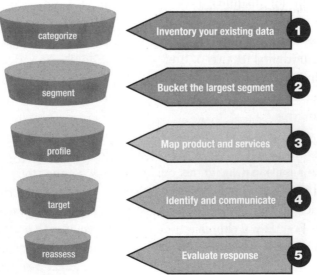

categorize	Inventory your existing data — 1
segment	Bucket the largest segment — 2
profile	Map product and services — 3
target	Identify and communicate — 4
reassess	Evaluate response — 5

>> **Categorize**

First, categorize your customers, dividing them according to whether they view your brand, product, or service favorably, somewhat favorably, or unfavorably. Use whatever you already know about your customers. Whether you have sales histories, purchase data, or survey results, you'll quickly find that the swing group will almost always be the largest category in whatever data set you're studying. The point is that you want to categorize your customers in such a way that you maximize the differences between the groups—that is, categorize them so they are as distinct from one another as they can be.

And keep the size of the middle group in mind the next time you're in a meeting in which the Swing Voters are being ignored, or the "somewhat favorables" or "neutrals" are being treated as if they were just another part of the indistinguishable contents of a large bucket, of little or no interest to the business. If that's the case, it means that all the plans and energy of the team are focused on preserving the business of the very favorable customer or attracting the unfavorable customer. It takes considerably more time, effort, and money to change a dissatisfied customer into a satisfied customer. In other words, the team's energy is directed toward the two groups *least likely* to change their behavior with respect to the brand.

THE GIRL YOU JUST CAN'T GET

Susan Schwartz McDonald's earlier story about the loyal customers Schlitz suddenly lost to Miller—from "Should You Believe the Squiggly Line?"—is relevant to the discussion of Swing Voters, too, but experience has also taught her that some Swing Voters will never stop swinging.

> With Schlitz and Miller, I guess you could argue that there were always a lot of Swing Voters out there. But no one really knows who the Swing Voters are from a distance, because the definition depends on the market. If, for example, you have a person who drinks Beer A, and only that beer, you know you have a loyalist. Of course, you could piss them off, but for the time being they're loyal. If you have someone who's splitting his vote already, sometimes

drinking one beer, sometimes drinking another, that individual obviously has more volume to give you, and so clearly is a great opportunity for growth. On the other hand, you haven't established a clear value proposition for them, and if you're honest, you have to admit the possibility that you may never be able to do that.

So once again, while conducting a serious effort to separate the market into segments, you must be prepared to separate the fundamentally irrelevant, or unobtainable, customer. Let's call her the girl you just can't get. But that doesn't change the fact that you have to continue to identify the customers who will drive more volume. Still, as we said above, always keep in mind that while this subgroup may be using your product today, they are by nature fundamentally promiscuous. That was our name, by the way, for the Swing Voter in the brewing industry. We referred to him as promiscuous, because, while he might occasionally buy from us, he would never become a true convert. It could be because he's too adventurous, or too fickle, but for whatever reason, you'll never get him to commit to a relationship.

In other words, when targeting Swing Votes it's important to understand that there will be some customers you'll be able to attract—albeit momentarily—but whom you'll never be able to hold. Again, the point is that the better your data selection is—that is, the more you focus on the relevant data, without being overwhelmed by the random numbers shooting out of the hose—the more successful you'll be in categorizing the most promising targets for your marketing efforts.

>> Segment

Keeping those sound insights in mind, when you start to break each group down into segments of leaners, undecideds, and at risk, it's best to start with a single metric. That metric could be overall customer satisfaction, willingness to repurchase, how satisfied they were with the products and/or services they recently bought, their willingness to recommend those products or services to others, the likelihood they'll purchase products or services from you again, or their perception of your brand's total value. Or you could segment them by frequency of purchase or average transaction size. And those decisions, about which metrics to target, will often be driven by the Fire Hose Questions we've already covered. What's the Essential Question, both for your customer and for your business? Where's the customer's North Star? And what, in the data you've already collected, surprised you?

Again, in keeping true to the Fire Hose principles, ours is not a rigid model that dictates specific metrics, because you know your business better than we do. Whichever metric you start with, however, once you've segmented the larger groups, you'll know which subgroups are leaning toward becoming buyers and which are more likely to become defectors. You can then play "offense" or "defense" with each segment, as we will explain below.

A visual may help bring this technique to life (see Figure 26). The bar graphs under the "Current Situation" show that nearly six in ten consumers hold "somewhat favorable" views of our business, product, or service. As Swing Voters, these consumers constitute the business's greatest opportunity for low-cost growth.

[FIGURE 26]

RETHINKING GROWTH THROUGH "SWING VOTER" LENS

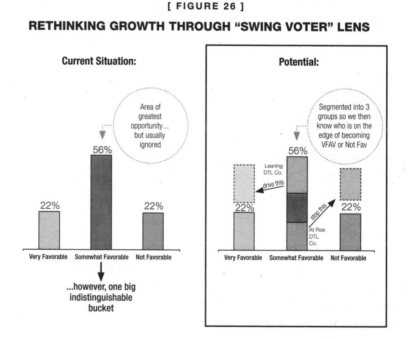

As you can see, the categories we introduced in Figure 24 become even more useful if you can segment them into more narrowly defined subgroups, determined by your chances of "tipping" them into a more favorable group or "losing" them to a less favorable category. This, clearly, is the most critical step in segmenting.

Note that the top segment of the "somewhat favorable" potentials constitutes the "leaners." Clearly, they're the easiest customers to win over, and the customers for whom the least amount of additional marketing is necessary. They're already leaning toward you, are somewhat satisfied by their earlier experiences with your brand, and so have fewer concerns. What's more, in this hypothetical case you'll see that that particular subgroup constitutes nearly *one-quarter of the total*. Put another way, if you were successful in moving the entire "leaning" segment of the "somewhat favorable" group into the "very favorable" group, you would instantly *double* your number of customers. And keep in mind that these buyers already know your brand and therefore have been affected, at least to some extent, by your current messaging.

The middle section, on the other hand, are "true neutrals"—i.e., on-the-fence customers who could tip either toward your products and services or away from them. Their issues with your company are more extensive and harder to define than those in the first group. Once again, looked at in terms of marketing costs, you'll need to do more work to make members of this group "leaners."

Finally, we see the "at risk" customers who are ready to switch to the "not favorable" group. Defectors are disillusioned with the product or service—across the board—and blame the company for all that ails them. With these "defectors," or potential customers who are about to be lost forever, you've got to play defense. To do that, you need data specific to them. You need to know why they feel the way they do about your product, service, or brand. But acting on that information will cost you more than it would to reach out to neutrals or leaners.

>> Profile

By generating additional, meaningful data for each of these group segments, you can move a step further and profile each group by their demographic, sales, and satisfaction ratings. Sometimes data isn't even necessary; the process can be informal, or simply a matter of common sense. What mini-portraits of your swing consumers emerge? In addition, figure out how each of these mini-groups tends to purchase. A leaner may be a frequent buyer of a single product. Neutrals typically make sporadic purchases over time. A typical at-risk customer, or potential defector, makes one or two purchases over an extended period. Next, create a profile for each group based on their demographics, their sales histories, the way they rate your business, and their total buying experience—including any contact you have with them after they purchase products or services from you. With these things in mind, you can then tailor your marketing messages accordingly, depending on your marketing budget and your short- or long-term goals.

And you don't need sophisticated software or a marketing degree, or the ability to crunch numbers, for this step. Imagine, for instance, that you're the head of a small law firm, marketing consultancy, architectural firm, design firm, or literary agency. At a law firm, for instance, you may have many one-time clients who hire you to write a family will—clients who can then be encouraged to review that document periodically. As a literary consultant, you might notice that queries from retired executives almost never result in manuscripts, and knowing that you can decide whether to shy away from such calls or to figure out how to put those kinds of callers' experience to work. Finally, an architect may discover a pattern among clients who frequently request information regarding renovations, but aren't good at following through.

You've now categorized your customers, segmented each category, and created profiles of each subgroup. As we've just shown, segmenting allows you to isolate both those groups of customers who offer greater opportunity and those who offer less.

This entire approach, by the way, can easily be applied to whatever sort of data you have at hand. It can begin with customer satisfaction ratings, sales reports, corporate financials, and even academic performance. Leaners, clearly, will be more receptive to your core message. At risk, who run the gamut from those who have had poor experiences with the product to those who have had unfavorable customer service experiences, will be much harder to reach. But the more accurate the profile, the more effectively you can target the customers it describes, with messages designed to address their specific concerns, dislikes, or misconceptions. As you segment, then, you match strategies to each subgroup and narrow your messaging down to one or two incisive points.

As with the entire Fire Hose program, these techniques are flexible, and may help you in whole or in part. And they can be applied to small, medium, and large businesses. For the small firms mentioned above, you might also look at client history. Which of your clients give you the highest ratings? Which clients have consistently requested your services, or referred others to you? These are your loyal, or your very favorable, customers. The neutral segment of the Swing Voter group might include clients with whom you haven't worked for some time but with whom you had a good relationship. Other neutrals might include smaller companies that have grown larger since you last did work for them, or allies in a close network who haven't been pitched yet. At risk profiles, instead, might include start-ups that can't yet afford your full services, poorly informed clients who didn't understand the role your company played, or clients who initially expressed low satisfaction, but for reasons beyond your control.

>> Target

Targeting has to do with being able to communicate with these customers, and the first question that will occur to your colleagues is "How do we find them?" Having categorized, segmented, and profiled your swing customers, start by going on the offensive with the leaners, because they'll require the least time, effort, and money to tip into your "very favorable" category. And for those who take the leap into the adjoining group, focus on the short list of items where this group gives you low marks. You know what the motivators are for people who purchase from you. Leaners have the same motivations, but there may be one or two things about which their feelings are lukewarm. The early steps in the process identified these concerns. The key is to build your strategy to specifically address these lower-rated items. By doing so, you are micro-targeting your efforts, and leveraging your existing assets to a group of folks who are already purchasing from you.

Then play defense with the next group of Swing Voters—the at-risk buyers. They're at the bottom on the middle bar for a reason, whether or not it's something you can control. And keep in mind that these customers are very close to becoming part of one of the groups you've already decided to ignore. Therefore, understanding that your success rate is going to be lower, start with positive messages about your brand

and your customers, so that potential defectors can see the benefits of doing business with your company. Also, try to clear up any misconceptions your research has revealed. But don't commit too large a portion of your budget or too much of your limited time and energy.

Then make sure your neutrals are well informed. These "true neutrals" are the folks whose positive and negative impressions are the most evenly balanced, so of everyone you measure, they'll have the least emotional engagement—again, either pro or con—with your product or service. With them you want to use fact-driven messages that appeal to their broader interests, and relevant promotions, like products that complement other items they've already bought (say, mixing bowls for someone who's just bought a mixer). A partner in the law firm we discussed above might write to a client for whom, years earlier, the firm drew up a will and, while stressing the importance of reviewing the will might then be able to turn the conversation toward new business, like estate planning. A Web designer, to take another example, might offer free consultations for former clients with older Web sites. Or an architect seeking work in the public sector might meet with local elected officials to document the firm's track record, efficiency, and on-time, under-budget performance in earlier projects.

>> Reassess

Finally, as you proceed with your varied campaigns and continue to gather information about the consumers in each subgroup, continually reassess your categories, segments, and profiles. How? By asking the *Fire Hose Questions over and over again*. Ask the Essential Questions for each group. Look to see if their North Stars have moved. Decide whether the latest Squiggly Line is meaningful, whether there are any new surprises, or whether there's any previously unseen Lighthouse data.

>> Data Underload

While we wrote this book to demonstrate that a few simple questions can help almost anyone see through the fog of data in today's business world, situations do exist in which there is little or no data available. This is most common with new products, and new businesses without track records or customer histories. It also happens when your business considers turning down an unknown path, or toward a new, unsegmented market with which you aren't yet familiar. What then?

In earlier chapters, we've proposed navigating by your customer's North Star or looking for surprises when data overload makes meaningful analysis all but impossible. But what about data underload? In such cases, when no North Star yet exists—or it's so small that you're still unable to see it—our advice is to try employing the Swing Voter approach.

Consider the emergence of the dot-com era in the 1990s. Think back to the pure rush of technological and business-model evolution. Was there data to segment? Could CEOs profile and create new, targeted markets? Would offensive and defensive priorities be obvious and clear? Perhaps surprisingly, the answer is yes—although the data is different in kind. Whenever you enter uncharted territory, dig down into your own data—that is, evaluate your own organization to understand its fundamental strengths and the range of its possibilities. And then put that information into even sharper relief, thinking about the extremes, about your business's natural boundary lines. What makes your company tick? What is the essence of your corporate DNA? What is your company willing and prepared to do profitably? What should you avoid, given the answers to all the questions above? Only then can you apply the five Swing Voter steps and, proceeding with caution, continue to gather information as you go.

During the 1990s, for example, how many technology firms boomed, then went bust, having lost their way as they followed every businessperson's dream? And while believing in the dream may be a necessary part of every successful start-up, most failed to listen to their potential customers' voices as they slowly became audible. So as their businesses built up momentum they were no longer able to hear what their markets were saying. As a result, they were unable to identify their customers' wants. They asked themselves if they should become Internet service providers, not whether that business matched their core competencies, or, put another way, whether they were capable of answering, and delivering on, the new business's Essential Question. Others thought perhaps we can get rich in the Web hosting business. Still others listened to consultants who said that the future is about applications, which is why all the smart players were getting into the application service provider game. No, said some, we want to monetize the entire ecosystem, so let's build an e-marketplace for consumers and businesses alike. Better yet, let's start a dot-com and corner the market for one particular service.

Over the years, entrepreneurs in both emerging and mature markets have taken a ride on the same boom-and-bust roller coaster, where the sounds and screams of the adrenaline rush blocked out the voices of potential customers, unwelcome surprises in the data, and unmistakable Lighthouse data. In the IT and telecommunication business, the current wave is cloud computing, application development ecosystems, and mobile applications for a growing array of wireless devices. The answer then was the same as it is now: Slow down. Check the data. Ask simple questions. Stop thrashing and vibrating. If you're an entrepreneur, executive, marketer, or venture capitalist, always start by following the five simple Swing Voter steps. Because even when an industry cannot yet be said to exist, its success or failure will depend on its ability to attract Swing Voters—even though, in this case, not one of them is a customer yet.

APPLYING THE LESSON

Step 1: Categorize your competitors according to their core competencies. Then consider your own core competency—or your corporate DNA—and try to understand how, or if, that competency differentiates you from the competition. Even more important, are you sure you want to be, or are qualified to be, one of the leaders in this domain? Do you have "brand permission"? That is, do potential customers acknowledge that you belong in this space? How many others might be thinking about jumping in, too? Which of your competitors are almost certain to stay out? Once you've checked the provider side, examine existing customer data—whether for this particular product or service or the nearest thing to it for which data is available. Always start with what is publicly available. Then talk in depth to thirty or more prospective customers focused on the emerging space—customers who demonstrate the characteristics of longevity. In other words, don't bet on feedback from two dozen also-rans; focus on what a representative set of market leaders care about. Then categorize the market in terms, once again, of both vendors and buyers.

Step 2: Segment the market's categories as described above, starting with the swing cohort, and calculate the percentage of leaners, neutrals, and defectors in it.

Step 3: Profile the emerging segment(s) to create portraits of demographics and purchasing behavior. This can be determined even in emerging segments, but remember that "perfect" is the enemy of "good" and will inhibit progress. We are looking for insight, not a doctoral thesis.

Step 4: Target an addressable subset of the emerging market and focus on early wins—that is, leaners convinced to join the "very favorable" category—to build momentum and demonstrate the financial rationale for targeted messaging by profile. Don't pursue neutrals or defectors yet, although you should always address negative feedback immediately, whether it comes from customers or competitors.

Step 5: Reassess: As you gather information about the emerging market(s) and collect customer feedback, apply the Fire Hose Questions to look for surprises, Lighthouses, and Squiggly Lines. At this point in emerging markets or start-ups, Swing Voters can suddenly become very visible. This can be incredibly iterative, because the feedback and insights can come from many directions and in multiple waves over a short period; therefore, remember to strive for flexibility, but without self-destructive course corrections, as you continually reassess the latest market conditions and feedback.

At this point, let's check back in with our experts in retail, starting with Jim Hilt.

I think more about the people who are *able* to become better customers of mine. That is, people who already buy from me but could buy more, and how I could convince them to be better customers. I've worked for companies that touch most American households, so we didn't have to approach this challenge the way most companies do. My problem, unlike theirs, wasn't to convince someone to be a customer; my problem was convincing them that they wanted to be a more frequent customer. And if I focus only on my loyal customers, I'm going to miss sales opportunities. And so using the data—and this is an area where we are incredibly focused—we can say [continuing the earlier analogy], we already offer bread, and these are the people who want milk and bread, and if we can figure out how to add milk, we can generate even more business from these existing customers.

So, for both the people who come into our stores and the people who come to us online, if we're able to add something a little more attractive than our usual offerings, I'll have a chance to grow the "intensity" of my customers' spending. So again, it's not really focusing on those people who might *become* our customers, but on those who are already customers. And if I understand what I need to offer them—that is, what they really want—then I've got a chance to make them even better customers, and more satisfied customers.

I think that most companies, unless they're really new, or really small, can use their own data, and their own assets, to find the low-hanging fruit among their own Swing Voters. Again, the old way involved thinking about whether I could get a bigger share of their wallet. But if a lot of your customers have wallets that aren't particularly big, or have already opened those wallets as wide as they can, there's still a lot of data and information and feedback you can get from that group that could help you to expand your business with customers somewhat like them.

The same thing is true of a lot of people who are still on the fence, who can give me really good insight if I engage with them just a little bit, and while I may not end up doing more business with *them*, they may help me understand my other Swing Voter customers even better, so that I can succeed in making them even more intense buyers.

Jim Dippold's outlook, given that he's tracking customers moving up and down the aisles in a grocery store, is slightly different.

It's much easier to sell more to a customer that you already have in your store than it is to acquire a new customer. Much more cost-effective. And there are two things that you look at to make that happen. One, you look at general data from someone like IRI, and then try to cross-check that data with what your customers tell you they buy *outside* your store. Believe it or not, there are thousands of people who, every time they come back from a shopping session and empty their grocery bags, they actually have a scanner gun at home, and scan everything they buy. So you can look at that data, check it against your own loyalty data, and try to figure out how to generate more of those sales in your store instead of someone else's. Two, you look at customers and put them into bands. One band will be your best, most loyal customers, and they'll be platinum. And then you go down the list and put the others in gold, silver, or bronze. And then you look at the platinum customers, and you try to figure out how to get as many of the others into that band as possible. At the same time, you look at your bronze customers and try to find out why you're missing with them. They're not shopping in this department. They're not shopping as frequently as customers in other bands. So how do I migrate them into another band? And the answer is, you migrate them by meeting more of their needs.

In the retail grocery business, though, you've got to keep one final, perhaps surprising thing in mind. And that is that the top 5 percent of buyers account for 30 percent of total sales, and the bottom 60 percent account for only 10 percent of sales.

Information like this—which certainly surprised us—makes it easier to choose your primary marketing target, no matter your business. The point, however, is *not* that if your "platinum" customers account for such a great proportion of sales, you want to sell *them* more, but rather that you want to create *more of them*—that is, bring more of your Swing Voters into their small but critical group.

We think you'll find—as we have over years of working through some pretty tough business challenges ourselves—that these concepts give you an edge that will quickly surprise your colleagues, and your competition. And the more often you follow these steps, the more you'll experience their power. Your small investment in time will quickly produce returns in the conference room, in presentations, and in performance reviews. Even today, with broad data collection and market tracking, too many marketers paint all their consumers with the same broad brush. Instead, continually ask yourself how you and your coworkers can paint a series of customer portraits and use them to refine your communication strategies.

PLAYING OFFENSE: HOW SALES EXECUTIVES CAN EXPAND THEIR PIPELINE

Sales provide the best opportunity to make a play for swing customers, particularly in the case of business-to-business sales. Sales managers already know how to manage their prospects and repeat customers with a pipeline report listing business they expect to book and business they're trying to book.

What's more, the sales pipeline is typically segmented by "odds to close" of low, medium, and high, as well as timelines (i.e., near term, current business quarter, within the fiscal year). Under pressure to meet sales goals, managers obsess over their high-probability prospects and clients, and ignore the swing prospects in the middle of the spectrum. They are playing offense with *committed customers* who are already satisfied with the relationship, and practically ignoring everyone else. That means they're missing the *leaners*—that is, the ones they could convert to highly satisfied, repeat customers.

By targeting the same group of reliable customers, or pulling longer-term stretch deals into the current quarter through incentives or extraordinary sales tactics, the sales leader—feeling the heat to make quarterly numbers—can understandably make the mistake of "eating the seed corn." This quarterly focus may provide immediate gratification, but where is the investment in and cultivation of new business? Furthermore, these sales blinders inadvertently introduce more risk into the revenue pipeline by narrowing the universe of prospects and opportunities to the same tight subset of core customers that constitute the company's cash cow.

That said, a privately owned, cash-rich firm with an organic-growth mind-set can operate this way—at least to some extent. Orvis, the outdoor clothing and fly tackle company, resells and markets its high-end merchandise to loyal, profitable customer segments. The outdoorsman/outdoorswoman or angler who buys from Cabela's or Bass Pro Shops—meaning that they have no more than a moderate interest in fly-fishing—is not likely to hear from Orvis, and for good reason. Orvis is a best-practice example. This is something to aspire to, high-lighting the potential of focusing on the Swing Voter to move customers into the loyalty bucket.

Having guided countless start-ups through this trap, we have shown sales executives how to achieve higher strategic growth by reinforcing core clients and cultivating low-key and new clients from adjacent markets. Knowing that this sort of swing client is receptive to good news and positive developments about the firm, sales managers can communicate frequently and decisively to move clients from suspects/defectors to prospects/leaners, and then eventually into the "firm pipe-line." By doing so, both newer and more mature businesses can invest their sales resources so as to yield the highest possible return.

PLAYING DEFENSE: HOW MICROSOFT CONVERTED HARD-CORE GAMERS

In 2008, when Chris was at Microsoft, he deployed a Swing Voter strategy in rapid-response mode, with insights that apply to steps two, three, and four—segment, profile, and target. A short, innocuous post about the Xbox game system hardware had broken through to the top-ten list on Technorati, a Web site devoted to social media and the blogosphere. Microsoft's public relations agency quickly flagged the post, and when Microsoft's marketing executives investigated, they were able to use an existing tracking system to score the continuing online discussion according to the *intensity* of positive or negative sen-timents. Using it, the team was not surprised to find that the initial "product defect post" was almost completely negative.

The investigators were, however, surprised to find that the initial "flame" post spurred a large number of reposts from bloggers express-ing more constructive, thoughtful views—the views, in other words, of true neutrals. These secondary bloggers quickly established a group of Swing Voters, or a far larger group between the two extremes. As a result, Microsoft encouraged questions, provided facts, and directed those bloggers to their service team—and the "swing bloggers" pushed the discussion in a more productive direction. This gave the company time and breathing room to address any outstanding issues and to put in place a customer support process to address them in a positive, productive way. Would it have been better if the problem had not existed? Perhaps. But the reality is that technology is complex, and therefore problematic, and that having the ability to evaluate a full set of data through a new lens helped create time to drive a smarter strategic plan. If the team had ignored the neutrals in favor of the "loudest voice in the room," using a typical public relations strategy such as "calm and control," Microsoft might have missed the opportunity to engage its most active customers, and the chance to steer the conversation. Finally, moving down the list of steps to "reassess," Microsoft worked at creating a longer-term relationship with these highly active *and* highly vocal customers, and in so doing created a new group of leaners.

In short, this enormous middle cohort presents the greatest opportunity for low-cost (and low-friction) growth—that is, for earning an extra dollar of revenue without having to spend a corresponding dollar on marketing. Swing Voter analysis yields deep insights regarding the nature and potential behavior of your customers. As you become more familiar with the approach, you'll become better at listening for the quieter voices that might have the largest effect on you and your business. It will show you how to bridge satisfaction and loyalty—and then loyalty and profits.

CHAPTER SIX TAKEAWAYS

1. Swing Voters, or swing customers, offer the greatest opportunity for growth with the smallest expense.
2. To find your Swing Voters, categorize. To identify those voters mostly likely to become customers, segment.
3. To reach your Swing Voters, profile your segments and target your messaging accordingly.
4. To drive sales demand among Swing Voters, identify the two or three factors that are unique to neutral customers and incorporate in your communications.
5. Once you've identified your leaners, neutrals, and defectors, continually reassess the Swing Voter category.

DELIVERY

What? So What? Now What?

"This is not the end. It is not even the beginning of the end.
But it is, perhaps, the end of the beginning."
—WINSTON CHURCHILL

This chapter is a bit different from the six that came before it. Here we complete the transition from filtering data to communicating results. By now you really shouldn't have to ask the Fire Hose Questions anymore; they should be asking themselves. You should automatically hear at least one of them whenever anyone presents a plan. One or two should come to mind whenever anyone reports results. In fact, almost no matter what you're doing or anyone else is doing, you should hear a familiar voice in the back of your mind asking, "What's the Essential Question here?" Or "Are there any surprises in this data?" One or more of these questions should come to mind whenever your business veers off course, too, or the numbers seem to cloud the discussion, instead of showing you the way. Finally, whenever you feel as if you're about to be buried under the data, you should ask the questions yourself—as loudly as you can.

In this chapter, we'll bring the process we've outlined in the earlier chapters to its logical conclusion, using a simple but pragmatic framework: the Three W's. The "What?" is the collection of data, facts, and figures. The "So what?" is a discussion about what the data really means. The "Now what?" drives the discussion about what you should do as a result. While the three W's have been around in different forms for some time, by using them in the sequence below, with the Fire Hose Questions embedded in the three sections according to purpose, you'll be able to create a framework for both investigation *and* presentation.

- What?
- So what?
- Now what?

Looked at in this way, the "What?" is the information you brought to light by asking the first three Fire Hose Questions, all of which are requests for *relevant* data:

- What is the Essential Question?
- Where is your customer's North Star?
- Should you believe the Squiggly Line?

The "So what?" asks you to explain the meaning of that data, and the numbers it produces, for your business. To do that you'll use the fourth, fifth, and sixth Fire Hose Questions:

- What surprised you?
- What does the Lighthouse reveal?
- Who are your Swing Voters?

Finally, you'll ask the "Now what?," which is a request for an overall plan, and a list of specific steps to drive your projects, or your entire business, forward—determined by the way you've answered the "What?" and the "So what?"

Together these three questions form a simple framework, with a beginning, middle, and end. They'll ensure that the data you gather plays its proper role—that is, the role of a supporting actor, and not the lead in the play, a role always reserved for strategy. Finally, your use of the Three W's, and the insights they yield, will serve as catalysts for change and empower the other members of your organization to use them, too.

CHAPTER LESSONS

1. Find the data that matters.
2. Ask yourself what that data really means.
3. Create action plans based on that meaning.

It's true that up to this point we've treated the Fire Hose Questions independently—that is, as a list of stand-alone questions introduced in a somewhat random order, questions that could be asked singly or in combination, depending on the situation or the stage of a project or strategic plan. In fact, earlier in this book we compared the questions to the notes of the C major scale, which songwriters and composers have rearranged to produce an inexhaustible series of melodies, or variations on a theme that revisit key musical passages, like extended jazz pieces or concertos. And while the questions can certainly be used that way, as we've demonstrated throughout the first six chapters of this book, the seventh question can be used to create a more structured approach.

To repeat what we've written above—for emphasis—you'll use the first three Fire Hose Questions (Essential Question, North Star, Squiggly Line) to sort and then to collect the information you need. You'll then sift through the answers to the next three questions (What surprised you? Swing Voter, Lighthouse) for the sort of insights that will allow you to make sound business decisions, something data overload commonly prevents. Finally, you'll use the last group of questions (What? So what? Now what?) to point to what you found, analyze the information, create a plan of action, and inspire people to act.

APPLYING THE LESSONS

Throughout this book we've begun each chapter by introducing one of the Fire Hose Questions, then applying them to one or more case studies. We've used them to see past the sales data for commodities (like Starbucks coffee), new products (like the Roomba), and global disasters (like the Icelandic ash cloud). Now, having introduced all of the questions, we'd like to try an even more ambitious approach, and apply as many of the questions as we can to a single business story over a much longer time frame, to further demonstrate their uses and the way they work.

Long-established companies, after all—whether they sell things manufactured or processed, or process things manufactured or sold, or manufacture things processed or sold—have compiled vast, unparalleled data sets that new entrants will have difficulty matching.* Sometimes, this history will work against long established companies, and for newer entrants, since they'll probably be far more alert to surprises than companies that have done business for years, and with some success, by collecting pretty much the same numbers—and expecting them to tell the same story.

But we still had to decide where, or in which industry, to look for this kind of showcase. We thought of computing, of course, but dismissed the idea, because so much has already been written on the topic. Wireless communication seemed like a good choice, too. So did broadcast and cable television. And then we both realized that the story of digital photography was almost made for our purposes. And who better to comment on the Fire Hose Questions as we review the advances made in the field over the past twenty-five years than Steven Sasson, the inventor, along with Gareth Lloyd, of the digital camera.

Why did we think digital photography was a good test case? Well, to start, we're going to risk our reputations as visionaries by guessing that every single person reading this book has a digital camera. And don't forget: Even if you don't have a device made only for that purpose, you'll have a mobile phone with an embedded camera, or a computer with a built-in camera. And if you don't, you've certainly been caught on digital surveillance cameras at one time or another in your life, whether standing at an ATM or passing through an airline terminal. In fact, from security cameras to Facebook photos, digital photography has practically defined a generation. And digital cameras all have one thing in common: They can trace their origin to Steve Sasson. How did it happen? Kodak supervisor Gareth E. Lloyd asked Sasson, one of his engineers, if he thought a camera could be built using solid-state electronics, imagers, and an electronic sensor known as a charge-

*This was Nancy Smith's opinion, at iRobot, when discussing Lighthouse data showing competition for the company's products growing.

coupled device (CCD). Now, more than thirty-five years later, let's look back on these events, using the Three W's as our guide.

>> **What?**

Why would Kodak, the company that first brought photographic film to market, the company that was still the undisputed leader in global film sales, the company whose cameras, just like Gillette's cartridge razors, were simply mechanisms for selling their most profitable product (film) and services (film processing), be interested in "filmless" photography?

Fortunately, we don't have to guess. Listen to what Sasson, the inventor of digital photography, has to say about that critical moment in 1975 when Lloyd asked him if he could somehow cobble together the world's first digital camera. And note how he begins not with the Essential Question but with the customer's North Star. What he had to say may surprise you, given the revolution in which he played such a major part.

> In 1975–76, when I built and demonstrated the camera, I don't think the customer was dissatisfied in any way with the photographic process. Actually, I think it had been honed and developed and optimized over the last hundred years, such that the average person could pick up a camera, use it without much training, get excellent pictures, and display them in any way they wanted—that is, as slides or prints.
>
> So Kodak wasn't missing what customers wanted; they were thinking about what customers might be able to get, about what kind of advantages they might be able to get, because of the big technological discontinuity occurring around 1975, which was still in the future but turned out to revolutionize not only the photography business but just about every business—that is, the digitization of information.

So Kodak, according to Sasson, had never lost sight of its customer's North Star. Instead the company recognized that the wind was about to change, technologically speaking, so they asked themselves two questions (the second of which could be considered the Essential Question). One: What would the next age of photography look like? And two: Could Kodak remain relevant and profitable in that new world?

Sasson notes the difference between inventing the camera itself and the way it would affect the photography industry's business model. To understand that difference, it helps to remember that Kodak, in Sasson's words, was primarily an "imaging company," dedicated to "capturing people's memories," not a manufacturer of film. Therefore, the digitization of images, or of memories themselves, didn't represent a change in the company's mission.

> Back in '75 and '76, the challenge I got was How can this thing ever be commercially viable to a consumer? Their view of digital technology was . . . oh, let's just say they thought of it as esoteric, and unreliable. So there was the idea itself, and then the technology I used to demonstrate it. The idea was electronically capturing images—a camera with no moving parts—and then displaying them on a television set. And the technology I used, which was digital technology, helped me eliminate a lot of mechanical complexity I really couldn't deal with in building this prototype.
>
> That idea implied capturing images without using a consumable [film] and displaying them without using a consumable [photographic paper]. That was really the concept. I even called it "filmless" photography back then, if you can believe it.

In December 1975, Sasson and his team built a digital device about the size of a toaster, then persuaded a lab assistant to pose for the first digital photograph ever taken. The black-and-white image, captured at a resolution of .01 megapixels (ten thousand pixels), took twenty-three seconds to record onto a digital cassette tape and another twenty-three seconds to read off a playback unit onto a television. That the television existed—that is, that a device existed on which you could display an electronic image—might seem pretty lucky in hindsight, but Sasson debunks the notion.

> By the late eighties we were sure that whatever this form of electronic photography was going to be, it was not going to involve, or revolve around, the television set and its image format, even though most of the video people who were involved at the time

thought so. They thought, everyone's going to see photographs on a TV. And we thought, that's just not going to be acceptable. Film will always be better than this.

By "this" Sasson meant NTSC standards, which regulated transmission, resolution, and the means by which color images were created on a television screen. Now, more than thirty-five years later, it's tempting to see the earlier optical chemical process as somewhat unfriendly to the customer. But that's true only in hindsight. We think Sasson's argument is compelling—that is, that the customer was remarkably well served, and by a company that might have cared far less, and made just as much money, given its share of the market (which hovered around 90 percent).

Having created the first prototype, Sasson basically spent the rest of his career working on and staying abreast of advances in the various fields of electronics and computing that would finally allow digital photography to overtake Kodak's film-based process. There were three advances in particular, and you might say that, together, they could be regarded as the fledgling industry's Essential Question.

The first was the development of a solid-state imager that was economical, that had high resolution, and that could faithfully reproduce color. Over the decades that followed, Kodak spent many millions of dollars refining the charge-coupled device, and remained an industry leader in that technology, introducing the first megapixel sensor and the first color filter array technology.

The second was the development of a secure, reliable means of storing an image. Again, while the CCD was a great image-capturing device, it was a terrible storage device. So some sort of solid-state film, as Sasson called it, had to be developed. That eventually took the form of digital memory—that is, something that would retain the integrity of whatever information it stored without any power applied to it. Of course, at the time that Sasson put the first digital camera together, that sort of memory didn't exist.

In retrospect, it seems as if film-based photography didn't stand a chance against emerging digital technologies. But Sasson, who was there during the entire story, still has great regard for the earlier technology's strengths.

You know, film really was amazing, and whenever you're involved in a technology discontinuity like this, you really gain a tremendous appreciation for the technology you're displacing, because it's often really good. Think about a piece of film. One thirty-five-millimeter slice of film, you know, manufactured by anyone in the world, stored for years, and then put in anybody's camera and exposed for a few milliseconds, holds that latent image indefinitely until it's developed, and then the same piece of film is used to make an exposure on a piece of photographic paper. And that piece of film only cost a few cents. And so you take a look at that and you say, How can we come up with an electronic imaging chain that can compete with that?

Sasson also points out that consumers trusted the system. They weren't afraid of losing their images once they had captured them on film, as complicated as that whole process was—i.e., light moving through the moving mechanical parts in the camera to strike the film, followed by a series of chemical operations that could easily go wrong. And yet the technology was so well understood, and had been improved upon so continually, that the market trusted it implicitly. Consumers trusted their cameras, they trusted their film, and they trusted that once an image was captured it wouldn't somehow disappear. At the time, digital memory didn't have that sort of reputation, and even the suggestion that you could somehow come up with a form of digital memory that didn't require batteries, that would hold your images indefinitely, without losing any information whatsoever, was quite a stretch.

The third piece of the puzzle was the development of microprocessors, which led to the appearance of personal computers. That technology allowed consumers to move digital data rapidly and inexpensively, and without a great deal of technical expertise.

>> So What?

In the seventies and eighties, though, even with the primary technology in hand—that is, the technology used to make the camera itself—the market for that technology wouldn't, or couldn't, appear until all three parts of the Essential Question had been answered. And Kodak, for the first time in the company's history, couldn't supply all the answers itself. The new technology, it seemed, would never have a single, primary element, like film, that captured an image, stored an image, and was also used to create a copy of that image.

This fact would take control of the process, including quality control, out of Kodak's hands for the first time in the company's history. According to Sasson, that loss of quality control was most troubling.

> Kodak was very proud, and considered it their obligation to provide the highest image quality to consumers. And in order to do that, they had to have a hand in the entire photographic imaging chain, from capturing the image all the way through printing. We had photofinishing operations, we sold chemicals, we sold paper, we did the algorithms for the photofinishers, we worked with camera manufacturers, and built cameras, and provided film formats, so we had our hands in the whole chain.
>
> And when digital photography finally came along, to actually get a good print from a digital camera was a real challenge. You used a camera that was made by one manufacturer, that stored images on a memory chip made by another, and then transferred it into a computer made by somebody else, using software made by yet another company. And none of these entities ever talked to each other. For that reason, back in the late nineties, we called it the "chain of pain."

Nor were there any generally recognized standards—at least not as all the parts of the process began to take shape, without any sort of coordination. And the system we enjoy now was not the only one considered. Sasson still remembers battling the entrenched interests of television.

> By then we thought that instead of [digital photography] revolving around the television set, it was going to revolve around the personal computer . . . even though the PC hadn't been completely developed yet. We just knew that that's where the image had to show up to meet the quality standards that people expected from their still photographs. We knew that people weren't going to take a step backwards, just because they could do this new thing right away, because if the outcome was a really lousy

image, what good does that do? So a bunch of companies that were comfortable with video technology tried to apply it to the world of still photography, and made some inroads, too, because it could put a presentable picture on a television screen. But it was never going to replace a film camera, in terms of quality.

Sasson also points out that the technological advances we now take for granted—that is, that now seem almost inevitable—almost never proceed smoothly, from one success to another. Instead, he says, long series of failures generally lead to incremental advances in technology. And even though most of the early efforts fail—think of Drei Tauben Ltd. trying to interest newspapers in a technology none of them could grasp—the early efforts get people thinking about the possibilities. And even before the technology has been refined, there are usually a couple of sectors that can use it, even in its crude forms. Think of security cameras or real estate listings. Quality wasn't nearly as important as the fact that the photos could be taken quickly, and transmitted quickly, too. And once even a few people start using the technology, others begin thinking about how, if the quality were just a little bit better, they might begin to use it, too.

Now that digital photography has become the dominant medium, we tend to take its advantages for granted, and consider its appearance almost preordained. But only twenty years ago, film was inseparable from photography. And yet by 1995, even though digital cameras couldn't yet match the visual quality of exposed, developed film, digital cameras already allowed both amateur and professional photographers to: (1) capture images easily and inexpensively; (2) review those images without having to take the time and trouble to "develop" them; (3) transmit those images to a personal computer, where they could be manipulated in a variety of ways (again, for contrast, color, etc.); (4) print only those images they selected; and (5) securely store those images. As a result, the sale of conventional cameras peaked around 2000 and rapidly declined in the next decade as the sales of digital cameras skyrocketed.

Now, it's difficult to read about the development of this technology story without wondering why film manufacturers didn't see the digital rocks along the shore. As Sasson reveals, the digital revolution was anything but predictable. Shining a light on the information did allow

Kodak to navigate a disruption and major transformation in the market. Recall that Kodak was a pioneer in digital camera technology. Yes, they are a very different company today in terms of size, products, and services, but they remain a $7 billion entity.

After I'd built the prototype, I wrote a report that described it, and I even tried to predict what would happen in the next couple of decades. But of course I wasn't allowed to talk about it outside the company, for a couple of reasons. One was that nobody knew where it was all going to go at that time. Nobody was predicting the birth of the Internet, or the fact that everyone would have a personal computer at their disposal, or that it would be easy enough for anyone to use, to say nothing of photographic desktop printing. All of those things were in the future, so we were just looking at it like an experiment, and I was just looking at it as a way to demonstrate a camera without film, and without any moving parts.

Maybe the closest analogy I can use, thinking back to the time, was the digital calculator, which was coming out around then. People had used slide rules for decades, when you were an engineering student, and all of a sudden now you had a digital device that could compute. And I thought if a camera could ever become like these calculators—that is, like digital calculators with a lens—well, that was sort of my crude vision of what the future might be like.

And although there were many technical obstacles to this, I couldn't see any fundamental reason . . . you know, there was no fundamental law of physics that would say we couldn't do this.

So the company was interested in it, and pursued it very aggressively for many decades, but was not public about it for two reasons: One, we really didn't realize what the answer would be, that is, to the question of whether or not it would be commercially viable, and two, because people looked to Kodak, that is the way they would look to any company that is a leader in a field, to say "Hey, what's going to happen next?" And we didn't feel that we knew the answer very well. And I don't mean just a technical answer, but we also didn't know, for our purposes, what a good business model would be with this. We clearly knew what the business model was for photographic, that is for silver halide film, but it wasn't clear at all what the business model might look like with the electronic imaging chain.

Before concluding our interview, we asked Sasson if he saw any rocks ahead for the current technology, more than thirty-five years after he took the shot seen round the world.

> I often worry about our belief that, since we can capture images this way, it feels like we've got them forever. But will we always be able to find and view them, given the rapid obsolescence of one format after another? I often ask myself what the archivists think about this. How do they preserve these digital images? And not only how do they preserve the original images technically, but how do they make sure they're the original images themselves? Digital manipulation takes place everywhere. There are famous examples of people painting other people out of photographs, and painting other people in, and changing the original nature of the photograph. What's appropriate there? Sure, there's artistic license, but there's the integrity of the photograph, too. And so there are really interesting questions about whether or not you're really looking at reality, when you can't really be sure.

This fascinating case study of the birth of digital photography illustrates how the Fire Hose Questions can enable you to be agile in a dynamic environment. Beyond the core market research data, applying the Fire Hose Questions reveals the strategic choices from the vast information available to you. It amplifies the key areas to discuss. The Fire Hose framework will not give you the answer, but it serves as a bridge between the facts and figures and your business strategy.

>> Now What?

Luck, once again, played its part in the development of digital photography, and most likely will play a part in subsequent developments in the field. Sasson invented the digital camera at about the same time the first personal computers were being built. By then, the first crude Internet system—the ARPANET—had already been in place for more than five years. Ten years later, in the mid-1980s, the National Science Foundation oversaw the creation of the modern (TCP/IP-based) Internet. The World Wide Web followed in 1990, by which time the market for PCs was firmly established. Both were critical to the widespread use of digital cameras, the PC because it allowed users to manipulate and store digital images and the World Wide Web because it allowed users to transmit those images—something so surprising, it hadn't even been *imagined* during the century and a half that photographs were made using film.

As a footnote to this story, on December 29, 2010, *The New York Times* reported that the last Kodachrome lab in the country, Dwayne's Photo, of Parsons, Kansas, would no longer process the legendary color film.[*] First made available in 1935, Kodachrome was manufactured in a variety of formats for both motion picture and still photography. Its unique chemical design—which accounted for its renowned color fidelity—also made professional development a must. With the closing of the last Kodachrome lab in the United States, the triumph of digital photography is complete. It's worth noting, however, that in answering the Essential Questions of photography—i.e., how to make photographs easier to take, less expensive to print, and easier to send and store—the industry also made an implicit decision to deemphasize the North Star of professional photographers and focus instead on the much larger population of the casual photographer.

The same thing, of course, happened long ago in the recording industry, when large-width magnetic tape and pressed vinyl gave way to digital recording techniques, and for somewhat the same reasons.

FIRE HOSE EXERCISE NO. 3: TRENCH FANTASY FOOTBALL

Having used the history of digital photography as an exhibition game of sorts for the Three W's, we're now going to turn to another real-world example—one that is still "playing" itself out in the world of online fantasy sports. We like to think of this case study as a bookend to the one we introduced in the beginning of the book, that of Drei Tauben Ltd. (DTL). Christopher Frank was a principal of that business,

[*] A. G. Sulzberger, "For Kodachrome Fans, Road Ends at Photo Lab in Kansas," *New York Times*, December 29, 2010.

and Paul Magnone is a principal in the story of Trench Fantasy, to which we will turn now. And while DTL, like most start-ups, is a thing of the past, Trench Fantasy is very much a story of the moment, with its ending still unwritten.

Trench Fantasy Football was born of the conviction that traditional online football games make the same mistake that fans and commentators make. That is, they concentrate on the stars in the offensive and defensive backfields, and ignore the "trenches." And that, of course, as anyone who really understands the game knows, is where the game is won or lost. According to the site:

> In the NFL, games are won and lost in the trenches. Not by "skill" players tiptoeing down the sideline, but by strong, talented, 300-lb men with hands and feet quick as lightning who smash and grind for every yard of daylight. But you wouldn't know it from playing regular fantasy football, where the spotlight shines on the end zone and glamour guys with names like Chad, Peyton, Carson, and DeAngelo.
>
> Traditional fantasy football games take the ultimate team sport and reduce it to quarterbacks, running backs and wide receivers. Where, you ask, is the love for the guys who deal in pancake blocks, blindside sacks, goal line stands and holes you could drive a truck through? Does anybody care about the grueling, dirty work that wins football games?
>
> Now you can go beyond the pretty boys and their choreographed end zone celebrations. With Trench Fantasy Football you draft and manage a team of units instead of individuals. Then you score points off the every-down plays that win and lose games, like first downs, ball control, three-and-outs, sacks, picks, return yardage and more.*

Now let's put the reporting framework we introduced in this chapter to work, and take a look at Trench Fantasy using the Three W's, the first of which covers the Essential Question, the customer's North Star, and the Squiggly Line.

---

*www.trenchfantasy.com.

>> **What?**

Like most start-ups, Trench Fantasy began with a simple question: If real football was won and lost in the trenches, why couldn't fantasy football be approached from the same angle? With this Essential Question defined, Trench Fantasy founder and CEO Eric Koivisto turned eagerly to the market data. There was plenty to look at.

In Koivisto's words:

> You absolutely want to see data. Anyone who says that you can make these instinctual decisions, without anything to back up those instincts, is reading only half the story. You have to have data, because you need to know if there's a market there and, if there is, how you're going to position yourself in it. I think from a marketing and advertising standpoint, that's ultimately what it comes down to. It's how you're going to position yourself, and you've got to position yourself relative to something else. So you've got to have data that defines that something else.

The data was encouraging. According to market research prepared for the Fantasy Sports Trade Association (FSTA),[*] almost 30 million North Americans played some form of fantasy sports in 2007–08. So for Koivisto, a marketing man by profession, that meant shifting his focus to marketing.

> If you've got your marketing hat on, what you want to do is understand share. You want to understand demographics. Who purchases this thing? Why do they purchase this thing? What sort of influence model is at work during the purchase process? And also what length of time does the purchase process cover? Those really are the marketing questions, and they'll let you understand the sort of expectations you should have with any sort of marketing and communications campaign or sales efforts you direct at the market.

---

[*]As it turns out, the Fantasy Sports Trade Association commissions market research from Ipsos, the Europe-based market research company for whom Darrell Bricker works as CEO of public affairs in the North American office.

The Essential Question, according to Koivisto, was pretty simple, too.

It may sound simplistic, but the essential business question is always "Is there a business?" Is this thing a stand-alone, viable moneymaking business? Or is it really just a feature of some other product? That's what investors are always looking at. And if there is a business, is it a moneymaking business?

This, according to Koivisto, was an especially important question where online businesses were concerned.

A lot of online businesses are predicated upon a significant amount of their revenue coming from ad sales. But if you're going to make money selling ads, you need to be able to acquire customers for a cost well below what you're going to charge to sell advertising.

I don't mean you have to have all the questions answered. If you try to do that right at the beginning, you can end up suffering from data paralysis or, worse, analysis paralysis. Still, you've got to have something that either sizes or scopes or defines or gives you some kind of perspective on the market. Something that tells you if the water is hot or cold, or frozen or boiling. So data is critical; I can tell you that from my Microsoft days to my start-up days at Trench Fantasy. But you have to figure out what sort of data sets you want to look at, based of course on the resources you have available.

The initial data certainly made it seem as if there was room for Trench in the fantasy sports world. According to the same market research, more than 80 percent of fantasy sports fans played fantasy football. Not only that, but most of them had been playing for years, and played in more than one league. The bulk of them were white men around the age of forty, and approximately two thirds of them were college-educated. Surprisingly, more than 20 percent were women. Approximately 75 percent of them were married, and the same percentage owned their own homes. Finally, the income of the average player was more than $75,000 per year.

But those were just the hard numbers. Some of the more interesting data had to do with the social aspects of the fantasy sports. Friends tended to play together. Fathers and sons played together. Leagues were also common at work and, according to surveys, created team spirit in the workplace. Not only that, but more than 15 percent of respondents claimed that playing fantasy sports had led to valuable business contacts. Fantasy football players were also far more likely to attend live professional sports events than those who didn't play.

With that in mind, Koivisto and his team targeted a market segment of some three million rabid fans. These players demonstrated the propensity to spend regularly, and in greater amounts than casual fans. They played in multiple leagues and purchased a variety of online and offline fantasy football content (e.g., magazines, draft guides, player reports, etc.). If they could reach this market with the right message, thought Koivisto, success was far more likely, and marketing acquisition costs almost sure to be far less expensive. After all, these were players who were already playing in more than one league, so the marketing campaign for the new site only had to capitalize on existing behavior; it didn't have to change it. What's more, it seemed that a significant part of that highly committed market segment understood the importance of the offensive and defensive lines, and the artificial nature of existing fantasy football games built around the offensive stars. And this feeling was borne out by initial interviews with prospective customers, who consistently made comments like "We can't wait to try it."

The North Star, or perhaps we should say the North Stars, of these customers was pretty easy to find. To start, they all loved football. They loved playing it, and they loved doing the closest thing they could to Monday-morning quarterbacking—that is, running a team themselves. These were the kinds of fans who watched games at home and in stadiums, and after every unsuccessful play thought the same thing that some of the best professional commentators and knowledgeable former players were saying: What does the coach think he's *doing*? Why'd they run left? They should have gone right on that pass play to exploit the weak secondary. The guard needs to pull and get to the outside faster. And why isn't the running back following the guard into the hole?

So it seemed as if Trench Fantasy had all its ducks in a row. Management understood its business's Essential Question, had found its customer's North Star, and hadn't based its plans on data from a Squiggly Line. After all, the fantasy football market had been growing for years.

>> So What?

You can't always trust the survey, though, and once the site was up and running, players—and, even more important, players in leagues— didn't materialize as quickly as Koivisto, top management, and investors thought they would. In this respect, the stories of DTL and Trench Fantasy were similar. In DTL's case, it seemed that in spite of the size of the market, and its innovative marketing plan, it had simply been a little too far ahead of its time. Had newspapers used computers in the early nineties and had they been able to understand the value of the new system as well as job seekers and employers did, one of our authors probably wouldn't have developed his share of the expertise on display in this book.

In Trench Fantasy's case, the slow start may have been the result of the Great Recession of 2007–08 or the natural hesitation of the market to try something different. One thing was sure, though: The Trench Fantasy team was looking at a much longer marketing campaign than they had planned. And as with all start-ups, that meant their resources were going to be stretched thin. As it turned out, there were a lot of surprises ahead for the company, most of them the kind they hadn't wished for.

"The data points we had," said Koivisto, "showed there was a market, and that to succeed, based on certain economics, it wouldn't take a huge piece of that market. It was enough for us to be Diet Coke to Coke. What we didn't realize, though, was that—even though the data was there, and the market was there, and the size was there, and the initial response from analysts and experts and potential customers was positive—fantasy sports was a *group purchase decision*."

In other words, while Trench Fantasy was open to single players, the business model called for the creation of leagues, and for that to happen, whole groups of individuals had to decide to play together. While at first glance that doesn't seem difficult to manage, consider that among a group of ten friends, there are probably only two or three we could call "over the top" fans—that is, truly committed fans. The rest are mild fans or followers. (This, you may have noted, mirrors our discussion on Swing Voter.) For Koivisto, that raised the issue of the length of the marketing campaign.

> If my purchase process is twelve months, say for an enterprise IT solution, well, you better have a campaign that spans twelve months. If you're selling Windows PCs, and a consumer can walk into a store and buy it tomorrow, you could actually have three-month campaigns. So when you're putting your campaign together, you have to acknowledge the length of time it takes to purchase your product and then to install it and satisfy your customer.

In Trench Fantasy's case, that campaign was going to have to go on a lot longer—that is, if there was going to be any chance the site would stay on its feet. As it turned out, time itself had a lot to do with the need for an extended campaign. In fact, stepping back and looking at the reams of data from a Lighthouse perspective revealed that Trench Fantasy's main competitor was not another fantasy sports game; it was simply the ordinary demands of life, work, home, and family. In effect, the market was feeling saturated. There was not a burning need or compelling reason to buy an alternative game. It turned out that those multiple-league players were playing as many games as they could, given the time they had to play, but the big rock that was revealed was that the leap to a new approach to the game needed more user support, education, and migration tools to build a mass audience. However, the analytics created by Trench showed wide appeal.

What about Trench Fantasy's niche? That strategy, just like DTL's basic strategy—i.e., the creation of a virtual hiring hall that brought employers and job seekers together—was essentially sound. The data showed that on average, the three million rabid players played in three to four leagues at one time. And in order to work, the Trench Fantasy model needed only a portion of those rabid fans to add one additional league, or switch to a league with a unique and compelling form of play. However, despite all the early positive feedback, it turned out that most of the existing players needed more information and support in order to learn a new form of fantasy football, much less gather a group of friends all interested in this new form of play.

Still, not all the signs were bad. One early, pleasant surprise was the popularity of the new statistics Trench Fantasy produced. The Trench

Fantasy platform offered a fresh perspective on the game, driven by a new set of metrics that factored game play *by unit*. This mirrored the real results on the field. If your Trench Fantasy offensive and defensive team units did well, then chances were that the actual NFL team did well, too. This was far more interesting, and authentic, than a random star player's performance, reflected in actual NFL wins and losses. By asking what was surprising, the Trench team identified that the Trench statistics and Trench Ratings not only were popular with players in other fantasy football leagues; they even began to attract some attention in the NFL. So while the early business plan was focused on leagues, another revenue stream appeared in the kind of data the site produced in the course of its operation. This was part of the original business plan, but it wasn't expected to be a significant revenue stream until the second or third year of operation. And this new content could be sold not only to players but to media outlets (newspapers, radio, and TV) or to fantasy and non-fantasy sports magazine publishers.

Besides, there were still tens of millions of active fantasy players. And while it appeared as if the industry's growth had reached a plateau once the economy stalled, the simple fact was that there were players out there. Lots of players. So for management, the question became: How can we get them to move to Trench Fantasy? In other words, who were Trench's Swing Voters?

According to Koivisto:

> You can describe them pretty easily. They're the guys that are already playing the game. But finding the ones most likely to move is the hard part, because they're everywhere. For us, it slowly became clear that the Swing Voters of the fantasy sports world are what we call the "commissioners." These are the single players with the power to affect the opinions of six, eight, ten, twelve other people. They're the ones who do the hard work. They're the ones who do the research, set up the account, sign up for e-mail, set the password, and set up the league. Basically, they're the ones that say, Yeah, this is something me and my tribe will do.

This demographic tended to be a little older—say, twenty-eight to thirty-two years old. And Koivisto's research effectively zeroed in on what made them different.

When you're twenty-two and you're watching the game, you're watching the highlights. You're watching the red zone. You're drinking a beer and giving your friends high fives. If you're twenty-eight to thirty-two, though, you're already looking at the game, and the world, from a different perspective. You've loved once, you've lost your first job, you know life is more than touchdown dances, and you've started to appreciate the intricacies of the game. You realize that it's not just the quarterback. You've expanded your knowledge or your understanding of the game. You're a bit older, not just some fast-twitch gamer. You're out of the fraternity house. You've graduated, and you're really starting to pay attention to how the game works.

>> Now What?

In addition to targeting the "commissioners" of the fantasy sports world, one of the answers to "Now what?" seemed to involve the sorts of players who didn't have a major role in the company's initial plan—that is, single players. At first, management didn't pay much attention to them, since single players were far more likely to use the site's free product sample and so didn't drive significant revenues. As it became clear that Trench would have to change its business plan, however, management began to pay more attention to the sorts of players they had initially overlooked.

But that wasn't all they had to reconsider. Advertising and co-branding had been part of the game plan from the beginning, but they weren't considered primary sources of income. What's more, the slow growth in membership limited revenue from advertising. Co-branding, however, turned out to have far more potential than management had expected. Even if the site hadn't succeeded in attracting millions of players, it had succeeded in creating a brand. And that brand projected the persona of a covered-with-mud, tough-as-nails, flat-nosed, lunchbox-carrying, belly-over-the-belt trench warrior—the kind of player who appealed to brands like Prilosec, Ford, Coors, Walmart, Spike TV, and, in particular, Under Armour.

So while membership grows more slowly than originally projected, Trench Fantasy is beginning to generate revenue from co-branding campaigns tied to social media. These campaigns include adding a simplified free version preferred by individual users to other brand promotions that use free giveaways. And these tie-ins allow the site to reach out to their customers via Facebook throughout the entire season.

Management is also trying to leverage Trench Ratings, or the weekly statistics gathered from every game played on the site, which have turned out to be more interesting to consumers (and the media) than the game itself. What's more, those ratings are now beginning to be applied to NFL football, via Trench Recommendations. In other words, media outlets and traditional fantasy football players are now beginning to look at the significance of the stats generated by the site's rating system, and to use it to decide whether to start or bench a player given matchups created by the Trench Ratings. In fact, the Trench Ratings recommendations consistently yield at least 20 percent more points than the average player at all positions—i.e., quarterback, running back, wide receiver, and tight end—and the bench recommendations consistently score 20 percent fewer points than average fantasy. Simply stated, by looking at the upcoming opposition matchup through the Trench viewpoint, you could begin to predict which "skill player" (i.e., QB, RB, WR, and TE) would do well or poorly against an opposing defense. So, in focusing on a part of the game no other fantasy football site does—that is, the team game—it's now quantifying factors that pro-coaching staffs are beginning to watch. In other words, Koivisto and his team are in the process of leveraging the previously unforeseen strengths of the site, making the core game almost irrelevant or a loss leader—at least for the time being. And while the ultimate fate of this start-up is still unknown, Koivisto's model, and the analytics it drives, may yet make him the Bill James* of football.

Businessmen and businesswomen can make good decisions only if they have good information. But data itself, as we wrote at the beginning of this book, does not inform. Relevant numbers have to be teased out of the data, and then those numbers need to be analyzed. And only after that analysis has yielded some insight can anyone be truly prepared to make sound decisions.

*The father of Sabermetrics, which we discussed in Chapter Three, "Should You Believe the Squiggly Line?"

Capturing data, though, is often the endpoint of research; it should, instead, be the beginning. This is especially true today. We are so inundated with data, from so many sources, that we're exhausted long before we can comprehend even a small part of it. And that flood of data will continue.

If we're to have any chance, then, to make effective use of it, we have to learn how to focus our search. Toward that end, we have to begin by asking ourselves why we need the information to begin with, and select only the data that pertains to our needs. This reinforces that the Fire Hose process is natural and logical. Once we have it, we need to determine whether that data confirms what we know, reveals some hidden information, or provides new insight into the workings of our companies. Finally, we need to use that information to make plans. And then start right back at the beginning.

CHAPTER SEVEN TAKEAWAYS

1. The "What?" is the collection of data, facts, and figures. The "So what?" is a discussion about what the data really means. The "Now what?" drives the discussion on what you should really do about it.
2. Manage data overload by searching only for the data you need to answer your essential business questions.
3. Make data the supporting character, not the star of the show. Demote the raw data, the description of your methodology, and any supporting materials to the appendix.

CHAPTER EIGHT

Reporting Your Findings

"Finally, in conclusion, let me say just this."

— PETER SELLERS

When you opened this book, whether you knew it or not, you were walking into data rehab. Now, nearly two hundred pages later, we're happy to tell you that you've made it to the final session. In another twenty or so pages you'll close this book. But, of course, the problem of data overload won't have gone away. It'll still be there. The only question is how you'll take what you've learned in *Drinking from the Fire Hose* and put it to work.

We began by describing the implications of data overload, then we introduced the questions we've developed to manage the problem. We followed those introductory chapters with in-depth examinations of each of the Fire Hose Questions, along with real business-world applications. Now it's time to move to the last step in the process—presenting the results. Again, the relevant data leads to numbers, the numbers to information, the information to insight, and the insight to answers. But you have to communicate your findings to influence and inspire decision makers, and that's the focus of this chapter. All that said, we have good news: The end of the process is all about doing less, not more. Or, as Mark Twain once said, "I didn't have time to write a short letter, so I wrote a long one instead."

Similar to a movie director who shoots hundreds of hours of film to wind up with a ninety-minute picture, building an effective presentation means being comfortable with leaving data on the cutting-room floor. Ineffective analysts instead present every single number they collect—and what should be an award-winning film turns into a miniseries, without focus or purpose. In short, answering the essential business question is the goal, not producing a commercial on the time and effort invested in the presentation.

CHAPTER LESSONS

1. Employ a simple framework to report your conclusions.
2. Reduce the surface area of your presentations.
3. Present the numbers, but always in the context of other numbers.
4. Be confident enough to leave the "extra footage" on the cutting-room floor.

Whether you adopt a new approach to presenting, or whether you don't, there's still going to be too much data. There will always be too much data—sales data, customer survey data, and focus group data, and more of it coming in all the time. There isn't just more data than we need; there's more than we can possibly process. Using any one, or any two or three, or even all the questions introduced in this book, you should now be able to take a sip from the Fire Hose and not get knocked to the ground doing it. In other words, by now you should understand how to use these questions to get to the numbers you need to see, without being buried under the ones that just don't matter. Every time you accomplish that, though, you've got to keep one critical element of this process in mind: Even the right numbers will never be more than supporting actors in the play. The insights, learning, and answers should take the lead role in any presentation, not the facts and figures. While this gets an easy head nod of agreement, it is hard to do when you're faced with a mountain of data. Pause to consider how many data-heavy, chart-happy, unreadable small-font presentations you are asked to review.

HOW FREQUENTLY DO YOU SEE THE FOLLOWING DURING PRESENTATIONS?

1. Presentations that take refuge in detail.
2. A focus on the data, instead of the solution.
3. Irrelevant data (i.e., data that doesn't help answer the Essential Question).
4. A glut of data (so the substance drowns in the volume).
5. Data reported in the order it was gathered.
6. Headlines or bullet points for every single data point.
7. Too many slides devoted to setting up the presentation.
8. Too many messages on one slide.
9. Slide titles that don't explain the data on the slide.
10. An incomprehensible mix of bar charts, pie charts, graphs, and spreadsheets.
11. Decks that begin and end with data, instead of moving from data to insight to recommendations.

If you answered "frequently" more than five times, you'd better keep reading.

The most effective use of data is to be selective in what you show and move the rest to the appendix. Because no matter who uses them, and for what purpose, the numbers you worked so hard to get are just *means* to a wide variety of ends.

They might help you focus on the Essential Question, but only so you can *answer it*. They might help you find your customer's North Star, but only so you can *follow it*. They might warn you that you're developing long-term strategies based on short-term results, alert you to a potentially game-changing surprise, or help you identify your Swing Voters. But once the numbers have warned you, or alerted you, or picked your Swing Voters out of the crowd, *you need to make some decisions*.

That's why we go to all the trouble to collect the numbers, and to scrutinize them once we do. Is the drop in sales in one particular region a sign of trouble ahead, or just an aberration? Is our primary competitor's growing market share cause for alarm, or an indication that the market is growing fast enough to keep us all busy? The numbers are meant to answer questions, and those answers are meant to drive decisions—in particular, the answers to the fundamental questions, that is, the "what," the "so what," and the "now what." And unless you don't intend to ask anyone else what they think—a distinctly unusual style for the leaders of any successful company—you'll also use the numbers to inform others, to ask the opinions of others, and to convince others to act.

So once you've gathered the numbers you need, you've got to make the *results* of your inquiry understandable and available to your colleagues. Your job starts anew once the data is collected.

And that brings us to presentation.

One of the most effective approaches is a best practice developed by members of the American Express Global Marketplace Insights team. That team and its leaders have developed a well-defined program to improve reporting, and one that is in sync with the approach we've discussed in this book. We've pulled a few simple, practical tips from that program, all of which can be put to use without lengthy training. They'll help you *present* the answers you get to the Fire Hose Questions, whether you're putting them into your reports or your presentations.

1. Start with the essential business question.
2. Highlight the people you spoke to as part of the analysis; adding their names will give your results additional validity.
3. Use the lead statement to answer the "So what?"
4. Embrace white space.
5. Remember that getting to the "Now what?" is the point of the research, and of the presentation.
6. One slide, one message.
7. Use language that is clean, concise, and comprehensible.
8. Exploit opportunities to draw pictures of your ideas rather than describe them.

Putting these general rules to work, though, requires one important feature, something that's part of every successful presentation: a good framework.

FRAMEWORKS

Powerful presentations are delivered with clearly defined frameworks. We cannot overemphasize the need for a framework when communicating the results of your research. That framework can be either implicit or explicit, but you have to group your results in a logical manner and in a way the listener, or reader, can easily understand. Whether your audience is sitting in a theater, a university lecture hall, or a conference room, listeners want a clear narrative with a beginning, middle, and end. Plot twists, whodunits, and puzzles are for fiction, not fact.

Below are a few examples of some of the more commonly used frameworks.

1. The Problem/Method/Collaboration/Solution template. One of the most common forms. First state the problem. Then describe the method you used to address the issue (i.e., how data was gathered and analyzed). Then list those with whom you worked. Finally, describe your solution.
2. The Core Question template. Another common approach. First, take the time to identify the core question—which we call the Essential Question—and be sure to give yourself more than a few minutes to do it. Then identify the data you used to answer it. Discuss the implications of that answer, and the to-do list it implies.
3. The What/So What/Now What template. We introduced this in Chapter Seven. Share the data you've gathered. Reveal the insights that resulted from your analysis of that data. Present a plan for taking action as a result of those insights, and your company's goals.

No matter what structure you use, keep in mind that the initial task is to communicate the results of your research, not to describe the process. So don't start with methodology or blueprints. Your colleagues want to see photographs of the finished house, not video of the foundation being poured. And keep it simple: Start with the question, deliver the answer, and then serve some food for thought regarding what you think should be done next. And if you're using a deck, don't make each slide different, in a mistaken attempt to spruce up the results. The observer just has to work harder to understand. Your job, if you're presenting, is to make sure it's easy for them to understand. And if the audience members have to reorient themselves every time you bring up a new slide, it won't be easy. So if you're using bar charts with certain colors on slide one, don't use pie charts with a different color palette on the next slide.

FIRST DRAFTS

Focus time and energy on refining and honing, not rehashing. This book went through four drafts before we put the manuscript in our editor's hands. Two more revisions followed while the book was in production. In other words, when someone talks about writing a book—or a report or a PowerPoint presentation—he or she is really talking about "rewriting" it, because that's where all the work is. For that reason, a good first draft gives you a lasting advantage; that is, each successive rewrite will be that much easier, because you started with a sound structure. This is especially true when you're reporting results, because every hour of preparation pushes the first opportunity for "decision making" back by an hour, too. So we've included a short list of directions to follow when you *first* lay out a deck (see Figure 27). You can follow them to create a report, too, or a list of talking points for a conference call. Again, they won't eliminate the need for a rewrite, but your second draft will be much closer to your final draft, and you'll be far less likely to veer off in the wrong direction.

[FIGURE 27]
DEVELOPING A SUCCESSFUL FIRST DRAFT

GOAL	HOW TO ACHIEVE IT
Focus on developing a coherent, compelling story.	Answer the Essential Question.
Think about What?, So what?, Now what?	Put data in context.
Aim to convey key messages in sixty minutes.	Fifteen to twenty slides.
Deliver one slide, one message.	Lead statement.
Use language that is clean, concise, and comprehensible.	Edit meticulously.
Exploit opportunities to draw your ideas, rather than describe them.	Word pictures.
Include the one-pager Essential Question slide in every deck.	Use Essential Questions wisely.

Again, data is only a supporting character, so use it to shape the story, and to support the story's key points, but don't allow the data—or the means by which you collected it—to *become* the story. One way to do this is to write a "story outline" *before* writing the deck, and then use your results only where the story needs them.

We included several report templates above, but if you're using the Three W's, remember that the *"what"*—that is, the findings, or the data and numbers—should be used to answer the *"so what."* And as important as those findings are, make sure you devote at least as much time to the *"so what"* and the *"now what"* as you do to the *"what."*

Again, always remember that you're making a presentation to communicate *key messages*, not data. So focus on those key messages, and refer to the data only when necessary to support them. All other data—and bullet points needed to display them—should be moved to the appendix.

Each slide should contain only one key message. A slide with a single message, and nothing else but white space, is far more effective than a slide with two separate points. That message should be a vital component of the deck's overall story, and should be contained in the slide's lead statement. This also brings to mind the consultant deck technique, which ensures that if you just read the lead statement in the masthead or top line of each chart, you are actually reading the concise and clear full story as you move across the deck, irrespective of what is in the body of the charts.

Every word on a slide should be there for a reason. Don't take refuge in details. Less is more. Use precise terms and avoid language that will be understood by only one type of listener (such as acronyms familiar to those in marketing but not finance). The easiest way to do this, after your first draft, is to try removing every word on the slide, one by one, to see if it's necessary. Another technique is to force yourself to keep any lead statement or bullet point to a single line; this will make it necessary to precisely articulate your findings.

In addition to carefully chosen words, use pictures, diagrams, or charts to communicate your key points. If you find that your key points are too big to fit into a picture, break them down into smaller, more easily communicated points. And remember that while carefully chosen words are the most efficient and precise method of communication, carefully chosen images may create longer-lasting "message memories." Pictures or photographs or charts can also give the audience a much-needed break from complex theoretical constructs.

In addition to the general guidelines above, which you'll use to create the *structure* of the report, we've also included a more detailed checklist for each individual slide (see Figure 28).

[FIGURE 28]
CHECKLIST

OVERALL QUESTIONS
Is there a logical framework for the overall deck?
Does the deck map to the Essential Questions?
Does each page have a lead statement?
Does each header have a focus?
Is each header meaningful?
Have you pushed thinking from insights to implications?
Cut as many words as possible?
Exploited opportunities to use word pictures?
HAVE YOU . . .
Checked spelling and grammar?
Checked and checked again for words you can cut?
Checked for consistency of font; color coding; slide shape/design?
Added fieldwork documents, full survey details, weighting scheme, sample structure, etc., into the appendix?
Explored all opportunities to add more white space to the slides?
Supported your points with customer verbatims?
Added the study name, month, and year as a footnote?
Added base descriptions for all charts?
Included the question (description, not just number) on all charts?
Checked for consistent scales where appropriate?
Checked for chart annotations: axes; percentage signs; currency notes?
Checked all keys and legends?
Removed unnecessary repetition (e.g., percentage sign at top of column, not next to every value)?
Checked that appropriate chart is being used (e.g., full stack bars add up to 100 percent, etc.)?
Charted all data not shown in the core deck in a separate appendix/data deck (annotated by question)?

These directions begin with a few general questions (Is there a logical framework to the overall deck? Does the story follow the Essential Questions? Have you pushed thinking from insights to implications?) and move on to more specific directions (Does each page have a lead statement, a meaningful header, and as much white space as possible?) Only after you've laid your deck out according to those guidelines will you turn to more mechanical considerations—like grammar, spelling, consistency of font, etc. Most important, with every rewrite you should look to cut any words you can do without. Only after you've come to the point where every single word counts can you consider the deck "written." Then you'll turn to the graphic details—like consistent scales, keys and legends, and your appendices (where the background data belongs).

Finally, keep in mind that every deck—and the research and recommendations it contains—is part of a larger strategic plan, generally set at the front of the year and not modified for at least twelve months. So your final slides should always refer your findings and suggestions back to those goals, big bets, and priorities. To do that, make sure that the Essential Question slide—in longer, strategic terms—is present in every deck (see Figure 29). Simply adopting this example will enable you to easily apply all the lessons just discussed. It starts out with the business question, thereby signaling that this is about answers, not data. The middle column provides the answer, and the final column discusses the potential implications (a.k.a. So what?). One slide, three columns—a simple, practical way to immediately change how you communicate data. Think of this slide as a valve on the fire hose, enabling you to easily regulate flow. Include the EQ slide in every deck.

[FIGURE 29]

Answer the EQs and provide direction via implications.

Business Question	Answer—What Should You Do?	Food for Thought
Essential Questions	Conclusions/ Recommendations	Key Findings/Support

Finally, remind viewers of the general flow of activity—from leadership to strategy to execution—by concluding with a slide that puts your report inside the entire enterprise (see Figure 30).

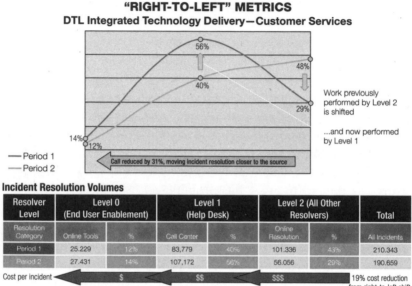

[FIGURE 30]

"RIGHT-TO-LEFT" METRICS
DTL Integrated Technology Delivery—Customer Services

Incident Resolution Volumes

Resolver Level	Level 0 (End User Enablement)		Level 1 (Help Desk)		Level 2 (All Other Resolvers)		Total
Resolution Category	Online Tools	%	Call Center	%	Online Resolution	%	All Incidents
Period 1	25.229	12%	83,779	40%	101.336	43%	210.343
Period 2	27.431	14%	107,172	56%	56.056	29%	190.659

Cost per incident — $ — $$ — $$$ — 19% cost reduction from right-to-left shift

JUST THE FACTS

We all know what it's like to listen to people who don't—or can't—use a simple, clear-cut framework. And listening to them, we all come to pretty much the same conclusion—before nodding off. The speakers either have asked the wrong questions or haven't come up with any clear answers. Or they've come up with answers they didn't like, or answers they couldn't understand. So they can't present their findings with any confidence. But rather than admit that lack of confidence, they present every single data point they can, hoping to hypnotize their audience, not enlighten them.

Worse, they often treat presentations as advertisements for themselves, or for the way they do business, not as a means of delivering results. And this leads to even more wasted time. After all, if a number appears on a slide, everyone in the audience presumes there's a reason for its being there. And so they consider it fair game for discussion, even though it has no legitimate bearing on the topic. Too much data is a problem in itself, but when unnecessary data makes its way into a presentation, the problem mushrooms, creating more questions—and more distractions. And of course that sort of misinformation can't possibly lead to sound decision making.

So use a framework to pose the Essential Question, include only the numbers decision makers need to see, and then answer the question as simply as possible. Start with yes or no: Is the market large or small? Yes or no? Is it growing? Yes or no?

With those general ideas in mind, let's return to the scene of the first crime in this book—the conference room we described at the beginning of the introduction. The scene was probably recognizable to every businesswoman and businessman in the world. A darkened conference room, illuminated by a never-ending succession of slides, each one more complicated and more bewildering than the one before it (see Figure 31).

[FIGURE 31]

SUMMARY: MARKETPLACE LANDSCAPE

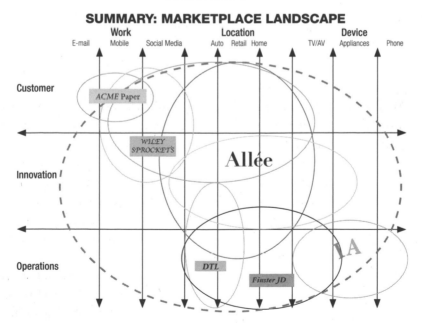

That, once again, is what we don't want to see. Ever again. And so building on what we've discussed since then, let's see if we can't rewrite that scene in order to drive the point home that the presentation of results—whether to justify a decision you've made or to influence decisions that have to be made by others—is the logical conclusion to everything we've discussed up until now in this book.

That's why we told you right from the start that we didn't have any answers—not for *your* particular business. Instead we've got questions. So we wrote this chapter to make sure that once you check out of data rehab, you never forget that the data, and the numbers, and the information that come from it, and the insights they provide, *are just cast members in the play.* That means you need them onstage, but you don't want them hanging around, trying to steal the scene. Find them, put them in costume, and have them read their lines—then get them offstage as fast as you can. And when they're onstage, make sure they're not lost in the scenery. In other words, reduce the surface area so that the information stands out—but we'll get to that point a little later in this chapter. For now, let's see what made the difference between the meeting we've sketched below and the one we wrote about at the beginning of this book.

TREATING MEETING MADNESS

Days before it took place, you took several small but critical steps to improve the chances the meeting would be a success. And by *success* we don't mean you getting a round of applause when it's all over, because for all you know the audience is celebrating the end of the meeting, not congratulating you on what you had to say. By a successful meeting we mean one to which the right people were invited and in which the material was presented as effectively and judiciously as possible. As a result, meaningful discussion occurred. People considered the new information. Of course, this doesn't mean they will accept all of your recommendations, but it will almost certainly make them pause, and will probably lead them to factor the information into their final strategy. And that's okay. That's enough. You were just trying to be sure that everyone had the information they needed to make sound business decisions. And if you've done that, you've already exceeded expectations.

You also realized that you were far more likely to create an ideal meeting if you started with an ideal invitation. And so the e-mail you sent to those you wanted at the meeting did the following:

- Described the type of meeting.
- Designated the expected outcome.
- Defined your role.

Figure 32 is an example of this sort of invitation.

[FIGURE 32]

Meeting called by:	Gussy Friegang
Subject:	Strategic Learning Plan + Insights
Type:	Brainstorming
Date:	Early January
Duration:	90 minutes
Your Role:	No prereading. Bring copies of 2011 priorities.

If you're using this template, you have one very important decision to make: What type of meeting are you proposing? This may seem obvious at first, but the *type* of meeting is a critical up-front callout. It not only guides the organizer—regarding the location of the meeting, what he or she needs to provide, whom should be invited, and how long the meeting should run—it also sets the expectations of the participants.

Meetings can be classified into one of three broad types:

- Brainstorming meeting: Expected to generate ideas for the solution of a problem via a working session; data synthesis is incomplete; the report is a work in progress; everyone should be involved in the back-and-forth; longer deck.
- Information-sharing meeting: Meant to pass on new, interesting, relevant facts and figures; no call to action; no preparation on the part of attendees required; everyone but the presenter is in listening mode, there only to receive new information; only once the presentation is complete should the presenter ask for questions, and those should be restricted to the need for clarification; shorter deck.

- Decision-making meeting: Meant to produce a final decision. Not the time for new information or to request additional analysis; finalize the path forward—i.e., yes or no, and if yes, how; very short deck.

As you can see, the type of meeting sets the tone and the agenda for the meeting. And depending on the responses the invitation gets, it also determines whether the meeting can be held at all. If, for example, you're setting up a decision-making meeting, and a key person declines at the last minute, then the meeting should be rescheduled. The same thing is true if a key person sends a proxy, but that person doesn't have the authority to make the final call. Under those circumstances—again, for a decision-making meeting—you should reschedule. Implicit in this approach is the understanding—communicated via your invitation—that if *any* of the key attendees can't make it, the meeting is going to be canceled. And this will not only make those key attendees think twice before accepting the invitation; it will make them think three times before they skip it.

If, on the other hand, the meeting is a brainstorming session, you'll need to recalibrate *your* expectations. Whether or not one or two key people decline the invitation or have to beg off at the last minute, the meeting should go forward. You don't need decisions approved; you need ideas exchanged. There may still be a great deal of data but not much analysis. Your role in this sort of meeting is to facilitate conversation between everyone who attends, to identify and record any key ideas or insights, and then to prepare everyone for the next steps.

Finally, a word about duration. Today's e-mail and calendar applications usually set meetings at one hour by default. Think about what that means. An hour is roughly 10 percent of the average businessperson's workday. So the question becomes: Is the meeting truly important enough for you to ask everyone to give up such a large chunk of their workday?

You'd be wise to consider that question in terms of your rung on the corporate ladder, too. Inviting those to whom *you report* implies a certain risk. Is the meeting truly important enough to justify your request for an hour of their time—time they are happy to "use" but undoubtedly reluctant to "lose"? As for your own direct reports, is the meeting important enough for you to pull them away from the work you've already assigned them?

Finally, one-hour meetings are much harder to justify, and schedule, given the stream of requests that come across everyone's desk, every day of the week. So think it over carefully, then talk it over with the organizer. Is an entire hour really needed, or could you reach the objective in thirty minutes?

Toward that end, if you change the way you collect and analyze data and the way you present your findings, you can take a lot of the unnecessary stuffing out of your presentation. Do this often enough and those who attend your meetings will wonder why all the meetings they attend aren't run the same way. In other words, your approach will serve as a Lighthouse for other presenters.

As we pointed out above, preparation for the "ideal meeting" began long before anyone sat down at the table. Again, you defined the meeting by "type" before you sent any invitations. And then you took care to invite everyone who needed to be there, and no one who didn't. And you sent any prereading materials twenty-four hours before the meeting was scheduled. Finally, keep in mind that the hypothetical "ideal meeting" we've sketched out below isn't a purely theoretical construct—i.e., we've tried to infuse it with a bit of the reality we've experienced on the front lines the past couple of decades.

Again, what we've tried to do in this book is to provide practical, workable solutions you can easily adopt. Finally, you'll note that we've put "ideal meeting" in quotes for a reason, since we know that not everyone will get around to the prereading, not everyone will be on time, and those in attendance won't necessarily interpret the information the same way you did or come to the same conclusions you have. On that note, before taking a look at what a Fire Hose meeting might look like, we're going to bring Darrell Bricker in again.

It's sort of what I said before: The survey sets you free. You don't have to be brilliant. You don't have to be Einstein. As long as you have the proper level of humility and you organize the research process the way it's supposed to be organized, and you ask the questions that you really need to have answered, and you ask them of the population you need to target. When the answers come back, pay attention to them. Like I said, my best presentations are when I stand up and say, "Take a look at this." And then "Here's my opinion." And if everyone else doesn't come to the same conclusion I did, then *I'm* probably wrong.

REDUCED SURFACE AREA

The meeting starts about five minutes late.

The first slide in the deck frames the issue, so everyone is on the same page. And because your invitation defined the type of meeting, only the people who need to be there are there—for example, for a decision-making meeting, only decision makers are present.

Since you've called for a smaller, shorter, decision-making meeting, everyone you invited assigned the meeting a high priority, because they knew a decision was going to be made, and none of them wanted to have to live with that decision without having had a part in making it.

Your deck contains only eight slides. It's organized to facilitate a decision, not a discussion. Each slide contains critical information. Slide one frames the issue and identifies the preferred outcome (see Figure 33).

[FIGURE 33]

PROBLEM
While research is effective in providing data and insights to support individual business decisions/needs, creating an integrated and impactful story for key milestones is currently a difficult and time-consuming process that has a detrimental impact on work/life balance.

POINT OF ARRIVAL (GOAL)
Realign **processes**, **people**, and **tools** to enhance research's capacity for delivering integrated insights in a painless and timely fashion to inform big bets in the next 12 months.

Slide two lists those who have already weighed in on the issue (see Figure 34). This gives your findings credibility and makes it easier for those attending the meeting to support your conclusion.

[FIGURE 34]

WHO WE TALKED TO
This solution is informed by 24 interviews

MARKETING	FIELD	CORPORATE
✓ Luke Francis	✓ Lauren Catherine	✓ Alexander Ryan
✓ Stephanie Walker	✓ Kevin Case	✓ CASRO
✓ Ina Gamble	✓ Nicolas Diego	✓ ESOMAR
✓ Kim Shelton	✓ Ina Mariette	✓ Reviewed MREB
✓ Karen Smith	✓ Renee Shell	● Vince Vawe
✓ Neil Bette	✓ Leo Ericsson	● Anthony Case
✓ Jeff Tracie	✓ Julia Take	✓ Deven Willem
✓ Jerry Hashi	✓ Riley Bishop	
✓ Erik Renne	✓ Zoe Sinead	
✓ G. Betty Jones		

Slide three briefly summarizes the nine solutions you considered, then outlines the three final options. It then summarizes the pros and cons of each, and finally, it highlights your recommendation.

Slide four discusses barriers and bridges, and what might happen if the company doesn't change its present course. Slides five through eight are supporting slides—they contain data, facts, and figures. While they are covered with numbers, each starts with a statement articulating the impact of the information they contain. Therefore, only those who want to look at the individual numbers have to. Furthermore, each of the four "data slides" has numbered points corresponding to callouts on its graphic. So as dense as those slides are, they're easy to navigate. There are no footnotes.

In addition, the data slides all follow a similar format, all of them use bar charts, and all the charts use the same colors, scale, and layout. That said, color and bold fonts are used sparingly—that is, only to highlight key takeaways. Most of the text is black, and there's a great deal of white space.

When you glance around the room, you can't help but feel that something's different. Everyone seems to be engaged, and listening to you as you present.

In the end, not everyone is satisfied with your recommendations, but those whose suggestions didn't make it into slide three know their views were considered, and they know *why* their suggestions didn't make the final cut. They also know that quite a few members of their teams were a part of the process, having seen slide two, and they feel comfortable with the level of rigor and the logic string you used to arrive at your solution.

You didn't drown them in data. You just presented the important information and based your recommendations on it. If it had been necessary, you were ready to go deeper—using the data slides—but since the important numbers had already been presented in earlier sessions, that wasn't necessary. And once the decision was made, you ended the meeting by outlining a Plan B going forward (see Figure 35).

Okay, that's not just a look at what a Fire Hose meeting is supposed to look like, but what an ideal meeting would look like. So the next time *you* receive an invitation to a meeting, try thinking back over the fundamentals we've discussed.

First of all, ask yourself if you really need to attend the meeting. What about your role? Is it clear? And does this meeting *really* require a full hour? Or put another way, does it *deserve* an hour of your day? What's the agenda? What's the desired outcome? Who's already seen the material, and what did they have to say about it? If the answers to any of these questions are unclear, then shoot an e-mail back to the organizer and ask for specific answers.

[FIGURE 35]

SOLUTION
Process / People / Tools

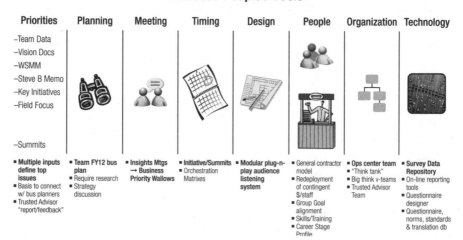

Priorities	Planning	Meeting	Timing	Design	People	Organization	Technology
–Team Data –Vision Docs –WSMM –Steve B Memo –Key Initiatives –Field Focus –Summits							
▪ Multiple inputs define top issues ▪ Basis to connect w/ bus planners ▪ Trusted Advisor "report/feedback"	▪ Team FY12 bus plan ▪ Require research ▪ Strategy discussion	▪ Insights Mtgs → Business Priority Wallows	▪ Initiative/Summits ▪ Orchestration Matrixes	▪ Modular plug-n-play audience listening system	▪ General contractor model ▪ Redeployment of contingent $/staff ▪ Group Goal alignment ▪ Skills/Training ▪ Career Stage Profile	▪ Ops center team ▪ "Think tank" ▪ Big think v-teams ▪ Trusted Advisor Team	▪ Survey Data Repository ▪ On-line reporting tools ▪ Questionnaire designer ▪ Questionnaire, norms, standards & translation db

CONTEXT IS KING

As we've said from the beginning of this chapter, even if you've learned how to drink from the Fire Hose—if you've gotten to the essential data you need, and have used it to gain some new insight—it won't mean much if you don't include the right numbers in your presentation. So let's spend a moment describing the sorts of numbers that *should* make it into your deck, and how your presentation can confirm their importance.

No matter the data source—and we'll use social-media data for this example—you'll be far more likely to convince your audience if you present your findings and recommendations from the following three points of view.[*]

1. Absolute position—e.g., total unique visitors to your business's Facebook page.
2. Relative position—e.g., your company's visitors relative to your competitors', and relative to industry volume as a whole.
3. Position over time—e.g., the trend in visits over time for you, your competitors, and the market.

Social-media data is actually a great example of the importance of this approach. Why? Because people think of the data social-media sites generate as something they've never seen before. It isn't. It's like any other data stream. So don't bolt some sort of exclusive filter for it onto your existing framework, and don't come up with a separate process of measurement and analysis. You already do focus groups. You do quantitative surveys. You do online surveys. Social-media sites just generate another stream of data, and while it's going to take people awhile to get used to that, our position is that you should still use the same approach to evaluate it. And you should still use the same model to present the results.

First, track the absolute position. Are total volumes up or down? Next, assess your position relative to your competitors'. Are visits to their sites falling while yours are climbing, or vice versa? Are more

---

[*]We've covered this approach in several other sections of the book, but it's so important we want to reemphasize it here.

people posting to their pages? Finally, track these relationships, and the changes in them, over time. That's the only way you're going to tell an effective data story; because there's so much volume, it's hard for people to get their heads around it. So you have to present the various streams relative to one another. You're up five hundred tweets . . . or your traffic increased 300 percent in December: That's great, but what are other sites doing?

Just remember: Counting is easy. Evaluating is hard.

Finally, remember that while there are all sorts of *data* you can use, oftentimes there's nothing like the answers you get from your customers themselves—whether you're selling outside or inside the company. So don't forget to include their input.

FIRE HOSE EVANGELISTS

Once you've completed your fact-finding and you've chosen the framework you're going to use to present those findings, you've got to think about persuading the key stakeholders to act on them. Scott Penberthy has a great story that speaks directly to that issue, a story in which he played a part, involving the early days of the Internet at IBM.

There's a very common term used in management called "wheelbase," and everyone thinks about managing their wheelbase. And what your wheelbase was, was your network of contacts. And whenever you had a decision, it was all about getting your corporation to move. There are some people from whom you always had to have approval, and more, to convince them to become sponsors of the idea. Even if the idea's yours, you kind of have to give up the ownership to actually make the corporation move forward.

I've personally seen it action, and in a big way, a couple of times. One was around 1995. We were a small band of people doing Web stuff, in IBM Research. And we were really enamored of this thing called Oak. It was a technology invented by James Gosling, and we thought, Oh my God, this brings object-oriented computing to the Internet. And we all wanted to put it into our browser. And they told us, "No, no, we can't get licensing rights—don't put this in the browser." We couldn't get them to pay attention to us.

Well, a woman in her twenties who was in marketing renamed it Java. At that time IBM was thinking about buying Lotus, and we were just a band of engineers in love with this thing with a strange name that no one had heard of. So we couldn't get anyone to move. And I remember the head of research called me, a great mentor named Jim McGroddy, and here he is telling this twenty-year-old—me—that you can't just go face-first at the executives and in essence call all of them idiots, and tell them they've got to embrace Java and dump this thing called Lotus script. You've got to get somebody they'll believe, and who has the authority, to say it's *his* idea. If you don't, you're not going anywhere. Ask yourself this: Do you want the corporation to win, or do you want to win?

So we found a couple of really smart senior technologists in the IBM Academy and invited them down, and then we walked them through it, in a very meek way, holding our tongues as much as we could, and saying "Here's something we found that you might be interested in." They analyzed it, did a lot of work on it, and realized, you know, this could have some merit. And then they made some presentations, saying this thing called Oak, or Java, could be pretty interesting. And lo and behold, now that management was hearing this from a senior executive, not some kid or a bunch of kids from research but from a very senior guy they trusted, a guy who managed billion-dollar businesses in the technology field, they said "This *is* interesting." And that Swing Voter became the head of Java.

One of the other executives at the time, when we were trying to get the company interested in using Java, took me aside and said, "You're going to kill your career, Scott. Don't you know our investments are in C, C+, C++, Cobalt, and Fortran? We've got no time for this Java nonsense, and if you say we should give it time, you're going to push yourself off the cliff at IBM." As it turned out, though, after we'd enlisted the support of the senior technologist, that executive eventually became known as the number-one Java GM in the company.

And so we all learned that you can have a great idea yourself, but in order to get the corporation to consider it, and to move on it, you've got to figure out who you need to become your supporter, or I guess what you would call your Swing Voter in the corporation.

In other words, in addition to using a solid framework to report your results, be prepared to name the people you've already talked to, or the people you consulted, or the people who have already reviewed the material. This is especially true, as Penberthy noted, when you're talking to the general manager. He's going to want a list of the executives you've run it past, and to know that you have informed those people about what's coming so that the results don't come as a surprise. In other words, make it easy for decision makers to act on your results.

In presenting your results in a way that will drive decision makers to act, you can also show management, your colleagues, and your employees how the Fire Hose Questions work. That is, as we pointed out earlier, your successful presentation will serve as a Lighthouse. And by presenting your results clearly and effectively, you'll provide a forceful example of how the Fire Hose approach clears the fog of data and leads to a better understanding of the situation and, as a result, to more focused plans of action. And by doing that, you'll encourage everyone in the company to embed the approach in their routines, and they in turn will encourage others to do the same.

CHAPTER EIGHT TAKEAWAYS

If you're writing a report or speaking in front of an audience, you really need a six-point checklist.

1. Decide the type of meeting up front: decision making, information sharing, or brainstorming.
2. Organize your deck around a framework, e.g., what, so what, now what.
3. Start by answering the Essential Question.
4. Always put data in context—show absolute score, the change over time, and/or competitive data.
5. Be a ruthless director, leaving data on the cutting-room floor.
6. Make data the supporting character, not the main character.

A Final Thought

"Data is a means to an end. It is the supporting character.
Too often it takes center stage."
—CHRISTOPHER FRANK AND PAUL MAGNONE

An amazing journey is coming to a close, and we thank you for taking part in it. Our day job is to help our companies grow, but often we felt a bit naked out in front of our colleagues. Heretic or evangelist or perhaps just wrong? Well, as the saying goes, in the land of the blind the one-eyed man is king. Often our eyes were shut and then opened by very bright colleagues we were fortunate to work with and learn from. We've taken those lessons to heart and shared the learning with you.

Time and again, we saw patterns whenever we talked to our colleagues, all of whom are constantly generating, consuming, requesting, and analyzing facts and figures. To return to one of our favorite quotes, by Andrew Lang, "People use statistics as a drunken man uses lampposts—for support rather than for illumination." Data overload is here to stay. We live in a time when information is exploding and often feels invasive or intimidating. In reality, we are fortunate to have this staggering amount of information at our fingertips, but we need to master the flow from the Fire Hose.

We have become a world of data hounds. It does not matter what size the entity is: Small business or large, well-funded start-up or garage business—they all have one recurring theme. People want answers, but a constant refrain we hear is "I have data but don't know how to make sense of it. Can't we break this down into a handful of simple points? I know what I need but don't have the time to roll around in the numbers to find the answers—answers about how to drive growth, introduce new products, or figure out how to keep the lights on." We often ask ourselves: Is there a market for this product? How do we win the account? How much will people pay? How do we get new subscribers? What do customers want? What features do we cut? How do we increase satisfaction? What functionality do we add? What is our value proposition? What do people think of our brand? These are the fun, hard questions to answer. However, the fun seems to come to a screeching halt when the data arrives. Instead of being a well-arranged piece of music, it's a mash-up of sounds. The volume drowns the substance.

Our intent was to make sense of this noise. Documented in these pages are the things we've learned over the course of our careers that help focus the data. We have been part of some terrific successes, we've been part of some failed start-ups, and we've been fortunate enough to be on the inside of some of the most respected companies in the world. Had we known how to ask the right questions a little sooner—that is, the Seven Questions in this book—they might have put us on a different career path. Just the same, we've been lucky enough to have sat at the same table with some amazing leaders. And it was during those sorts of meetings that we observed, developed, and created this toolbox of tips, tricks, and techniques for drinking from the Fire Hose of data. In short, to thrive in the Spray and Pray nature of business today, and to navigate the steady stream of information that characterizes the modern business world, we all need some sort of guidance. This book was our attempt at creating a sort of guidebook for dealing with information overload.

We have seen what it takes to lead. How to motivate and inspire a group of people to find the answers. To think differently. To see what everyone else has seen but to think what no one else has thought. Our goal was to put down on paper a set of deceptively simple, easy-to-apply questions to help readers make sense of the data deluge. Our intent was to teach and hopefully launch an ongoing dialogue. To write a sort of how-to book grounded in practical examples and real-life scenarios that you would recognize. To show how to use, consume, and engage with data and facts, in a meaningful way, to shape real-world answers. To serve up some intriguing concepts, in a genuine voice, to enable you to use what you just read in your next meeting.

At the end of the day, it is the golden few who understand the power of data, know the questions to ask to separate the wheat from the chaff, connect it to business, and then use it to engage the customer to achieve revenue objectives. We have seen innovations missed, opportunities passed by, and customers lost because people did not know how to create and deliver insights. The goal of this book was to be the gear in the machine that connects the business with the customer. It's a "translation guide" bridging the gap between data and strategy. If you take it to heart, we think you can be a catalyst for new thinking, spurring new conversations through smart questions that will put you well ahead of the game.

Who Was Your Favorite Teacher?

At this point we'd like to offer a small reward—you can think of it as a bonus lesson—for those who hang around to read this final section. And conveniently enough, in order to share that lesson we'll need to recognize the many people who have supported us on our journey. To know who we are, in fact, you need only read down this short list of friends and mentors—their values are our own.

As we indicated above, we have always believed that the acknowledgments should be renamed "Who Was Your Favorite Teacher?" Why? Because we couldn't have written the following pages without the coaching, constructive criticism, support, and advocacy of a few core people in our business lives. And now, as authors, we finally get to exercise that belief and acknowledge our favorite teachers.

(Disclaimer: By design, there is not one mention of *"le nostre famiglie"* in this section. While an irreplaceable constant in our lives, we preferred to recognize their love and support in the dedication.)

Before we name business names, however, we'd like to offer one small bit of advice: Don't look for a job you'll like; look for a leader you'll love working for. Anyone can find the perfect job. But if it comes with a manager you cannot follow, then that perfect job will quickly become a prison sentence, no matter how well it pays. Even a mediocre job with a wonderful manager—that is, someone who will partner with you, help you power through the job, help you grow, and insist that you have fun—is vastly preferable. The lesson we've learned from doing countless job interviews—which we think of as Interviewing 101—is that too many candidates direct their questions toward understanding their roles in the job. Instead, we advise them to flip this around: Put greater focus on learning about the style, principles, and values of the manager doing the hiring. Ask open-ended questions about what surprises the manager. Put greater weight on the quality of the leader when making a job selection. It is the rocket fuel that will make a job soar to the level of career management and sustain your passion for the business.

We have been fortunate to work for some outstanding leaders, and so the bar has been set very, very high, but after all these years each of us can point to one that stands above all the rest.

>> CHRISTOPHER FRANK

For me that person, that one great teacher, is Ann Redmond, my former manager at Microsoft. Ann is an amazing person and a manager who epitomizes leadership. Ann always established a high bar, creating an environment that fostered creativity and enabled me to think bigger, fly further, and accomplish the impossible. She taught me the art of critical thinking—that is, she taught me how to interrogate data, think strategically, and communicate effectively. She served as coach, mentor, and partner, providing perspective and guidance. Her opinion was always worth having. Above all else, she demonstrated that a positive attitude is a great multiplier. Nothing is impossible when you work with Ann. She is a positive, dynamic person, and working with her made me a better researcher, a more successful professional, and, most important, a better person. She has been an inspiration to me and remains so. I consider myself fortunate to call Ann my friend.

As I mentioned, there has also been a select group of people in my career who served as mentors, each of whom I am indebted to. This includes Jim Minervino, Jeff Hansen, and Mich Mathews. Each of them has had a tremendous, positive influence on me, and it was from them that I learned the arts of precision questioning, precision answering, and effectively reducing surface area when presenting data. I'd also like to thank my dear friends at Microsoft, with whom I spent many hours crunching data and smoke jumping: Doug Doyle, Kelsey Vaughn, Helen Hopper, Neil Shah, Anne Groom, Thomas Walker, and Toni-Ann Lupinacci; Steve Ballmer, who taught me that it is all about satisfying the customer, loving the customer, delighting the customer—in other words, tailoring everything you do to the customer. Nor can I leave out Kevin Turner, who showed me that the most important "go-do" for market research was to serve as the customer steward—to jump up and down on the table until people listen to the voice of the customer. I'd also like to send a big thank-you to Toby Richards, M3 Sweatt, Kathleen Hogan, and Kevin Johnson, with whom I spent many tireless hours using data to shape an outstanding customer and partner experience. Other friends, new and old, deserve a mention. Jim Suzansky and Gerry Crispin, my two fellow pigeons in Drei Tauben Ltd. Bonnie and Joe Post, who ran the first research agency I worked with and fielded my endless questions and data requests. And especially Darrell Bricker, of Ipsos, and Susan Schwartz McDonald, of National Analysts, who were my confidants, helping me to widen my thinking as I embarked on the journey that culminated in the writing of this book. A book would not be in your hands, in conclusion, if it were not for my dear friend Joseph Cositore, who connected us with our extraordinary agent, Joelle Delbourgo.

Finally, the story of my almost unbelievably lucky business associations continues at American Express with John Hayes and Adam Rothschild, two outstanding leaders who both foster a culture of innovation and teach the art of being "irritatingly objective" when it comes to analysis. I have deep respect for both of them and am grateful for all they continue to teach me.

>> PAUL MAGNONE

For me that favorite teacher is Jim Corgel, my former manager at IBM. Jim is a great leader who gave me my first real opportunity to spread my wings. Maintaining high standards while remaining practical, he is a surprisingly creative entrepreneur with a calm presence and a constant focus on core values and the bottom line. Jim created an environment of teamwork, innovation, respect, and, most important, straight talk. Employing these principles, he taught me the art of building a business from scratch, which involves finding out what matters in the boardroom and then focusing the power of individuals. Jim's voice is reflected in the voice of this book—he's the leader who asks the deceptively simple questions and inspires you at the same time. I was fortunate to work for him and lucky to learn from him, and I continue to appreciate our friendship.

I've also been fortunate to learn from a select group of colleagues I've been privileged to also call my friends—a group that includes Tom Hawk (another true business builder) and Mary Garrett, Matt Friedman, Jim Hilt, and Dan Powers, each of whom taught me how to grow a brand. I also have to mention Scott Penberthy—the smartest man I know—who has been a peer, manager, client, mentor, and general co-conspirator. Each of them has had a deep influence on my approach to business, and to life. Finally, special thanks to my friends at IBM who asked all the right questions in Piscataway, Somers, and Armonk and during our world travels—Liz Stafford, Kerrie Holley, Luba Cherbakov, Mark Ernest, Ken Khouri, John Mullaly, Gerry Mooney, Rick Qualman, Joe Ziskin, George Welleck, Jim Gallagher, and Joann Duguid. Ever onward.

My journey continues at Openet, where I've been fortunate to find new colleagues like Niall Norton, Apollo Guy, and Mike Manzo—all outstanding leaders, in a dynamic market, who exemplify the lessons of this book. I'd also like to add a special word of thanks to Chris Hoover for his encouragement and enthusiasm regarding this project. He was, in fact, one of the first to hear about this book, while we were both stuck in Dublin during the Icelandic ash cloud.

We would both like to thank a few shared friends, beginning with Don Merino, who was a mentor to both of us at the Stevens Institute of Technology. Dr Merino was our first coach—though he worked in a classroom—and taught us leadership and accountability. We would also like to thank Marjorie Everitt and Hal and Elizabeth Ravaché, who encouraged our creativity and enthusiasm as young alumni. We want to mention Eric Koivisto, too. Both of us have worked with Eric, and we've all shared in one another's lives. Far too many stories to share and each one a gem—thanks, Sugar.

Before closing, we would like to thank all the contributors to this book, including those previously mentioned, as well as Herb Schaffner, David Moldawer, Cory Williamson, Steve Sasson, Nancy Dussault-

Smith, Jim Dippold, Dave McLurg, Jessica Bernow, and Emma Streatfield. To Jillian Gray and the fabulous team at Portfolio / Penguin, thanks for a terrific partnership. Thanks for asking your questions and sharing your insights.

Finally, our last words are reserved for our parents, who worked tirelessly from the docks to construction sites and on factory floors. They sacrificed much, asked for little, and provided constant love and support. We thank you with all the gratitude in our hearts.

Index